Refining Sound

Refining Sound

A PRACTICAL GUIDE TO
SYNTHESIS AND SYNTHESIZERS

Brian K. Shepard

OXFORD
UNIVERSITY PRESS

OXFORD
UNIVERSITY PRESS

Oxford University Press is a department of the University of Oxford. It furthers the University's objective of excellence in research, scholarship, and education by publishing worldwide.

Oxford   New York

Auckland   Cape Town   Dar es Salaam   Hong Kong   Karachi
Kuala Lumpur   Madrid   Melbourne   Mexico City   Nairobi
New Delhi   Shanghai   Taipei   Toronto

With offices in

Argentina   Austria   Brazil   Chile   Czech Republic   France   Greece
Guatemala   Hungary   Italy   Japan   Poland   Portugal   Singapore
South Korea   Switzerland   Thailand   Turkey   Ukraine   Vietnam

Oxford is a registered trade mark of Oxford University Press in the UK and certain other countries.

Published in the United States of America by
Oxford University Press
198 Madison Avenue, New York, NY 10016

Library of Congress Cataloging-in-Publication Data
Shepard, Brian K.
Refining sound : a practical guide to synthesis and synthesizers / Brian K. Shepard.
p. cm.
Includes bibliographical references and index.
ISBN 978-0-19-992294-9 (alk. paper) — ISBN 978-0-19-992296-3 (alk. paper) 1. Electronic music—Instruction and study. 2. Synthesizer (Musical instrument) 3. Music—Acoustics and physics. I. Title.
MT723.S44 2013
786.7′4—dc23   2013000232

1   3   5   7   9   8   6   4   2

Printed in the United States of America on acid-free paper

To Jenny, my love and my life

FOREWORD

Synthesizers are wonderful musical instruments that come in many shapes, sizes, and capabilities. From monstrous modular setups to minimal iPhone apps, they all sound good and are great fun to play. But right there is a big disconnect: How can there possibly be any relationship between the two? The common elements are oscillators, filters, and other basic building blocks, all clearly explained in Brian Shepard's *Refining Sound: A Practical Guide to Synthesis and Synthesizers.*

Synthesizers are easily the most versatile musical instruments ever invented. The wide range of sounds they are capable of generating is simply amazing. With this ability comes a certain amount of complexity, so learning the basics of synthesis will go a long way when you want to produce a sound.

My company, Dave Smith Instruments, faces a dilemma shared by other manufacturers of synths: we continuously design and release new instruments, and at some point have to write an operation manual for the new product. We try to fully describe all the features in a clear manner, but we simply cannot go into depth providing a tutorial on the basics of synthesis. That's where this book is invaluable! I can highly recommend it to any musician who wants to go beyond playing factory presets.

Software synthesizers have become a good resource, providing a great feature-to-price ratio. *Refining Sound* takes advantage of this by presenting numerous examples that the reader can try using free software. You can go as deep as you like, using these instruments to first understand the basic concepts and then go in whatever direction you would like.

Even better, a companion website gives the reader numerous resources to learn more or explore other synthesis concepts (sounds like "extra credit"). Needless to say, these are all resources I would have loved to have access to forty years ago!

As a designer of hardware analog and digital-analog synths, my hope is that you the reader will want to go beyond software and apply your synthesis skills to hardware synths. There are few things as fun as turning knobs on an instrument, hearing the results, and letting the sound lead you into new musical directions!

Dave Smith
Dave Smith Instruments

PREFACE

Like many musicians who grew up in the 1960s and 1970s, I have long been fascinated with synthesizers and electronic instruments. The musical—and often literal—pyrotechnics of rock synthesizer virtuosi such as Keith Emerson and Rick Wakeman as well as the gorgeous classical interpretations of artists like Wendy Carlos and Isao Tomita were a great inspiration to this young musician and composer. As I was beginning to purchase and use my own instruments, synthesizers were in the midst of a huge transformation from the large, modular, analog instruments made famous by performers such as those listed above to the smaller, all-in-one, digital instruments we commonly see today.

Although these newer instruments offer numerous amazing sound-making capabilities, they usually do so with an increasing complexity that tends to obscure how the sound is actually created. On the older analog instruments, it was quite easy to see what elements were creating and modifying a sound; you simply followed the patch cables. If a module didn't have anything plugged into it, it wasn't doing anything. If the output of a module was plugged into the input of another module, the second module was modifying the output of the first. For most of us making the transition to digital instruments, we kept that cable "picture" in mind as we dealt with the software connections in our new synthesizers.

Now, having taught synthesis for more than twenty years, I find that most of the people with whom I work do not have that earlier model on which to base their experience and understanding. They tend to see the inner structure of a synthesizer as a "black box" that mysteriously makes its sound, and they usually have no concept of the individual elements in a synthesizer and how they work, much less how they interact with each other, to produce those wonderful sounds. Without this understanding, users might tweak some settings and controls in a trial-and-error approach until they have something they like, but in most cases they just settle for the presets that come on the instrument.

Part of the problem has been the design of the instruments themselves. At times it seems as if manufacturers have gone out of their way to cloud the internal workings of their instruments by giving new names to standard elements. (I've long suspected that some manufacturers have a "Department of Silly Names" that comes up with these monikers.) Until the development of computer-based software synthesizers and their large graphical user interfaces (GUIs), the internal workings were further obscured by the tiny LCD displays and confusing navigation systems found on most hardware instruments. Thus, it is little wonder that many users found their synthesizers confusing and intimidating to program, and gave up on the idea of creating their own sounds.

Although every synthesizer model has its differences, in most regards they are actually quite similar to each other. Regardless of the manufacturer or model, there will be oscillators, ways to combine the oscillators, envelope generators, filters, modulators, and effects processors. The name, number, quantity, quality, and arrangement of these elements may change from one instrument to another, but the elements themselves, and their operation, are quite consistent from device to device.

I wrote *Refining Sound* as an attempt to demystify the synthesizer and its elements as well as to illuminate the sound-making process from start to finish. In teaching synthesis over the years, I have found many wonderful resources that cover different aspects of synthesis at all levels of knowledge and skill. Many of these resources are listed and described in Appendix I of this text and on the companion website pages.

What I have not found is a text that introduces and illustrates the entire synthesis process to the college-level musician who may not have a strong math or engineering background. In this book, I have attempted to provide detailed information on synthesis appropriate for college students, yet without requiring a strong background in mathematics. Concepts are explained with numerous illustrations and interactive demonstrations and a minimum of mathematical formulae. For students and instructors wishing to delve deeper into the math and science of synthesis, additional resources and links are provided on the companion website.

I think of synthesis as the process of creating and refining sound. Much like the jeweler or metallurgist who refines raw materials through numerous stages to create a beautiful work of art, the synthesizer artist begins with raw sound waves and transforms them through multiple refinement stages to create the exciting new sounds for which these instruments are famous.

My goal is to help you understand the stages of that refinement process by—metaphorically speaking—taking the synthesizer apart to explore its inner workings. As we do so, we will examine each stage of synthesis, its contribution to the sound, and how it interacts with other elements and stages. In every chapter, there will be opportunities to get "hands-on" with the individual elements so that you can see and hear—and most importantly, understand—what each of these refinement stages is contributing to the finished product. In the final chapter, we will "reassemble" the synthesizer as we create some of the most common types of synthesizer sounds from start to finish.

Whether you work with hardware, software, analog, or digital instruments, the synthesis process is immensely rewarding and a lot of fun. My hope is that working through the pages of this text and exploring the interactive demonstrations will clarify that process, giving you a much keener understanding of your own synthesizers. I also hope it will inspire you to create wonderful new sounds on those instruments.

Have fun!

CONTENTS

Contents

ACKNOWLEDGMENTS

A work like this does not happen in isolation. A number of people have contributed to this book in many ways, and I would like to take this opportunity to acknowledge those individuals.

Thank you to Jeanette Shepard for being such an amazing—and amazingly patient—first reader and editor. Everyone should be so lucky to have such a smart and talented partner in life. Thank you also to Steve Cunningham and V. J. Manzo for the expert readings of my initial draft, and to Dave Smith for not only reading the text but writing such a supportive Foreword to the book. The feedback and comments I received from all of you about the book and its content were immeasurably valuable.

Norm Hirschy at Oxford University Press has been incredibly enthusiastic and supportive of this project from the outset, and I appreciate his assistance on so many levels in seeing this through to completion. I must also thank my OUP production editor, Erica Woods Tucker, and copy editor, Thomas Finnegan, for their mastery in clarifying my manuscript and helping bring my ideas and words to life.

Creating all the demonstrations for the companion website was nearly as large and daunting a task as writing the text for the book. Most of the questions and challenges I encountered while creating those demonstrations were answered by the participants—often anonymously—on the Cycling '74 Forums (http://cycling74.com/forums/). Thank you all for your many suggestions and creative ideas.

Before I even began writing the text to this book, I knew I needed a software synthesizer that sounded great, provided a lot of flexibility, was available for both Windows and Macintosh computer platforms, and was inexpensive so cost would not be an impediment to the learning process. When my research led me to Glenn Olander's software synthesizer, Crystal (http://www.greenoak.com/crystal/), I was astounded. Not only did it meet, or exceed, every one of my requirements; it was available free of charge. I would like to thank Glenn for making such a fantastic piece of software available and for his kind, generous replies to all my questions and inquiries.

Finally, I want to thank my many synthesis students over the years. Your energy, enthusiasm, questions, and discussions both inside and outside the classroom continue to keep me on my toes and were the inspiration for writing this book.

ABOUT THE COMPANION WEBSITE

http://www.oup.com/us/refiningsound

Oxford has created a password-protected website to accompany *Refining Sound*, and the reader is encouraged to take full advantage of it to get the most out of this book. Throughout the text, icons in the page margin, like the ones at right, indicate available content (synthesis demonstrations, animations, recordings, additional readings, website links, etc.) that further explains and illustrates the specific topic at hand. The website is organized with separate pages for each of the book's chapters, and the URL for each page will be found at the beginning of each chapter. You can also move directly from page to page with the links at the top and bottom of each page on the site.

To access the companion website, use the username **Music1** and the password **Book5983.**

INTRODUCTION
GETTING THE MOST OUT OF THIS BOOK

Online Materials for the Introduction:

http://www.oup.com/us/refiningsound/Introduction.html

Refining Sound is not just a book for reading; it's a book for *doing*. As you progress through each stage of the synthesis process in this book, it is vitally important that you also experience the sound that the process creates. To this end, in addition to the companion website there are two supplementary elements to the text that are as important to the concepts in this book as is the text itself. These resources are designed to help you gain the deepest understanding possible by providing interactive, hands-on demonstrations and examples for nearly every aspect of synthesis.

Using the Interactive Demonstrations

Icons like the one in the page margin at right indicate an interactive demonstration on the companion website that allows you to experience the topic of that section and explore it in greater detail. The corresponding web page for most chapters has a set of demonstrations that may be downloaded as a group, or individually as desired. The demonstration icons are numbered to allow you to easily locate the correct one on the site. Each interactive demonstration also includes further information about the topic, as well as step-by-step instructions for effectively using that demonstration.

In order to use the interactive demonstrations, you must have the free Max Runtime software from Cycling '74 installed and configured on your computer. Max Runtime is available for both Macintosh and Windows platform computers. If you already own the full version of Max, you can also use that software for the demonstrations instead of the runtime version.

Installing Max Runtime

To install Max Runtime, go to the Cycling '74 downloads page by pointing your web browser to http://cycling74.com/downloads/runtimc/, and download the appropriate version for your computer's operating system. There is also a link from the Introduction page on the companion website. After downloading and uncompressing, follow the instructions in the Max Runtime installer.

Once you have Max Runtime installed, you can download the interactive demonstrations as compressed .zip files (for convenience, you will have the option of downloading the demonstrations individually or downloading all the demonstrations from a chapter as a group). Uncompress the downloaded files, and then double-click the .mxf file to launch Max Runtime and the individual demonstration.

xx

TIP

Note to Macintosh Users

Some Macintosh users may find that another program such as Avid's Pro Tools—not Max Runtime—attempts to launch when double-clicking these interactive demonstrations. If this happens, use the following steps to configure your Macintosh to open the demonstrations properly with Max Runtime.

Figure 0.1
The icons for the interactive demonstrations should look like the icon on the left when displayed on your computer desktop. If your icons look different, such as the one on the right, use the following steps to assign Max Runtime as the preferred application to open these demonstrations.

1. Highlight the icon for one of the .mxf files (do not double-click or open it).
2. Select **Get Info** from the File menu (⌘+I)
3. In the window that opens, click the little triangle next to "Open with:" to expand the panel so that you see a dropdown menu with a list of applications.
4. Select **Max Runtime.app** from the menu and click the "Change All . . ." button.
5. An alert window will open asking if you want to change all similar documents to open with Max Runtime.app. Click the "Continue" button to confirm this choice.

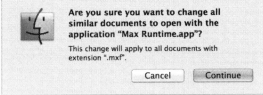

Figure 0.2
After highlighting the icon of one of your downloaded .mxf files and opening the Get Info window, select **Max Runtime.app** as the "Open with:" application and click "Change All . . ." to configure your computer to always open these demonstrations with Max Runtime. Confirm that choice by pressing the "Continue" button in the alert window that opens when you press the "Change All . . ." button.

Now that you have Max Runtime installed, there is one final bit of configuration you need to do before actually using the demonstrations. Download and open the Audio/MIDI Configuration utility from the companion website. Select the appropriate audio driver for your computer from the top menu, and the audio interface you wish to use for your input and output from the second and third menus. In most cases, the driver will be "Core Audio" on the Macintosh, and either ASIO or MME on a Windows PC. If you have installed a hardware audio interface or sound card, be sure to select the appropriate driver for that device. If you are unsure of the correct driver for your installed interface or card, consult the installation instructions that came with the device.

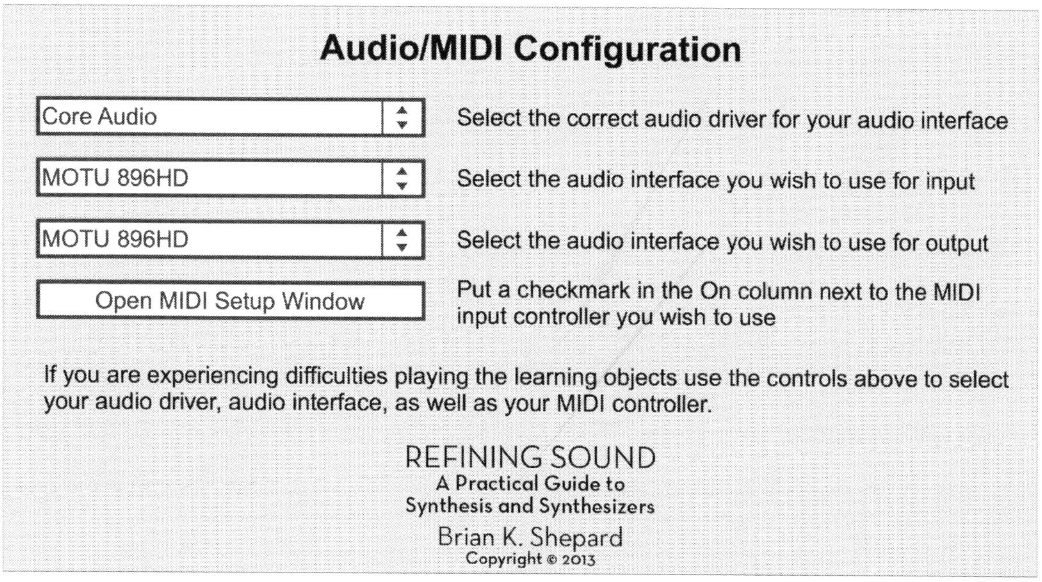

Audio/MIDI Configuration

Core Audio ⬍	Select the correct audio driver for your audio interface
MOTU 896HD ⬍	Select the audio interface you wish to use for input
MOTU 896HD ⬍	Select the audio interface you wish to use for output
Open MIDI Setup Window	Put a checkmark in the On column next to the MIDI input controller you wish to use

If you are experiencing difficulties playing the learning objects use the controls above to select your audio driver, audio interface, as well as your MIDI controller.

REFINING SOUND
A Practical Guide to
Synthesis and Synthesizers
Brian K. Shepard
Copyright © 2013

Figure 0.3
Use the Audio/MIDI Configuration utility to select the appropriate audio driver and interface for your computer as well as to choose your MIDI controller.

If you have a MIDI keyboard connected to your computer (highly recommended), click the Open MIDI Setup Window button, and confirm that there is a checkmark in the "On" column for your preferred MIDI input(s). When in doubt, check them all.

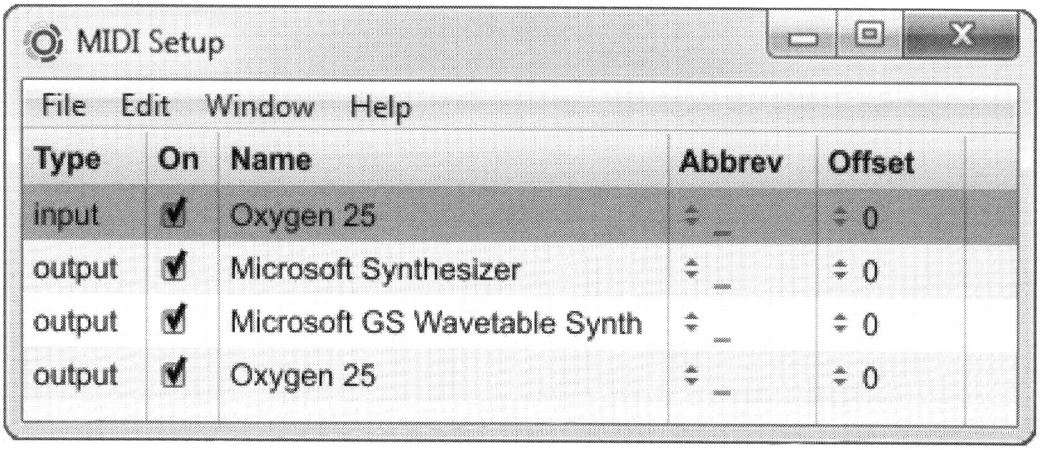

MIDI Setup

File   Edit   Window   Help

Type	On	Name	Abbrev	Offset
input	☑	Oxygen 25	⬍ _	⬍ 0
output	☑	Microsoft Synthesizer	⬍ _	⬍ 0
output	☑	Microsoft GS Wavetable Synth	⬍ _	⬍ 0
output	☑	Oxygen 25	⬍ _	⬍ 0

Figure 0.4
Confirm there is a check mark in the "On" column of the MIDI Setup window for any MIDI Input(s) you wish to use with these demonstrations.

Your computer is now configured to let you take advantage of the many interactive demonstrations accompanying the text in this book.

Using the Crystal Software Synthesizer

At the end of every chapter, you will find a Your Turn section that guides you through putting the chapter's topics into practice on an actual synthesizer. For the sake of uniformity for all readers, these activities are done with the Crystal Software Synthesizer, available free for both Macintosh and Windows computers from Green Oak Software. Downloads of Crystal for both platforms, as well as installation instructions, are available from the Green Oak downloads page (http://www.greenoak.com/crystal/dwnld.html). Links to Crystal as well as all the associated files and applications you will need for this text may be found on the Introduction page of the *Refining Sound* companion website.

Running Crystal with the Crystal Player

Although Crystal may be used from within any audio/MIDI application that supports either VST or AU virtual instrument plugins (see below), the Crystal Player, available from the *Refining Sound* companion website, is probably the simplest way to work with this software synthesizer. To use the Crystal Player, follow the steps below. These steps, and all download links, are also available on the companion website.

Please note that these instructions are specifically for installing Crystal with the Crystal Player. If you wish to use Crystal with a different VST or AU host application, please consult the instructions that came with your software for installing plugin instruments.

Windows Computers

1. Download and unzip Crystal for Windows from http://www.greenoak.com/crystal/dwnld.html.
2. Download and unzip the Crystal Player and the Crystal Support Files from http://www.oup.com/us/refiningsound/Introduction.html.
3. Copy Crystall.dll and both the CrystalPatchBanks and CrystalSoundFonts folders into your C:\Program Files\Cycling '74\Max Runtime directory.
4. Copy the CrystalPlayer.mxf file to a convenient location on your computer. You may want to create a folder on your desktop called "Refining Sound" for all downloads associated with this book. (*Note*: in order for Crystal and the Crystal Player to work correctly, *it is important to complete all of the previous steps before continuing.*)
5. Launch the CrystalPlayer.mxf and position both the keyboard and Crystal windows so that you can see both. (*Note*: the Crystal Player should automatically load the Crystal software synthesizer if you have followed the instructions above. If it does not, you can manually force the player to load Crystal by clicking the Find Crystal button in the keyboard window of the Crystal Player. Search for, and select, Crystal.dll.)
6. If you have already configured your audio and MIDI for Max Runtime with the Audio/MIDI Configuration utility (above), then you should now be ready to use Crystal.
7. Select whether you will use the on-screen keyboard or your external MIDI keyboard from the dropdown menu at the top of the Crystal Player Keyboard window.
8. Turn the Audio On by clicking the Speaker button and adjust the Output Level to a comfortable listening level as you play some notes on the keyboard.
9. You may also wish to download the Crystal User Manual to a convenient location on your computer, from http://www.greenoak.com/crystal/Crystal 24UG.pdf.

Macintosh Computers

1. Download and run the installer for Crystal for Mac OSX from http://www .greenoak.com/crystal/dwnld.html,

2. Download and unzip the Crystal Player and the Crystal Support Files from http://www.oup.com/us/refiningsound/Introduction.html.

3. Copy the CrystalPlayer.mxf file to a convenient location on your computer. You may want to create a folder on your desktop called "Refining Sound" for all downloads associated with this book.

4. Copy both the CrystalPatchBanks and CrystalSoundFonts folders into <system disk>/Users/<your user name>/Library/Application Support/Crystal. (*Note*: if the "Crystal" folder does not exist inside Application Support, create it and then put the two folders inside. Some recent versions of Mac OSX hide the <your user name>/Library directory. If you cannot locate this folder using the path above, hold down the Option key while clicking the "Go" menu and you should see a new option in the menu called **Library**. Select this option and the computer will take you directly to your Library folder. In order for Crystal and the Crystal Player to work correctly, *it is important to complete all of the previous steps before continuing*.)

5. Launch the CrystalPlayer.mxf and position the keyboard and Crystal windows so that you can see both. (*Note*: the Crystal Player should automatically load the Crystal software synthesizer if you have followed the instructions above. If it does not, you can manually force the player to load Crystal by clicking the Find Crystal button in the keyboard window of the Crystal Player. Search for, and select, Crystal.vst. The installer places both VST and AU versions on your computer. However, the Crystal Player is designed to work with the VST version of Crystal, so be sure to select that one.)

6. If you have already configured your audio and MIDI for Max Runtime with the Audio/MIDI Configuration utility (above), then you should now be ready to use Crystal.

7. Select whether you will use the on-screen keyboard or your external MIDI keyboard from the dropdown menu at the top of the Crystal Player Keyboard window.

8. Turn the Audio On by clicking the Speaker button, and adjust the Output Level to a comfortable listening level as you play some notes on the keyboard.

9. You may also wish to download the Crystal User Manual to a convenient location on your computer, from http://www.greenoak.com/crystal/Crystal 24UG.pdf.

Figure 0.5

The Crystal Player provides a simple VST host and interface to the Crystal software synthesizer. Once opened, you can control Crystal either from an external MIDI hardware controller or with the on-screen controller. (Crystal and the Crystal logo © copyright 2010 Glenn Olander, used throughout this book with permission)

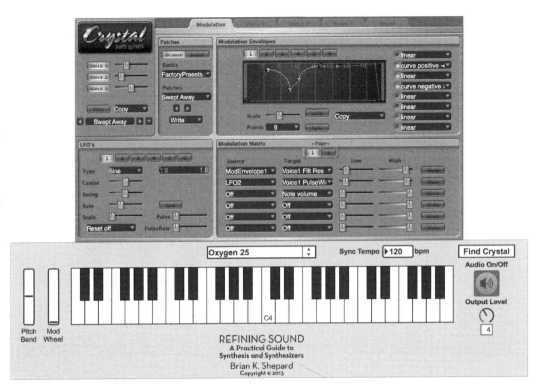

Practicing Safe Synthesis (Can You Hear Me Now?)

The National Institutes of Health in the United States estimate that nearly 15 percent of Americans between the age of twenty and sixty-nine (that's nearly twenty-six million people!) have high-frequency hearing loss as a result of exposure to loud sounds or noise.[1] Most researchers expect those numbers to rise in the coming years as a result of the use of earbud headphones with portable music players. Exposure to loud sounds, especially for long periods of time, will damage your hearing. As a musician, your ability to hear accurately is one of your most important assets.

Synthesizers have the potential for creating extremely loud sounds that can damage your hearing. Please be careful when playing these instruments and always follow the steps below, especially when using headphones.

- Before making any sound with a synthesizer, turn the volume all the way down.
- Start playing the instrument and *then* slowly turn the volume up to a comfortable level.
- Always turn the volume down before making any configuration or cabling changes, as these often produce loud pops and clicks.
- Give your ears a break. For every hour of listening, give yourself ten to fifteen minutes away from the sound. Not only will you avoid "ear fatigue," but even at moderate volume levels, long exposure to sound can cause hearing damage.

In the spirit of these steps, all of the interactive demonstrations in this text launch with audio processing turned off, and the audio level set at 0. Once you open a demonstration,

---

1 "Noise-Induced Hearing Loss," http://www.nidcd.nih.gov/health/hearing/pages/noise.aspx (accessed July 21, 2012).

click the speaker icon to turn audio processing on and *then* slowly raise the output level to a comfortable listening level.

Our hearing declines naturally with age. Don't accelerate the process! For more information on how you can prevent hearing loss, see the National Institutes of Health's Noise-Induced Hearing Loss website at https://www.nidcd .nih.gov/health/hearing/pages/ noise.aspx.

Audio On/Off

Output Level

Figure 0.6

Before using any of the interactive demonstrations, turn audio processing on by clicking the speaker button, and *then* slowly raise the output level to a comfortable listening level.

Refining Sound

1

Synthesis and Synthesizers

Digging Beneath the Surface *of Your Synthesizer*

Online materials for this chapter:

http://www.oup.com/us/refiningsound/Chapter1.html

syn·the·sis |ˈsinθəsis| noun: the combining of the constituent elements of separate material or abstract entities into a single or unified entity.

Derivatives: *syn·the·size* |ˈsynθəˌsīz| verb; *syn·the·siz·er* |ˈsynθəˌsīzər| noun

Quick: what's the first thing that comes to mind when you hear the word *synthesis*? As a reader of this book, it is probably safe to say you imagined the process of creating sound. However, for many people, the concept of making sound is not what comes to mind. Instead, the word might bring back memories of chemical reactions such as *photo*synthesis, or the philosophical resolution of two conflicting ideas (following thesis and antithesis), or some other logical, mathematical, or grammatical process. Regardless of the particular recalled memory, most people think of the word *synthesis* from the more abstract perspective of combining ideas or materials, and not from the viewpoint of creating sound. In fact, most dictionaries do not even include sound creation as one of the alternate definitions for the word.

Now, what comes to mind with the word *synthesizer*? My guess is that for nearly every reader of this book—and probably for most nonreaders as well—the term *synthesizer* creates a mental image of some type of electronic musical instrument—most likely one with a piano-style keyboard. Thus, even though nearly all of us think of a *synthesizer* in a musical sense, only a few of us think about music and sound creation when we hear the word *synthesis*.

Figure 1.1

To many people, the word *synthesizer* brings to mind some sort of electronic keyboard instrument like the Roland GAIA SH-01. (photo printed with permission of Roland Corp.)

Why, then, is there such a disconnect in our use and understanding of the two terms? If synthesis is about combining elements together, and a synthesizer is a device that *does* synthesis, then the process of creating sound with a synthesizer must, somehow, be about the combining of separate electronic and sonic elements into a single or unified entity, i.e., the finished, synthesized sound.

Perhaps this disconnect is due to our lack of understanding about how a synthesizer synthesizes. People often think of these instruments as magical "black boxes." They press a key, turn a knob, move a slider, and a cool sound comes out, but they have no idea how the sound is made. Ask many synthesizer users how they create their sounds, and you will frequently hear something like, "I don't really understand how it all works, I just tweak things until it sounds right." Unfortunately, many of the newer, more powerful instruments make things even more difficult to understand, as the multiple layers of the synthesis process are often difficult to navigate and shrouded in complexity.

TIP ### Synthesizer or Sampler: What's in a Name?

Many users of electronic instruments lump the synthesizer and the sampler into the same category. And why not? They often look alike, and both are electronic instruments that play sounds when you trigger them. In reality, though, they are two different animals. A synthesizer generates (synthesizes) raw sound waves that are then manipulated through the rest of the synthesis process. A sampler records (samples) other sounds and plays them back when triggered. Although some synthesizers use prerecorded waveforms, or samples, as a sound source, those waves are still treated as raw material to be further developed in the rest of the synthesis process. Many samplers also have the ability to process their samples with synthesizer-like tools. However, the end result is often meant to still be recognizable as the original sound. As these instruments continue to evolve, the boundaries between synthesizer and sampler become more and more blurred. For the purposes of this text, we will focus on the synthesis process, and not the recording and editing of samples.

TIP *continued*

It is the goal of this text, then, to dig beneath the surface of the synthesizer and peel back all of those mysterious layers. In doing so, we will not only reveal the constituent elements of the sound-making process, we will explore them in depth. And, as we journey through the different layers, we will examine the many ways those elements combine and interact to create the refined, unified sound that exits the instrument in all its sonic glory.

Before we begin our journey, it will be helpful to have a little familiarity with sound and audio, the history and development of synthesizers, as well as a bit of understanding of the design and operational differences in hardware vs. software and analog vs. digital synthesizers. No single chapter can begin to do justice to these topics, but a brief overview will help set the stage for our journey through the synthesis process and the refining of the individual elements into the final, polished product.[1]

Sound and Audio

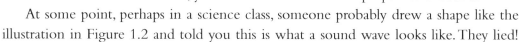

Demo 1.1

The word *sound* refers to the natural acoustic phenomenon of vibrations moving—usually through air—to our ears. *Audio*, by contrast, refers to the capture, storage, and reproduction of sound through electronic means. In general, audio equipment represents the changing air pressure of sound with a changing electrical voltage inside the components. Since this is a book about making sound with an audio device (a synthesizer), a brief review of sound and audio properties will be helpful. After all, before you can truly understand how to create a sound, you need to understand the properties of sound.

At some point, perhaps in a science class, someone probably drew a shape like the illustration in Figure 1.2 and told you this is what a sound wave looks like. They lied! First off, you cannot see a sound wave; but even if you could, it would not look like the up-and-down undulations that you see on the surface of a body of water.

If you could actually see a sound wave, it would look more like what happens when you blow up a large beach ball. Imagine that you blow

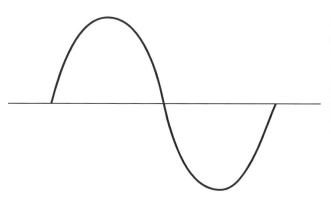

Figure 1.2
A two-dimensional representation of a sinusoidal (sine) wave is often used to represent the three-dimensional motion of a sound wave.

---

1 Any one of these topics could be the subject of an entire book by itself. In fact, most are already the subject of multiple books, along with numerous articles, both online and in print. Rather than repeat what others have so eloquently written, I encourage readers unfamiliar with these subjects to investigate and review these areas on their own. Many of the available resources are listed, along with annotations, in the online supplement to this text. This brief overview is intended as a review for those who are already familiar with these topics and will focus primarily on areas that lay the foundation for understanding synthesis and synthesizer operation.

6

into the beach ball and it expands outward in a spherical shape. However, when you take your mouth off the nozzle to take another breath, the ball slightly deflates. As you blow the next breath into it, the ball expands further, and then slightly deflates again as you take the next breath, and so on, until the ball is completely inflated. In a similar manner, sound radiates away from the sound source in a sphere, moving outward and then recoiling inward, then outward, and inward, and so on.

Figure 1.3

If you could actually see a sound wave, it would look much like a beach ball being blown up as it alternately expands and contracts with each breath.

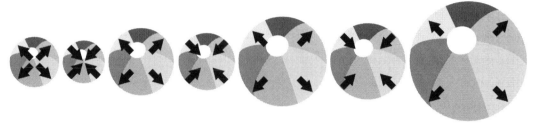

The sine wave drawing in Figure 1.2, then, is an illustration of that outward-inward movement shown in Figure 1.3. Think of the upward curve of the sine wave as when you are blowing into the beach ball, and the downward curve as when you are taking a breath and the ball contracts. In reality, sounds in the physical world are much more complex than the simple shape indicated by the sine wave, but the illustration provides a good reference for describing the elements of a sound wave.

Figure 1.4

Sound wave basics: the wave period consists of the complete cycle of the compression and rarefaction phases. The wave's amplitude is the amount of change in air pressure, either high or low, away from ambient pressure.

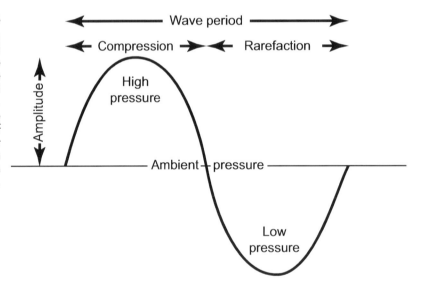

Every sound wave consists of two parts, or phases: compression (when the air pressure is greater than ambient air pressure) and rarefaction (when air pressure is less than ambient air pressure). A complete cycle, or wave period, consists of both compression and rarefaction phases. The amount of change in pressure—an increase or decrease from ambient air pressure—is the sound wave's amplitude. In general, the larger the amplitude, the louder the sound.

Demo 1.2

Figure 1.5

Large changes in pressure equal high amplitude, and small changes, low amplitude.

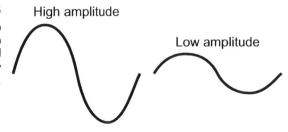

For both physical and psychoacoustic reasons, humans tend to hear certain frequency ranges as louder than other frequency ranges, even if they have the same amplitude. If we are hearing two simultaneous frequencies—one to which our hearing is sensitive and another to which it is not—it is possible that the frequency to which we are sensitive will sound louder even if it has a lower amplitude. So, while amplitude can be measured with a precise value, often in *decibels*; loudness tends to be much more subjective.

Demo 1.3

TIP The Decibel

When we describe amplitude in sound and audio, the standard unit of measurement is the decibel (abbreviated dB), a logarithmic measurement of the power ratio between two energy sources—in our case, sound waves. Named in honor of Alexander Graham Bell (1847–1922), the decibel is equal to one-tenth (deci-) of a *bel*, a rarely used unit that increases by a factor of ten for every unit of measurement. For example, a force measured at 2 bels has ten times the power of a force at 1 bel, 3 bels has ten times the power of 2 bels (a hundred times the power of 1 bel), and 4 bels has ten times the power of 3 bels (a thousand times the power of 1 bel), etc. (By the way, the bel is the unit used in the "Richter Magnitude Scale" to measure the intensity of shaking in earthquakes.) Since the decibel is one-tenth of a bel, it increases by a factor of ten for every *ten* units of measurement (i.e., 20 dB is ten times the power of 10 dB, 30 dB is ten times the power of 20 dB, 40 dB is ten times the power of 30 dB, etc.).

The other thing to remember about decibels is that the measurement is *always* a comparison between two values. In other words, there is no fixed scale that has a value of, say, 50 dB. The value 50 dB is always a comparison, as in "50 dB greater" or less than some other level. Using 50 dB by itself would be like a cashier in a store telling you that the price of an item is $50 more. More than what? Do you mean $50 more than free, or that much more than it was last week, or more than some other item, or more than what you have in your billfold? Without a reference level to compare, the term *decibel* is ambiguous, if not meaningless.

Unfortunately, there are several forms of the decibel (each with its own meaning, reference level, and identifying suffix), and this can lead to a bit of confusion, especially since many people are not so precise with the term and often just say "decibel," or simply "dee bee," without adding the appropriate suffix. Here, then, are brief descriptions of the types of decibels frequently encountered when discussing sound and audio.

- *dBm* (decibels in milliwatts) is referenced to 1 milliwatt. The dBm unit is typically used when describing a signal's power or flow through a circuit.
- *dBu* (decibels in volts) is referenced to $\sqrt{0.6}$ volts. The dBu was originally dBv, but the *v* was changed to *u* for "unloaded" in order to avoid confusion with another type of decibel, dBV (below). This unit is often found on mixer faders and other volume knobs. These controls typically have a reference level of 0 dB (often labeled *unity*, or simply *U*) that indicates the incoming signal is being neither boosted

TIP *continued*

nor attenuated, but passed through with no change in strength. Values above 0 dB are indicated as positive (+3 dB, +7 dB, etc.), while those below 0 have negative values. Since decibels use a logarithmic scale, there is no theoretical limit to how far a control can be turned up or down. Most amplifiers begin to distort the signal rather severely if boosted more than a few dB above unity, but you could theoretically keep turning the signal down forever. For obvious reasons, faders can move only so far. Thus many devices have an infinity sign (∞) at the bottom of their travel indicating that the signal has been attenuated so far that, for all practical purposes, it is nonexistent, or silent.

- *dBV* (decibels in volts) is referenced to 1 volt. The dBV is often used, along with dBu, to describe the line level voltage of audio signals. A level of −10 dBV is commonly used for "consumer" audio equipment, while +4 dBu is used for "professional" equipment.

- *dB SPL* (decibels in sound pressure level) is referenced to the so-called *threshold of hearing*. Technically, this reference value of 0 dB is 20 µPa (micropascals) and is frequently described as the quietest sound an "average" person with "good hearing" is capable of detecting. The dB SPL is used to describe how loud a sound is in the acoustic world. Providing a further distinction, dB SPL values are frequently indicated with "A," "B," or "C," to indicating a particular weighting scale that more accurately reflects the asymmetrical nature of human hearing.

- *dBFS* (decibels full scale) is referenced to the maximum allowable amplitude in digital audio, the point at which clipping occurs. The dBFS is used to describe the amplitude of a digital audio signal. Because 0 dBFS represents the point of clipping, dBFS values will almost always be below zero and negative.

To complicate matters even more, depending on the type of force being measured, there are two formulae used when calculating decibels.

- *Power quantities* (dBm) are the "original" decibels and are used to measure the intensity of a force, or the amount of power flowing through a circuit.

$$dBm = 10log_{10}\left(\frac{P_1}{P_0}\right)$$

- *Field quantities* (dBu, dBV, dB SPL, dBFS) are the actual manifestations of the force's power. Since power quantities are directly proportional to the square of field quantities, we have to square the ratio of the measurements in the field quantity formula.

$$dBu = 10log_{10}\left(\frac{V_1^2}{V_0^2}\right)$$

Thanks to the power property of logarithms, we can take a formula like $log(a^2)$ and simplify it to $2log(a)$. Thus the formula

> **TIP** *continued*
>
> $$dBu = 10log_{10}\left(\frac{V_1^2}{V_0^2}\right)$$
>
> is usually simplified to
>
> $$dBu = 20log_{10}\left(\frac{V_1}{V_0}\right)$$
>
> Because the dBu formula multiplies by twenty rather than by ten, as in the dBm formula, the dBu scale moves twice as quickly as the dBm scale. In other words, a doubling of a signal's voltage is a change of +6 dBu, while a doubling of a signal's power is a change of +3 dBm.
>
> The good news is that unless you decide to go into acoustics or electrical engineering, you will most likely never have to calculate decibels. The bad news is that because some audio engineers refer to power when using decibels and others refer to markings on the audio mixer's fader, there can be some confusion. If someone asks you to "turn it up 3 dB" (no suffix) you have to ask yourself whether they mean to turn the signal power up 100 percent (+3dBm), or to increase the fader level by 3 dBu (a 41 percent increase in voltage).

The number of times the sound wave completes a cycle (both compression and rarefaction phases) in a second determines the sound's frequency. In musical terms, a higher frequency produces a higher pitch. Much like with amplitude and loudness, though, frequency is a precise measurement while pitch is a subjective valuation. If you are a musician, you may be familiar with the term "A-440." This designation refers to a specific tuning level where the pitch A4 (A above middle C) is tuned to a frequency of 440 cycles per second. However, musicians commonly use other tunings as well, both higher and lower. Thus even though a wave frequency of 440 cycles per second is a precise value, the pitch A is rather subjective. With synthesizers, we will be working with both frequency *and* pitch, so it will be helpful to remember the distinction between the two terms.

When we describe the frequency of a sound, we use the unit Hertz (Hz) to measure the number of cycles the wave completes per second.[2] Therefore a sound wave that completes 100 cycles in a second has a frequency of 100 Hz. When frequencies rise into the thousands of cycles per second, we commonly use the kilo (k) prefix (i.e., 10,000 Hz = 10 kHz).[3]

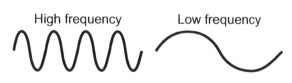

High frequency   Low frequency

Figure 1.6

More cycles per second equal high frequency (left), and fewer cycles equal low frequency (right). Note that both waves have the same amplitude, though.

2 The Hertz unit is named for the German physicist Heinrich Hertz (1857–1894) and is almost always abbreviated as Hz. Because the abbreviation is based on his name, the H is always capitalized.

3 Note that it is a lowercase k for 1,000. An uppercase K is used for the binary value of 1,024 commonly found in computer file sizes such as Kilobits (Kb) and Kilobytes (KB). When kilo is used with Hertz, it is abbreviated kHz (lowercase k, uppercase H, lowercase z).

Now that we have reviewed basic elements of sound and audio, there is a concept that is often difficult to comprehend but vitally important to our understanding of sound and the synthesis process. *Neither our ears nor our audio equipment captures a sound's frequency. They capture a sound's changes in amplitude.* Our brain interprets those changes in amplitude (large changes = loud, small changes = quiet, frequent changes = high frequency, infrequent changes = low frequency), but it is amplitude change to which we physically respond and that we capture with audio equipment. It is extremely important to remember, then, that when we discuss the way sound waves behave in the coming chapters, we will be talking about how their amplitude values add to, subtract from, and interact with each other.

A Brief (and Highly Subjective) History of Synthesizers

You might think of synthesizers as being a fairly new entry into the sound-making arena, but the use of electricity to create sound actually dates back to the eighteenth century, when scientists were first beginning to understand how to harness its power. A Czech theologian, Václav Prokop Diviš (1698–1765), is credited with creating the first electric musical instrument, the *Denis d'or* (*golden Dionysus*) in the 1740s.[4] This instrument, like nearly all that followed for the next 150 years, did not use electricity to directly create sound, but to manipulate the mechanical devices that physically made the sound. The first known account of using electricity to directly create musical sounds is with an instrument known as the Singing Arc, invented by the British physicist and engineer William Du Bois Duddell (1872–1917) in 1899.[5] Duddell was attempting to reduce the noise created by the carbon arc lamps frequently used as streetlights at the time, and found he could control and change the audible frequency of their electric arc by adjusting the current flow through the carbon electrodes. In a demonstration to fellow engineers in 1900, he connected a piano-style keyboard to his control mechanism and played "God Save the Queen" in what is thought to be the first public musical performance with an instrument creating its sound entirely with electricity.

Telharmonium

The dawn of the twentieth century brought numerous advances in the use of electricity, and with it a number of musical developments. Perhaps the finest example, and certainly the largest, from this era was the Telharmonium of Thaddeus Cahill (1867–1934). Although Cahill received a patent for it in 1897, the first working model did not appear until 1906.

The Telharmonium was a massive (the final version weighed almost 200 tons!) instrument using huge rotating tone wheels called dynamos to create musical sounds. The instrument was played with a traditional organ-style keyboard and pedal board and had a range of more than seven octaves, as well as the ability to change timbre through com-

---

4 Hugh Davies. "Denis d'or". *Grove Music Online.* http://www.oxfordmusiconline.com/subscriber/article/grove/music/47638 (accessed December 7, 2012).

5 Hong, Sungook Hong. *Wireless: From Marconi's Black-Box to the Audion.* Cambridge, MA: MIT Press, 2001, pp. 164.

binations of dynamo outputs.[6] Unfortunately, no recordings of the Telharmonium exist, yet listeners at the time describe the instrument as having a sound that was very clear and pure. Because it could add harmonics to sounds, it was also noted for its ability to reproduce the sounds of common orchestral instruments such as the flute, bassoon, clarinet, and cello.

Figure 1.7
(from left to right) Thaddeus Cahill, inventor of the Telharmonium; two musicians operating the Telharmonium's keyboard; the large dynamo room beneath the keyboard; one of the massive rotating dynamos, capable of producing a single note plus seven harmonics. (*McClure's Magazine*, July 1906)

Cahill imagined his instrument as an early form of Muzak, whereby subscribers could receive music through their telephone lines via large paper cones connected to the telephone handset (a forerunner of the modern paper cone loudspeaker). The amplifier had not yet been invented, so the only way to transmit these signals at such a great distance was to generate them with an incredibly powerful current. This had the unfortunate byproduct of creating "crosstalk," which overpowered normal telephone conversations, and the public quickly grew tired of hearing music on their telephones rather than the person they were calling.

In spite of its all-too-short career—it was last heard in 1918—the Telharmonium was a revolutionary instrument in numerous regards and can rightfully be considered the first modern synthesizer. Through its massive tone wheels or dynamos, it could create complex timbres by combining multiple harmonics in a process we now call additive synthesis. In fact, after the invention of the vacuum tube amplifier, Laurens Hammond used this same tone wheel system in 1934, only on a *much* smaller scale, for his famous Hammond Electric Organ. The Telharmonium was both polyphonic and "touch sensitive," features that would not appear again on synthesizers until the 1980s. And, in perhaps its most revolutionary aspect, the Telharmonium foreshadowed the distribution of musical performances through a network.

As revolutionary as the Telharmonium was, though, the main drawback was its massive size and power requirements, which were due to the two primary limitations of electrical sound creation at the time. First, in order to create multiple pitches, the instrument needed a large number of dynamos spinning at different speeds to generate alternating currents at specific frequencies. Second, because there was no method for amplification, the current had to be generated on a large enough scale to transmit the sound long distances through telephone lines. Little did Cahill know that, by the time the last version of the Telharmonium was dismantled, the beginnings of a solution to both problems had already been discovered in an odd-looking light bulb.

---

6 Weidenaar, Reynold. *Magic Music from the Telharmonium*. Lanham, MD: Scarecrow Press, 1995.

The Vacuum Tube Amplifier

Although first reported by the British scientist Frederick Guthrie (1833–1886) in 1873, Thomas Edison (1847–1931) "discovered" the thermionic effect—where certain metals, when heated in a vacuum tube, emit electrons—in 1880, while working to improve the design of the incandescent light bulb. Although he did not understand the significance of his find at the time, he nonetheless applied for a patent on the effect in 1884. However, it fell to later engineers to realize the potential of the "Edison effect" in vacuum tubes for controlling electricity.

The initial vacuum tubes looked much like the light bulbs of the day. Inside the glass tube, they had a negative-charged filament called the *cathode* that, when heated, released electrons into the vacuum, where they were captured by a positive-charged metal plate known as the *anode*. Since electrons would only flow in one direction (negative to positive), these early two-element tubes, known as diodes, were typically used to convert alternating current into direct current.

In 1907, the American inventor Lee de Forest (1873–1961) discovered that changing the voltage applied to a small metal *grid* placed between the anode and cathode allowed him to control the flow of electrons between the two original elements. With this new three-element vacuum tube, known as a triode, he discovered that raising or lowering the grid's voltage by a small amount produced a disproportionately large change in the flow of electrons to the anode. Thus, a small, fluctuating voltage could cause a large fluctuation in the flow of electrons, thereby producing an amplification of the grid's original signal.

Figure 1.8
When the cathode is heated in a triode, it releases electrons into the vacuum of the glass tube. Applying a small positive charge to the grid causes a large flow of electrons to the anode, producing a strong current from the anode's terminal (left). A negative charge on the grid disrupts the flow of electrons to the anode (center). A small, oscillating signal applied to the grid causes the electron flow to oscillate as well, but on a much larger scale (amplification) than the original grid signal (right).

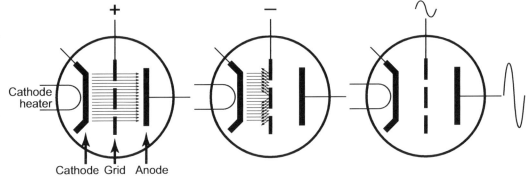

Cathode heater

Cathode Grid Anode

Numerous refinements of the triode occurred over the years to improve its efficiency and lifespan. However, the basic concept of signal amplification through superimposing the voltage fluctuations of a weak signal onto a much stronger signal remained the same and spawned the rapid growth of the electronics age in the twentieth century.

In addition to the ability to produce amplification, it was also discovered that sending a tube's output back to its input created a feedback loop that produced a high-frequency sine wave, much like what occurs when holding a microphone directly in front of a loudspeaker in a public address system. By first passing the amplifier's output signal through a few basic electrical components—typically, a resistor and a capacitor—before sending it back into the tube, one could control and adjust the frequency of that sine wave. Vacuum tubes thereby not only created the amplification needed in a circuit but also formed the very core of the synthesis process itself as the original sound-making elements known as oscillators.

By the middle of the twentieth century, solid-state devices such as transistors, and eventually integrated circuits (ICs), began replacing the venerable vacuum tube. These new components exhibit many of the same characteristics as tubes, but they have a number of advantages. Transistors and ICs are considerably smaller and less fragile than glass vacuum tubes, and they do not generate heat as tubes do. However, vacuum tubes have some unique characteristics in their behavior that continue to make them popular for a variety of amplification uses, and you still often find them glowing inside a number of electronic devices today.

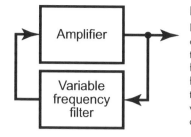

Figure 1.9
By passing the output of a tube amplifier through an adjustable frequency filter and feeding the signal back to the tube's input, a variable-frequency oscillator is created.

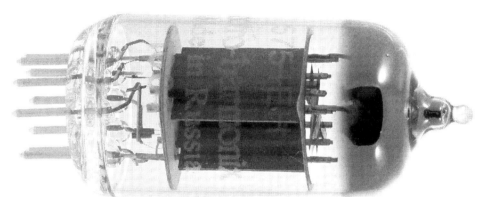

Figure 1.10
Modern vacuum tubes such as the Electro-Harmonix 5751 Gold Pin Preamp are still used in a number of electronic devices. (photo courtesy of Electro-Harmonix, used with permission)

When you consider that nearly every aspect of sound production on a synthesizer is either controlling and amplifying a signal or creating an electrical oscillation, you quickly realize how important vacuum tubes (and their solid-state cousins) are to the history and development of the electronic synthesizer. Following the commercialization of vacuum tubes, synthesizers in all shapes, sizes, and designs began to spring up around the world. Although it is well beyond the scope of this chapter to examine the many synthesizer models of the twentieth century, a few made such a significant impact on our perception and use of these new instruments that a quick overview of them will help position the modern synthesizer in its historical window.

Theremin

Perhaps no electronic synthesizer from the early twentieth century had a greater impact than, and inspired so many other instruments as, that invented by the Russian engineer Lev Sergeyevich Termen, or, as he was known in the United States and Western Europe, Léon Theremin (1896–1993). Although he initially called his 1920 invention an "etherphone," he changed the name to Theremin when he patented the instrument in the United States in 1928.

Theremin was working on a motion detector and proximity alarm for the Soviet government when he noticed that a person's distance from the device's sensor caused the frequency of the alarm sound to rise and fall. By gently moving his hand in relation to the sensor antenna, he could produce different notes; being an amateur cellist, he began trying to play some of his favorite cello repertoire. Initially, the loudness of the instrument was controlled with a foot pedal, but Theremin decided to make that aspect controllable with a proximity antenna as well. Thus, the "classic" Theremin design of a wooden box with a vertical antenna on its right side and a horizontal-loop antenna extending from its left side was born.

The Theremin remains unique among instruments in that the performer does not usually touch the instrument. As the player's right hand moves closer to the vertical antenna the pitch of the instrument rises. The left hand hovers above the horizontal-loop antenna to control the volume. Moving the left hand closer to the loop lowers the volume (silencing the instrument if it touches the antenna), and moving away raises the volume. With

Figure 1.11
A young Léon Theremin (ca. 1928) performing on the instrument that came to bear his name. Moving the right hand closer to the vertical antenna causes the Theremin pitch to rise, while moving the left hand closer to the horizontal loop antenna causes the volume to drop.

a great deal of practice, a musician can perform with wonderful expressiveness and lyric sensitivity. A number of Theremin virtuosi have recorded and toured extensively with this instrument, including two of Theremin's own protégées: Clara Rockmore and his grand-niece Lydia Kavina.

Although the original commercial model of the Theremin, produced by the RCA Company, was not a huge success, the instrument's sound has continued to fascinate performers and audiences alike. In recent years, several companies (most notably Moog Music) have produced Theremin instruments, as well as assembly kits for home hobbyists, spurring a resurgence of interest

in this wonderful instrument. Today, more than ninety years after its invention, the Theremin still makes occasional appearances on stage and in recordings and film soundtracks.

Ondes Martenot

At about the same time Theremin was patenting his instrument in the United States, the French musician and inventor Maurice Martenot (1898–1980) was developing an instrument capable of producing many of the same types of sounds as the Theremin, but with the aid of a piano-style keyboard. The ondes Martenot (Martenot waves), like nearly all synthesizers at the time, was monophonic, capable of playing only one note at a time. As with the Theremin, pitch was controlled with the right hand and volume with the left, although the processes for both were completely different. In the years after its invention in 1928, the ondes Martenot underwent a number of important refinements in both sound-making capabilities and ability to respond to player expressiveness, before ceasing production in 1988.

In addition to playing on the keyboard (*au clavier*) for fixed-pitch intervals, the performer wore a metal ring on the right hand that could slide along a metal ribbon (*au ruban*) positioned at the front edge of the keyboard to produce continuous glissandi between notes. The ring's position on the ribbon produced the pitch of the corresponding adjacent key, but with the ability to slide between notes. Pressing a key, or placing the ring on the ribbon, produced no sound, though, until a large volume button (*touche d'intensité*) located in the control drawer (*tiroir*) was pressed with the left hand. The depth to which the button was pressed increased the volume level from soft to loud.

Several other refinements to the instrument further heightened its expressiveness. While playing a note on the keyboard, the player could wiggle the key slightly left and right to produce a vibrato effect. Later versions of the ondes Martenot introduced a set of four different loudspeakers (*diffuseurs*) that changed the timbre of the instrument. From the same drawer that contained the volume button, the player could select the *Principal* (a standard loudspeaker), the *Résonance* (a loudspeaker with metal springs attached to produce a reverberation effect), the *Métallique* (a loudspeaker that used a small metal gong as its diaphragm to produce a rich set of harmonics), or the *Palme* (a lyre-shaped loudspeaker with guitarlike strings stretched across the face to produce resonance).

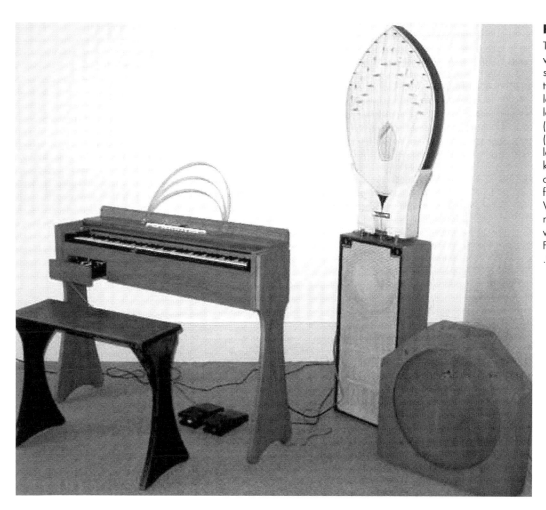

Figure 1.12
The ondes Martenot with three of its speaker (*diffuseur*) types: *Palme* (top left), *Principal* (bottom left), and *Métallique* (right). The drawer (*tiroir*) is open at the left end of the keyboard. (photo courtesy of unidentified Wikipedia user, Wikimedia Commons: http://en.wikipedia.org/wiki/File:Ondes_martenot.jpg)

Although the ondes Martenot ceased production more than twenty years ago, many of the original instruments still exist, and a few companies produce modern replicas. As with the Theremin, ondes Martenot are occasionally used in performances, recordings, and movie soundtracks.

Moog Synthesizer

No history of the synthesizer—even one as brief and subjective as this—would be complete without discussing the numerous contributions of Robert "Bob" Moog (1934–2005). There is no *one* Moog (pronounced *mohg*) synthesizer but more than twenty models that revolutionized synthesis in the second half of the twentieth century.

Bob Moog's interest in electronic synthesizers began at an early age. While still in his teens, he began manufacturing and selling vacuum tube Theremin kits for hobbyists and enthusiasts to build. He went on to receive multiple degrees in electrical engineering and physics, including a Ph.D. from Cornell.

With the development of the transistor in the 1950s, Moog realized he could make synthesizers that were smaller, cheaper, and more sophisticated. He also began teaming up with some of the most prominent synthesizer designers of the time, including Herbert Deutsch (b. 1932) and Vladimir Ussachevsky (1911–1990), to develop a number of refinements and improvements to the synthesis process. Along the way, Moog had a hand in the development of voltage-controlled oscillators (VCOs), amplifiers (VCAs), filters (VCFs), envelope generators (ADSRs), step sequencers, and effects processors—all fundamental elements in the modern synthesis process.[7]

Moog also recognized that the synthesis process itself worked through a number of steps or stages, and he began to design instruments with separate sections, or modules, for these various stages. In the early versions of his modular synthesizers, the modules were connected with the same type of cables that telephone and radio engineers used to make temporary connections, or "patches," in their equipment. The connections and configurations of these "patch cords" created the various sounds on the synthesizer, and so the sound itself began to be known as a "patch." And even though synthesizers no longer use these cables, the term is still commonly used to describe an individual sound or preset on a synthesizer.

---

7 We will explore all of these synthesizer processes in the coming chapters.

Figure 1.13
Dr. Robert A. "Bob" Moog, surrounded by a number of his legendary creations, each configured for a "patch." (photo used with kind permission of Ileana Grams-Moog/Estate of Robert A. Moog)

In the 1960s, the sound of the synthesizer was still considered a novelty, and not taken seriously by most traditional musicians. However, the musician, composer, and engineer Wendy Carlos (b. 1939) became fascinated with the Moog synthesizer and began composing for, and performing with, the instrument in the 1960s. In 1968, she released *Switched-On Bach*, an album of works by J. S. Bach, performed entirely on the Moog synthesizer. The album won three Grammy Awards and eventually went platinum, becoming the highest-selling classical LP at the time. Not only was the album a huge success, it helped establish the electronic synthesizer as a legitimate musical instrument, introducing its sound to millions of new listeners.

Even though *Switched-On Bach* was a classical recording, it also had a profound influence on many of the popular and rock musicians of the time who were looking for new sound sources to explore. The sound of a Moog synthesizer, in all its many variants, became so ubiquitous to pop and rock music that you could find one (or several) in nearly every major stage or recording studio in the late twentieth century. Other companies such as Sequential Circuits, ARP, Buchla, and many more created great synthesizers at the same time, although arguably none have garnered the same cachet as those designed by Bob Moog and the company he founded, Moog Music.

RCA Mark II Sound Synthesizer

One of the biggest limitations of synthesizers—including those from Moog—through the middle of the twentieth century was the fact that they were all monophonic and monotimbral; they could play just one note with one sound at a time. The only way to get polyphony, or simultaneous sounds, was by recording overdubs onto multitrack audiotape, an incredibly difficult and time-consuming process.[8] Because vacuum tubes, which required a lot of physical space, were needed for nearly every stage of a synthesizer, manufacturers were faced with a dilemma: make their instrument small enough to move around, but with only single-voice capability, or give it the ability to play multiple notes and sounds, but at the cost of being both huge and hugely expensive. Even with solid-state instruments, most manufacturers took the first approach of keeping the electronics simple (monophonic and monotimbral) and relatively inexpensive.

In contrast, the RCA Mark II Sound Synthesizer took the latter approach. It was installed at the Columbia-Princeton Electronic Music Center in 1957 and featured a whopping four-note polyphony using as many as twelve oscillators! Because of the complexity of setting up and controlling the instrument, it also featured a binary sequencer that read data punched into a paper roll—similar to that used by player pianos—to send instructions to the synthesizer. In fact, one did not "play" the Mark II so much as one programmed it. Since the Mark II used vacuum tubes for all its processing, it required a large room with substantial air conditioning to prevent overheating. In an ironic twist, the first polyphonic and multitimbral synthesizer since Cahill's Telharmonium shared large space requirements similar to those of its early cousin.

Because of its size, cost, complexity, and limited availability, the Mark II Sound Synthesizer never became the commercial success for which RCA had hoped. The company, whose primary business was electronics contracts for the military (the Mark II had a decidedly "military" look to it), dropped out of the synthesizer manufacturing business soon thereafter. However, for a small group of composers and electronics engineers, it pioneered the idea of polyphonic, multitimbral synthesizers and the use of computer-based sequencers to control these instruments.

Figure 1.14
The RCA Mark II Synthesizer at the Columbia-Princeton Electronic Music Center in 1958. Pictured (left to right), three of the pioneers of computer-based electronic music: Milton Babbitt, Peter Mauzey, and Vladimir Ussachevsky. (photo courtesy of The Columbia University Computer Music Center)

8 This was exactly the technique used by Wendy Carlos to create *Switched-On Bach*.

Sequential Circuits Prophet-5

While RCA opted for the large-computer approach to controlling a synthesizer, Sequential Circuits, a California company founded by another legendary synthesizer designer, Dave Smith, went in the opposite direction and began producing a small, affordable analog synthesizer called the Prophet-5.[9] What made the Prophet-5 revolutionary was the fact that it incorporated a digital microprocessor allowing the user to quickly program, store, and recall presets (*patches*) on the instrument. In addition to its computerized operating system, the Prophet-5 had a five-voice polyphony and featured a complex sound-making structure capable of producing incredibly rich sounds. With its lush and exotic sounds, patch management system, small size, and affordable price, the Prophet-5 became one of the most successful early synthesizers, selling approximately eight thousand units during its production from 1978 to 1984. Its design and structure also became the model on which most later instruments were based.

Figure 1.15
The Sequential Circuits Prophet-5 synthesizer combined a five-voice analog synthesizer with a digital microprocessor, allowing the user to program, store, and recall presets. (photo courtesy of Dave Smith, www .davesmithinstruments .com, used with permission)

Digital Synthesizers

Whenever we are presented with some sort of historical timeline, there is a temptation for us to think that all of the events on the timeline occurred one after the other: first A happened, then B, then C, etc. In reality, historical events frequently overlap one another quite a bit, and such is the case with our brief synthesizer history.

All of the synthesizers mentioned thus far have been *analog* instruments that create and modify sounds via continuous electrical currents. Even as analog instruments continued to flourish, by the middle of the twentieth century, new types of so-called digital devices had already begun to emerge.[10] Initially, most synthesizer designers felt the technology to be too impractical and expensive for synthesis purposes, but by the latter decades of the twentieth century, the size and cost of digital components had dropped dramatically, leading to a number of digital synthesizer designs.

---

9 We will talk about Dave Smith again in Chapter 7 when we discuss the development of MIDI for controlling networked synthesizers.

10 More on the differences between analog and digital synthesizers follows below.

These early digital synthesizers of the 1970s and 1980s were essentially musical computers that used momentary states of either on or off (binary) voltages for their computational and sound making purposes. In fact, the first digital synthesizers, like the Synclavier by New England Digital and the CMI (Computer Musical Instrument) by Fairlight, looked much like an early computer, but with the addition of a piano-style keyboard.

Figure 1.16
Early digital synthesizers such as the Synclavier II (1981) from New England Digital looked more like computers, but with the addition of a piano-style keyboard. (photo courtesy of Cameron Jones, used with permission)

Digital synthesizers offered the distinct advantage that, since every sound value and setting on the synthesizer was an individual number, the data could be easily captured, recorded, and edited. Although the computational power of these instruments gave them an amazing sound-making power for the time, they were incredibly expensive. Depending on the model and its various options, the cost of these instruments could easily exceed $200,000, placing them well beyond the reach of most musicians.

Yamaha DX7

The first digital synthesizer to make it into the studios of everyone else, the Yamaha DX7, became one of the most commercially successful synthesizers of all time. At a price of around $2,000 (or about a hundredth of the cost of a professional Synclavier), Yamaha is estimated to have sold more than 150,000 DX7s during the instrument's production from 1983 to 1989.

This all-in-one instrument packaged the entirety of its processing power into the same case that held the sixty-one-note keyboard. Although the DX7 was monotimbral, it could play as many as sixteen simultaneous notes and featured *MIDI* (Musical Instrument Digital Interface), the networking protocol that allowed synthesizers to be connected to increase their timbral and polyphonic capabilities. The DX7 was also the first commercial synthesizer to use a revolutionary new sound-making process called *FM Synthesis*, which gave it an incredibly rich and sophisticated sound.[11]

11 We will explore both MIDI and FM Synthesis in great detail in the coming chapters.

Figure 1.17
The venerable Yamaha DX7 Digital Synthesizer featured a new process known as frequency modulation synthesis to create its amazingly rich sounds. (photo courtesy of Yamaha Corporation of America, used with permission)

Even though the DX7 was produced for only six years, it had a huge impact on the development of synthesizers and spawned an explosive growth in digital instrument design on the part of nearly all the prominent synthesizer manufacturers. More than two decades after production stopped, the DX7 remains a popular instrument for its sonic capabilities. It is frequently seen in online auctions, and multiple websites dedicated to this venerable instrument can be found with a quick Internet search.

Korg M1

Perhaps the only hardware synthesizer to achieve a wider reach than the DX7 was the Korg M1, the first commercially successful "music workstation." Korg sold more than a quarter of a million M1s during the six years (1988–1994) in which it was produced. The instrument was known as a workstation because, in addition to its sound-making capabilities, it offered rather impressive effects processing, and a built-in sequencer that allowed users to record, edit, and playback MIDI data from the instrument itself. Like the earlier DX7, the M1 could play sixteen simultaneous notes, but the M1 was also multi-timbral, capable of playing as many as eight simultaneous sounds.

Instead of using combinations of basic waveforms for its sound engine, the M1 used an approach first implemented by the Roland Corporation on their D-50 synthesizer that layered short, prerecorded samples of rich, complex sounds together as the raw sound material for the synthesizer. This process of using sampled sound waves, sometimes called wavetable synthesis, became one of the primary forms of synthesis in use today.

Figure 1.18
The Korg M1 music workstation was both polyphonic and multi-timbral. Using its on-board sequencer, performers and composers could do all their production work directly within the M1. (photo courtesy of Korg USA, used with permission)

Software Synthesizers

With the proliferation of the personal computer beginning in the 1980s, synthesizer designers recognized another huge opportunity for growth: software synthesizers. Since most computers already had more computational power than the typical hardware synthesizer, all that was needed was the ability to connect a keyboard, or some other controller, to the computer to be able to play the synthesizer. With the development of MIDI interfaces for computers, that easily became a reality, and the number of available software synthesizers grew exponentially.

Software synthesizers offer a number of advantages over their hardware counterparts. For example, software synthesizers (or softsynths, as they are often called) can usually be updated to a newer version with a simple Internet download. Although a few hardware synthesizers have the ability to be updated via a disc or memory card, most can be updated only with a hardware modification—if they can be updated at all.

In addition to taking advantage of the computer's large processing power, softsynths can also use the computer's file storage capabilities, allowing the user to create large libraries of sounds that can be instantly loaded into the synthesizer. The typical hardware synthesizer provides access to the instrument's data through a small LCD screen that is often cumbersome and difficult to read. Computers, with their large monitors and graphical user interfaces (GUIs), make it quite easy to access even the most complex of a synthesizer's capabilities.

Another major advantage of softsynths over their hardware counterparts is the fact that most of them now run as so-called plug-ins within other audio and MIDI programs known as digital audio workstations (DAWs). This allows the instrument's sound to be recorded and edited directly inside the DAW along with other softsynth, audio, and MIDI tracks.

Although software synthesizers offer a number of sound-making advantages, they also suffer from what many consider a critical disadvantage, their lack of physical and tactile controls. One of the joys of playing a synthesizer live is the ability to modify the sound of the instrument as you play it via the many knobs, wheels, and sliders found on most hardware instruments. With a softsynth, you usually modify the sound by clicking and dragging a mouse on various menus and other control functions on the computer screen, a task that is nearly impossible to perform while playing the instrument. To work around this problem, a number of manufacturers create hardware controllers that connect to the softsynth through a computer interface. These hardware, or "external," controllers usually give the user a variety of physical knobs and other such controls to tweak while playing. Unfortunately, most external controllers are not designed for a specific software synthesizer, requiring the user to assign, or *map*, all the knobs, wheels, and sliders on the hardware controller to the various functions within the software instrument.[12]

---

12 We will discuss hardware controllers and their connection methods in great detail in Chapter 7.

Figure 1.19
Native Instruments' Massive softsynth provides a huge array of sound creation and shaping tools and can run on its own as a stand-alone instrument or as a plug-in inside of most DAWs. Massive can also map the various knobs and other physical controls from an external hardware controller to the instrument's many functions via the Macro Control panel located at the bottom-right of the softsynth's window.

Since most recent hardware synthesizers are essentially music-specific computers, this makes it quite easy to emulate many of these instruments as softsynths, and a large industry has sprung up creating softsynth versions of all the popular hardware digital synthesizers. Recently, with only a twist of irony, companies such as Arturia have begun creating emulations of many of the old analog synthesizers such as the Moog, ARP, and Prophet models of the sixties, seventies, and eighties. By its nature, a digital instrument tends to be extremely precise and accurate in all of its computational and sound-making characteristics. Because most of those older instruments used vacuum tubes in their designs, these modern emulators attempt to put back many of the "imperfections" that gave those instruments their famous sound.

Today, even though nearly all synthesizer manufacturers are creating digital instruments, a few companies continue to de-

Figure 1.20
The Modular V softsynth by Arturia is an amazingly realistic recreation—complete with swinging patch cables—of the original Moog Modular hardware synthesizer, but with the addition of extensive file handling and storage capabilities. Compare this image to the photo of the hardware versions shown in Figure 1.13.

sign and build analog instruments. Many of these companies base their products on earlier instruments like the Moog synthesizers, but a few companies, among them Dave Smith Instruments (the same Dave Smith of Prophet-5 fame), continue to develop hardware synthesizers built with analog components.

Figure 1.21
The Mopho x4 from Dave Smith Instruments is a current production analog synthesizer with four-voice polyphony and microprocessor control for patch creation and storage. (photo courtesy of Dave Smith Instruments, www.dave smithinstruments.com, used with permission)

Since Thaddeus Cahill's work at the dawn of the twentieth century, there have been hundreds, if not thousands, of hardware and software synthesizers designed. This brief overview of synthesizer history is given not to be definitive but as a quick snapshot of some of the more important landmarks in synthesizer development. Many of the elements of synthesis that we will discuss in the remainder of this text may be traced to one of these important milestones.

For those interested in exploring this fascinating subject further, there are a number of both print and online resources exploring aspects of the history of synthesizers and synthesis in much greater detail. One website in particular, Vintage Synth Explorer (http://www.vintagesynth.com/), provides a nice overview of synthesizer history, along with numerous photos and audio examples of the instruments, and is a great place to begin.

Digital Audio and Synthesis

As with the other topics in this chapter, there are many excellent sources of information on digital audio, not to mention numerous online and print discussions about the pros and cons of analog audio versus digital audio. It is well beyond our scope to wade into that battle here, but no one can deny the huge impact computers and digital audio have had on the synthesis process. For our current discussion, then, we will focus primarily on the aspects of digitization that affect synthesis and synthesizers.

TIP *Analog* comes from the same root as the word *analogy*. In common use, an analog is a continuous, uninterrupted representation of something else. For example, an analog clock represents the passage of time with continuously moving

TIP *continued*

hands interconnected by gears so that, as the second hand sweeps around the face of the clock, the minute and hour hands slowly advance as well. With analog audio, the compression and rarefactions of air pressure are represented by continuous positive and negative changes in voltage. These changes can be recorded as grooves on a record, or as changing densities of magnetic flux on audiotape.

Figure 1.22
Just as the sweeping hands on the face of a clock create an analog of the continuous passage of time (left), the single spiral groove on the surface of a vinyl record (magnified 1,000 times at right) creates a continuous analog of the original oscillating sound wave. (analog clock photo: limpido/Photos.com, record groove photo: Chris Supranowitz/courtesy of University of Rochester-URnano)

Digital represents the concept that, instead of a continuous stream, the data are individual, momentary measurements. For example, a digital clock may show only the hour and minute, and remain in this state for sixty seconds until the clock updates at the next minute. With digital audio, the compression and rarefactions of air pressure are measured thousands of times every second to capture a momentary value. These measurements are recorded as groups of bits that can be stored as alternating high and low voltage on a digital tape, or as alternating pits (small indentations) and lands (flat spaces) on the surface of a plastic disc like a CD or DVD.

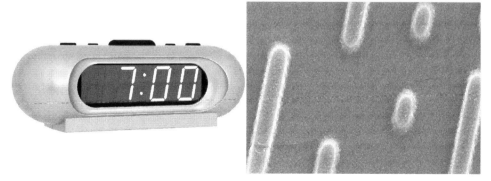

Figure 1.23
A digital clock displays a momentary measurement of the current time (left). The pits and lands on the surface of a compact disc (magnified 20,000 times at right) indicate the individual bits (zeroes and ones) that form the momentary measurement of the digitized sound wave. (digital clock photo: Artur Synenko/Photos.com, CD pits photo: Chris Supranowitz/courtesy of University of Rochester-URnano)

As with analog audio devices, digital devices first convert the acoustic energy of sound into electrical energy via transducers. Next, the electrical signal is passed through a process known as the analog-to-digital converter (ADC), where the signal's amplitude is measured thousands of times per second. Each individual measurement is recorded in digital words, or bytes, consisting of groups of eight bits (an elision of the words binary and digits), representing a single amplitude value at a discrete point in time.[13] Since computers and other digital devices cannot "read between the lines," they *quantize* the sample measurement by using the closest amplitude value on their internal scale when measuring the voltage.

Figure 1.24

In the digitization of a sound wave, sound is first converted to analog voltage (left), which passes through the analog-to-digital converter. At each clock pulse in the ADC, the amplitude of the voltage is measured, and quantized, to the nearest amplitude scale value (center). The discrete value of each individual measurement, or sample, is then recorded in digital bits (right).

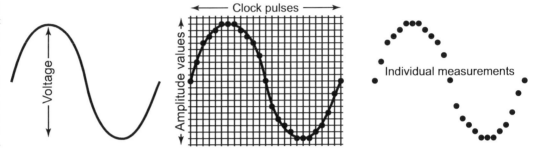

On playback, the individual samples are read into the digital-to-analog converter (DAC) and turned back into voltage levels to be transduced into sound by the loudspeakers. Although you and I might connect the dots with direct, diagonal lines, a computer cannot see the next value until it happens, so the voltage remains at the current sample value until the next sample, at which point it immediately jumps to that value. The resulting differences between the original sound wave and its digitized version are known as the *quantization error*.

Figure 1.25

Although humans tend to "connect the dots" with direct lines (left), computers wait until the next value before immediately jumping to that level (center). The difference between the original sound wave and its digitized version is known as the *quantization error* (right).

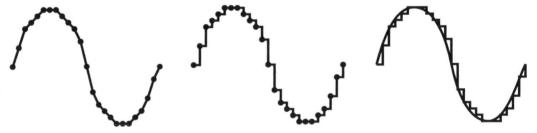

One way to reduce the quantization error is to increase the *bit depth*, or *bit resolution* (the number of zeroes and ones used in the amplitude measurements).[14] The typical digital audio device uses a bit depth of sixteen (sixteen zeroes and ones) to measure the amplitude, yielding a total of 65,536 measurement increments between the bottom and top of the amplitude range. However, increasing to twenty-four bits provides 16,777,216 measurement increments. Imagine you have two tape measures, with one being marked

13 These individual measurements are referred to as a *sample*, which often creates confusion with other common uses of this word. To some people, a sample refers to a sound, like a violin note, that is recorded and then triggered for playback. For others, a sample means a brief audio clip, like a drum groove or a guitar riff from another recording, used as a compositional element. In digital audio, though, the word refers to a single measurement of a digitized sound wave.

14 Do not confuse bit depth with bit rate. Bit depth is the number of bits in a digital audio sample. Bit rate is the number of bits transmitted per second, usually used when describing the streaming of audio between computers or computer programs.

only in inches, and the other marked in sixteenths of an inch. Which tape will give you the more accurate measurement? So it is with higher bit depths: the more bits, the more accurate the amplitude measurement.

Another way to reduce the quantization error in digital audio is to increase the *sample rate*, or the number of samples captured per second. The higher the sample rate, the closer together the measurements, and the more accurate the digitized version of the wave.

Since sound waves have both a positive and a negative phase (compression and rarefaction), a measurement must be made, at a minimum, in both phases. Thus one of the fundamental tenets of digital audio, known as the *Nyquist theorem*, states that the digital sampling rate must be at least twice as high as the highest analog frequency to be recorded. In other words, since most humans can hear sound up to about 20 kHz, the Nyquist theorem says our sampling rate must be at least 40 kHz in order to capture the frequency range. That "highest analog frequency to be recorded" (half the sampling rate) is similarly known as the *Nyquist frequency*. Thanks to a few historical and design quirks, most digital devices have settled on a sampling rate of either 44.1 kHz or 48 kHz, yielding Nyquist frequencies of 22.05 kHz and 24 kHz respectively. Today, many devices provide even higher sampling rates to improve the audio quality. Generally, these higher rates are either two or four times the two basic sampling rates, producing rates of 88.2 kHz and 96 kHz (2×), or 176.4 kHz and 192 kHz (4×).

Even with higher sampling rates, it is important to remember that high-frequency sounds have fewer measurements taken per wave cycle than do low-frequency sounds. So high frequencies are not recorded or reproduced as accurately as low frequencies. This issue becomes extremely important in digital synthesis as a great deal of the sound-making process is about combining partials and harmonics to create complex tones that have a lot of high-frequency content. With analog synthesizers, the combination of these harmonics is not a problem. However, with digital synthesizers, the same process that sounds fantastic on an analog instrument can sound quite different on a digital instrument because of how these inaccurately rendered high frequencies interact with each other.

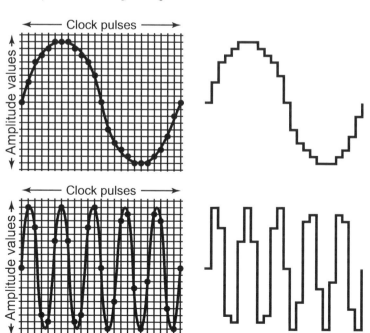

Figure 1.26

Given the same sampling rate, a low-frequency sound (top) is measured many more times per cycle, than is a high-frequency sound (bottom). Thus digital audio tends to produce more accurate representations of low frequencies than of high frequencies.

Demo 1.4

Aliasing

We mentioned earlier that human hearing goes up to about 20 kHz in frequency response. But are there sounds above 20 kHz? Of course there are; just ask your dog! What happens if a digital audio device tries to record or render a frequency higher than 20 kHz? Remember, according to the Nyquist theorem, our sampling rate must be at least twice as high as the highest frequency we are capturing. If it is not, then an artificial lower frequency called an *alias* is heard. Alias frequencies fold down symmetrically from the Nyquist frequency. For example, if your sampling rate is 48 kHz (Nyquist frequency is 24 kHz) and you attempt to record a frequency of 30 kHz (6 kHz above 24 kHz), you will hear an alias at 18 kHz (6 kHz below 24 kHz).

Figure 1.27

When the sampling rate is not high enough to capture two or more samples per wave period, artificial lower frequencies called aliases are produced instead of the original high frequencies.

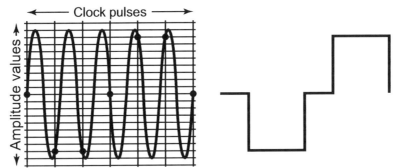

Digital recording devices avoid aliasing by using a lowpass filter to prevent sounds higher than the Nyquist frequency from entering the audio chain. However, with digital synthesizers, it is relatively easy to create aliasing. Many synthesizer sounds like sawtooth waves and pulse waves produce a great number of very high harmonics and partials. Even though the fundamental frequency of a wave might stay well below the Nyquist frequency, quite often those harmonics will exceed the Nyquist frequency, producing artificial lower tones that interfere with the desired sound.

Again, aliasing is not a problem with analog synthesizers, only with digital ones. To combat aliasing, most modern digital synthesizers use one of several complex algorithms to filter out the alias frequencies from their oscillators. Although these techniques reduce the effect of oscillator aliasing, they also tend to slightly alter the sound of digital oscillators as compared to their analog counterparts.

In spite of issues such as bit resolution, quantization error, high-frequency inaccuracy, and aliasing, digital synthesizers have become the standard instrument. No doubt the analog versus digital debate will continue, but we cannot escape the fact that nearly all synthesizers today are digital instruments. Most musicians have come to accept that the benefits of programming ease and the amount of available computational and sound-making power outweigh the issues associated with digital oscillators. In fact, as the amount of computational power increases, more of it is being applied to the quality of the oscillators, thus making the issue ever smaller.

Whether you are working with a hardware, software, analog, or digital instrument, you will find that nearly all of the basic functions of a synthesizer are the same from instrument to instrument. They may have differing names, but in general all synthesizers have oscillators and ways to combine those oscillators to create complex tones. They have ways of shaping both the amplitude and the frequency content of those tones and adding effects processing along the way. In addition to their wonderful sound-making, and sound-shaping, capabilities, today's synthesizers usually provide a large array of methods for dynamically altering and modifying those sounds as you play them. In the coming chapters, we will dig beneath the surface of our instruments as we examine every element of the synthesis process, and explore its role in sound creating and shaping. However, now that we have reviewed a bit of sound, audio, and the development of the modern synthesizer, it's time for you to start making some sound of your own.

Your Turn

Working with Crystal

Launch the Crystal file you created following the instructions in the introduction to this book.[15] Once Crystal is open, take a few minutes to explore the window. Note the five tabs across the top, which take you to different windows. Each window has a number of panels for controlling the various synthesis aspects in Crystal.

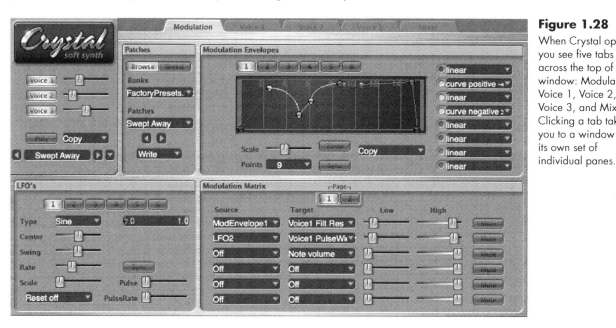

Figure 1.28
When Crystal opens, you see five tabs across the top of the window: Modulation, Voice 1, Voice 2, Voice 3, and Mixer. Clicking a tab takes you to a window with its own set of individual panes.

In the Modulation window, locate the Patches panel just to the right of the logo, and click the Browse button to bring up the patch browser for Crystal. Select the **Factory-Presets.fxb** bank from the Banks menu, and then choose the first patch, **Swept Away**, from the Patches menu.[16] Press, and hold, a note in the middle of your MIDI keyboard. You should hear a sound that begins low in the right speaker and then slowly evolves across

15 If you have not yet created your Crystal file, please do so now using the instructions in the Introduction to this book under the section labeled "Using the Crystal Software Synthesizer." You will use this file extensively throughout the book. Download links and instructions for Crystal are available from the "Introduction" page of the Refining Sound companion website.

16 If you happen to select the **RefiningSound.fxb** bank instead, you will see that it has only one patch called "default," with all the remaining slots unused. This bank and its single preset will be used in the coming chapters as you create your own sounds.

both speakers over a period of about fifteen seconds. If you do not hear anything, confirm that you have all your audio and MIDI connections properly configured as described in the Introduction in the section entitled "Using the Crystal Software Synthesizer."

Figure 1.29

To select a sound preset, or "patch" in Crystal, click the Modulation tab, and then the Browse button in the Patches panel. Select the Bank from which you wish to choose a sound (if you followed the instructions in the Introduction, you should have two banks in the menu: "FactoryPresets.fxb" and "RefiningSound. fxb"). Next, select the Patch you wish to hear. You can use the left-right arrow buttons to move back and forth in the patch list. Be careful with the Write menu! It overwrites patches with the current settings. We will use this feature extensively in coming chapters.

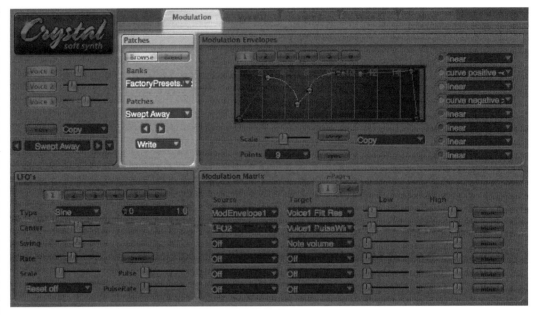

You can try out other sounds by selecting them from the Patches menu, or by clicking the left–right arrows immediately below the Patches menu. *Note*: the Write menu will overwrite the currently selected patch with any modifications you may have made in the various windows. We will use this function a great deal throughout this book, but for now leave this menu alone.

Take some time to listen to each of the FactoryPresets sounds. In most cases, these sounds are monophonic, so you will not be able to play chords just yet. Some sounds respond quickly, while others need to be held down for some time to completely develop. Try playing notes in different registers of your keyboard and note how this affects each of the sounds.

Once you have listened to all the sounds, select one and click on each of the remaining tabs at the top of the Crystal window. The three voice tabs allow you to configure the three sources available in a sound. As you switch between the three voice tabs, you will notice that the controls are identical for each voice.

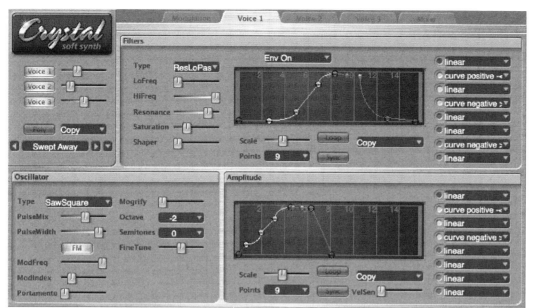

Figure 1.30

The three Voice tabs are identical and allow you to set the parameters for each of Crystal's sound sources.

Select the Voice 1 tab and turn off voices 2 and 3 by clicking their activation buttons directly underneath the Crystal logo in the upper-left panel of the window (when a voice is active, its button is illuminated). With voices 2 and 3 turned off, you will be able to easily hear any changes you make to voice 1. Feel free to experiment with the controls for voice 1 in the Filters, Oscillator, and Amplitude panels.[17] I will explain all of these functions in great detail later in the book, but for now just experiment and listen to the results. If you want to set voice 1 back to its original settings, simply choose **Revert** from the Copy menu in the same panel you used to deactivate the other voices.

After spending some time changing voice 1's settings, select the Mixer tab and you will see a window full of horizontal sliders. These controls allow you to combine the voices as well as numerous effects and delay lines in myriad configurations. All the sliders in this window may seem intimidating at first, but as we progress through the book we will get to all of them. Once you begin using them, you will see that this window is not very complicated at all, but actually rather straightforward.

17 You may find that some controls do not change the sound while a note is held down. If this happens, simply restrike the note on the keyboard to hear the new sound after moving the control.

    Many software synthesizers allow you to switch between "coarse" and "fine" resolution of a control by pressing one of the modifier keys (Shift, Control, Alt, Option, or Command) on the computer keyboard. In Crystal's case, pressing the Shift key while clicking and dragging a control puts the control into fine resolution mode, allowing you to make minute adjustments to the control's value. Even in fine resolution mode, however, you may find that some values—particularly the frequency and delay time values—skip rather than change smoothly. As we progress through the chapters, you will frequently be given a value for a specific control in Crystal. If the control does not allow you to set it to the exact value, just set it as close as possible. In most cases the small difference will not matter.

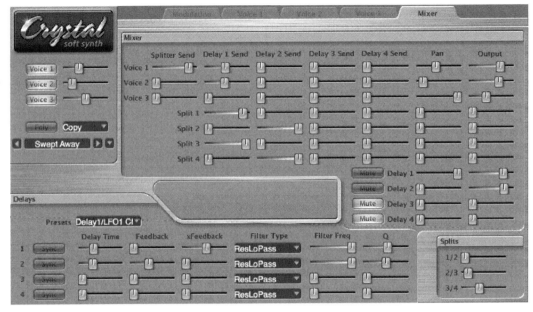

Figure 1.31

The Mixer tab allows you to combine all the voices and effects in Crystal to create the finished, composite sound.

Using Your Own Synthesizer(s)

Although the synthesizer sounds we create in the Your Turn sections of this text will be done with Crystal, readers are encouraged to explore and use their own synthesizers as well. It is impossible to write a text that fits every synthesizer model, but most synthesizers work in quite similar ways. In fact, some of the most confusing differences between synthesizers are not their functions but simply the names of those functions. Whenever appropriate, I will strive to clarify the terms commonly used to describe a particular synthesizer element or function.

If you do not already have it, get a copy of the user manual for your synthesizer. Most manufacturers make these available as a free PDF from their website. You will often find the manuals in the Support or Downloads section of the site. If your instrument is no longer manufactured, do an Internet search for it. Chances are a user group exists and will have links and references—and perhaps a downloadable manual—for your synthesizer.

Look at your synthesizer and its manual. How is your instrument organized? With Crystal, we saw that the Oscillator, Filter, and Amplitude Envelope Generator are all located in the same Voice window. Many instruments place these functions in different windows, requiring the user to switch back and forth between them. Before learning to create and edit sounds on your own instrument, you will need to learn how to navigate between these various functions, as well as how to select and store patches on the instrument. Switching between these functions on a software synthesizer is usually simply a matter of selecting a tab as in Crystal, or by selecting a function from the instrument's menu items. Hardware instruments, though, can often be more difficult to navigate. They typically have only a small LCD display showing just one element at a time. To navigate through the many functions, then, often requires numerous button presses and selections. Regardless of they type of synthesizer you use, be sure you know how to navigate through its various windows and functions and know how to save and recall patches on the instrument before proceeding.

2

Oscillators

Mining the Raw Materials *of Your Synthesizer*

Online materials for this chapter:

http://www.oup.com/refiningsound/Chapter2.html

os·cil·late |ˈäsəˌlāt| verb [intrans.]: move or swing back and forth at a regular speed

Derivatives: *os·cil·la·tion* |ˌäsəˈlā sʜ ən| noun; *os·cil·la·tor* |ˈäsəˌlātər| noun

> **TIP** The word *hertz* (abbr. Hz) is the standard unit for measuring frequency and indicates the number of oscillations, or cycles per second in a wave. When the number of oscillations gets into the thousands, it is often indicated with the word kilohertz (abbr. kHz). Therefore 20 cycles per second will be notated as 20 Hz, and 20,000 cycles per second will usually be notated as 20 kHz.

Without oscillation, there is no sound. Strike a tuning fork, pluck a guitar string, blow through a clarinet, sing, clap your hands, or even slam a door, and you create oscillations. These oscillations, also called vibrations, happen first in the device (the tuning fork, string, clarinet, throat, hands, door) and then transfer into the surrounding air, creating oscillating changes in air pressure. As that oscillating air pressure travels outward from the sound's source, it reaches our ears where the rapid changes in air pressure cause our eardrums to oscillate, sending nerve impulses to the brain. If the oscillations happen more than about twenty times per second (20 *hertz*), we perceive them as sound.

34

Figure 2.1

The oscillating tines of the tuning fork create oscillating changes in air pressure that travel to the ear. These in turn cause the tympanic membrane, or eardrum, to oscillate, sending nerve impulses to the brain that we interpret as sound. One oscillation, or cycle, of a wave is measured from one point in the waveform's features to the next occurrence of that same feature.

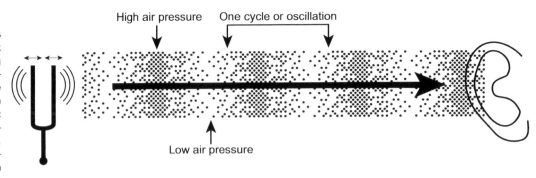

High air pressure   One cycle or oscillation

Low air pressure

TIP   A *transducer* converts one form of energy into another form. A microphone is a type of transducer that converts the oscillating air pressure of a sound wave into oscillating electrical energy, and a loudspeaker converts the electrical energy back into sound.

In the audio and recording world, oscillations go through several intermediate steps where they are converted to oscillations of electrical voltage by a microphone, or other type of transducer. Once the wave is converted to an electrical signal, it can be stored on electromagnetic media such as audiotape or a computer drive. When the audio is played back, the oscillations in voltage are converted back into changes in air pressure by an-other type of transducer called a loudspeaker.

Figure 2.2

Air pressure oscillations cause the diaphragm in the microphone to oscillate inside an electromagnetic field, thus creating rising and falling electrical voltage oscillations that correspond with the increasing and decreasing pressure changes of the original sound.

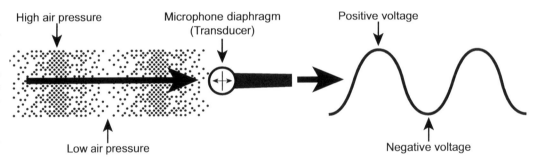

High air pressure   Microphone diaphragm (Transducer)   Positive voltage

Low air pressure   Negative voltage

Since a synthesizer *creates* a sound, instead of capturing it, the synthesis process begins by creating oscillating changes in electrical voltage. An electrical device known, appropriately enough, as an oscillator creates these voltage changes. The synthesis process begins with oscillators, and in this chapter we focus on these raw material resources that are found in every synthesizer.

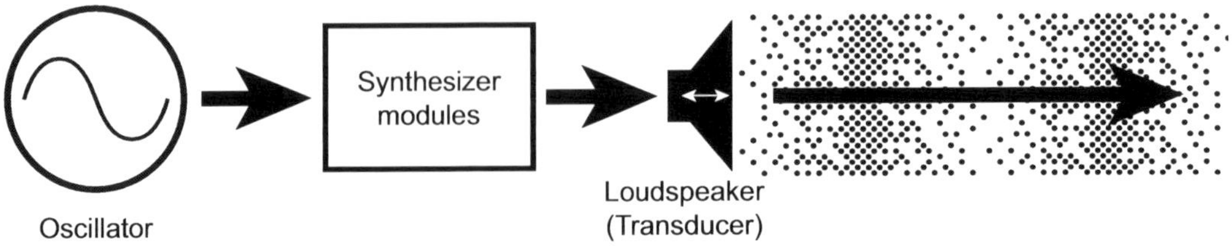

Figure 2.3

The synthesis process begins with oscillators.

Oscillator   Synthesizer modules   Loudspeaker (Transducer)

An important thing to remember about an oscillator is that it can make only one sound at a time. If you want to play four notes, you need four oscillators. If you want to produce three types of sounds, you need three oscillators. Want to play four-note chords with three different sound types? You'll need a minimum of twelve oscillators. As we will see in subsequent chapters, producing some sounds and notes requires more than one oscillator, and the need for numerous oscillators in a synthesizer quickly becomes apparent.

In the earliest synthesizers, oscillators were often a separate piece of hardware with a switch for determining the type of oscillation (more about oscillator wave types below) and a large knob for controlling the frequency of the oscillation. These oscillators tended to be rather large and expensive and were connected to the rest of the synthesizer via cables. Because of their size and expense, most early synthesizers had a small number of oscillators that were used in combinations to create more complex sounds, rather than for playing multiple simultaneous notes. Even as synthesizers evolved and oscillators became internal circuits instead of external devices, manufacturers still tended to focus on using the oscillators for complex sounds more than for increased polyphony. It was not until the mid-1980s that oscillator circuits got small enough, powerful enough, and most importantly cheap enough that manufacturers began, in earnest, to add polyphony to their synthesizers.

Today's modern synthesizer typically has the oscillator capacity to both make multiple, incredibly rich, complex sounds and play dozens—if not hundreds—of simultaneous notes with these sounds. On most instruments, you will see only a small number of oscillators, perhaps just two or three. It is assumed, however, that each oscillator you see actually represents numerous individual oscillators, all configured identically, allowing you to play multiple notes with the same sound. Therefore, the oscillators found on a contemporary synthesizer usually have nothing to do with polyphony. They are there to create sonic complexity.

Figure 2.4
A large, external oscillator such as the Mk1 'A' from MacBeth Synthesizers offers numerous controls for shaping and manipulating the oscillator waveform. However, like all analog hardware oscillators, it is capable of producing only one note with one sound at a time. (photo used with permission of Ken MacBeth)

Figure 2.5

MOTU's software synthesizer Modulo features two oscillators for creating sounds, with each oscillator capable of sixteen simultaneous notes with those sounds. (photo used with permission of MOTU, Inc.)

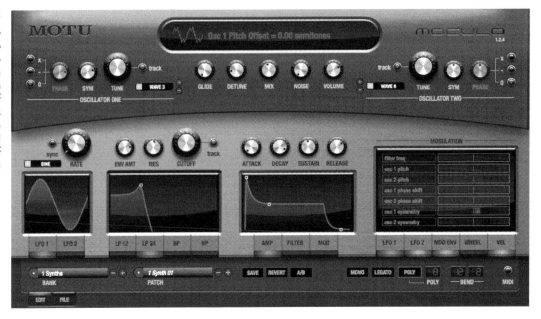

TIP

Changing Pitch

We discuss the use of keyboards to trigger and control the pitch of oscillators in much greater detail in subsequent chapters. For now, assume that all of the oscillator models described below use an equal temperament system like that on a piano. As you go up or down your keyboard from one key to the next, the synthesizer's oscillators (and all related oscillator functions) raise or lower their pitch by one semitone.

The very first link in the chain of the synthesis process is the oscillator section, and it can sometimes be difficult to see and hear what the oscillators are doing without them being affected by all the other processes that come later in the chain. In this chapter, we peel back all of those other layers to focus exclusively on the types of oscillators, their sounds, and their capabilities.

Over the years, synthesizer manufacturers have found a variety of ways to generate the raw material, or sound waves, for their instruments. These techniques generally involve one or more of three basic approaches: creating a repeating electrical waveform with an analog oscillator, repeating a digital representation of an electrical waveform, or reproducing a stored digital audio file. Technically, only the first one is an actual oscillator, but the use of digital representations of electrical waveforms and stored digital audio files as a sound source has become so ubiquitous and integral to the synthesis process that it would make no sense to exclude this approach here. It is well beyond our scope to examine every possible method of sound creation employed over the years. We do, however, in this chapter examine each of the main approaches. Before beginning, it is important to note that most synthesizers create their rich sounds by combining multiple oscillators in a variety of ways. We will explore oscillator combinations in great detail in the next chapter, but for the present let's focus on individual oscillators, the raw materials of sound creation in a synthesizer.

Meet the Oscillators

On most synthesizers, the oscillators are designated, appropriately enough, as Oscillator or perhaps by the abbreviation Osc. You may also see them labeled as VCO (voltage controlled oscillator) or DCO (digitally controlled oscillator). Other synthesizers use a rather ambiguous name like "Source" or "Sound Source" to designate their oscillators, so you may need to do a bit of reading between the lines in your synthesizer's manual to find its name for the oscillators. For our purposes, we refer to them all as oscillators.

TIP

How Low Can They Go?

On nearly every synthesizer, you will also see a module, or section, called Low-Frequency Oscillator, or LFO. Although these are, in fact, oscillators, they usually operate well below our range of hearing (less than 20 Hz) and are not used to make sounds but to control other aspects of the synthesis process. On some instruments, you will also see a set of modulation, or audio-rate modulation, oscillators. These, too, are oscillators, and as with the sounding oscillators on the instrument they operate in the audio-rate frequency range (greater than 20 Hz). However, like their low-frequency cousin the LFO, audio-rate modulation oscillators are not used for sound, but to control other elements in the synthesizer. LFOs and audio-rate modulation oscillators are important tools in synthesis, and we will discuss them in great detail in coming chapters.

Wave Type Oscillators

Demo 2.1

The simplest synthesizer oscillators usually create their voltage changes with one of four basic modes known as oscillator wave types. All of the types generate a repeating wave with equidistant positive–negative displacement from the center (or zero voltage) line. The primary difference between wave types is the rate at which the voltage transitions between the positive and negative poles, and the abruptness with which it changes direction. Even when these various oscillator types produce the same fundamental frequency, or pitch, their unique shapes produce extremely different qualities of tone for that pitch.

Sine Wave

The basic type of electrical wave created by an oscillator is one in which the voltage level changes smoothly and continuously between positive and negative poles without any abrupt changes in either direction. Because of its relationship to the motion around a circle, this type of energy wave is commonly known as a sine wave, although its technical name is a *sinusoidal* wave. Because sine waves have a smooth motion without any abrupt changes in direction, they produce only the tone of their root frequency and tend to be rather dull and dark sounding. Pure sine waves rarely occur by themselves in natural sounds, but are quite common in electronic devices like synthesizers.

Figure 2.6

A sine wave resulting from simple oscillation.

Triangle Wave

If the oscillator wave's voltage is allowed to transition from one pole to the other at a steady rate of speed, and then abruptly change direction and head toward the other pole at a steady speed, a triangle wave results. Because of the quick change of direction at the top and bottom of the wave, the sound tends to have a brighter timbre than the sine wave.

Figure 2.7

A triangle wave.

Sawtooth (or Saw) Wave

Like the triangle wave, the sawtooth wave begins at one pole and transitions smoothly to the opposite. However, when it gets to the opposite pole, it abruptly and nearly instantaneously jumps back to the first pole and starts the process over. With its abrupt directional change, the sawtooth wave tends to be considerably brighter, and "buzzier," than the triangle wave. Because of their timbral brightness, and the fact that sawtooth waves contain all of the harmonics of the fundamental frequency (more on harmonics below), these waves have been a favorite for creating synthesizer sounds for years.[1]

Figure 2.8

A sawtooth wave.

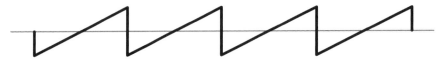

Pulse (or Square) Wave

The pulse wave is nothing more than a two-state wave: it's either fully positive or fully negative. There is no perceptible transition between poles; rather, it jumps abruptly from one pole to the other. Because of the two abrupt transitions per wave oscillation, pulse waves also tend to be rather bright-sounding, and because they produce only odd-numbered harmonics they have become popular for creating a number of woodwind-type instrument sounds.

Figure 2.9

A pulse wave.

1 The standard sawtooth wave ramps upward and then immediately jumps down, as shown in Figure 2.8. The reverse (or inverse) sawtooth wave ramps downward and then immediately jumps up. Confusion might occur with a few synthesizers that, instead, use the name *sawtooth* to refer to the inverted form and use *ramp* to describe the standard form of the wave. The harmonic spectrum of both wave versions is the same, and for practical purposes they sound the same when used as a single oscillator wave. However, combined with other oscillator waves, or used as a modulating low frequency oscillator, as we will explore in Chapter 6, there can be a considerable difference in the resultant effect of the two wave shapes.

Pulse Width

Most pulse wave oscillators also have a control to adjust the percentage of time spent in the positive phase versus the negative phase. If the pulse width (sometimes called the "duty cycle") is set so that both halves are equal to each other, the pulse wave is known as a "square" wave. The position of the pulse width is indicated variously by synthesizer manufacturers. Some use percentage, with 50 percent being the middle position, while others use zero as the middle position, with negative values meaning more time is spent in the negative phase, and positive values to indicate more time in the positive phase.

Pulse width adjustment can have a significant impact on the timbre of the wave's sound. In fact, as we will see in Chapter 6, a common technique for adding interest to a pulse wave is to sweep the pulse width adjustment back and forth while the wave is sounding, producing some interesting timbral-shift effects. Some oscillators also let you adjust the width of the triangle wave as well, to similar effect.

Figure 2.10
A square wave, a negative pulse wave, and a positive pulse wave.

Wave Phase

Oscillator waves are measured in degrees through their cycle. Like starting at the top of a compass and traveling all the way around the circle, the beginning of a wave is measured at 0°. Halfway through the wave is 180°, and the end of the wave (beginning of the next wave) is 360° (or 0° again). At first glance, the starting position of a wave may not seem important, but as we will see in the next chapter the starting phase position of a wave can have a huge impact on a sound when oscillators are combined together. Consequently, in addition to their wave type and frequency controls, most oscillators have a phase control that allows you to adjust the starting phase position.

As opposed to sound waves produced by oscillators, sounds in the natural world are generally quite complex, consisting of a rich spectrum of frequencies known as *partials*. Generally the loudest, and most prominent, of these frequencies is also the lowest one, called the *fundamental*. The partials above the fundamental, often called *overtones*, are usually much quieter, and typically they get even softer as they ascend in frequency until becoming inaudible. Some of these overtones

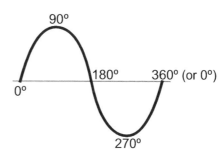

Figure 2.11
Phase positions of a sine wave.

have a distinct mathematical relationship to the fundamental frequency and are called *harmonics*. A sound that has a greater emphasis on harmonics tends to sound more "pitched," while a sound with more emphasis on the other partials tends to sound "unpitched," or as a "noise."

TIP Disambiguation

People often use the terms *partials*, *overtones*, and *harmonics* as if they are synonymous. They are, in fact, different; as a soon-to-be synthesis expert, you will find these differences to be quite important as you create your sounds. In the real world, when an object oscillates, or vibrates, to produce sound, it does so in a way that produces a large primary vibration called the *fundamental*, which we perceive as the basic audible frequency, or pitch. It also vibrates at an infinite number of smaller, suboscillations higher than the fundamental frequency.

- All of the vibrations associated with a complex sound, including the fundamental, are called *partials*.
- All of the vibrations higher—or over—the fundamental in a complex sound are called *overtones*.
- Depending on its mathematical relationship to the fundamental, we describe a partial as being either *harmonic* or *inharmonic*. Most people simply use the adjective as a noun, calling partials "harmonics" and "inharmonics."

A *harmonic* is partial whose frequency is an integer (whole-number) multiple of the fundamental frequency. For a given fundamental frequency of 55 Hz:

- Harmonic 1 (55 × 1) = 55 Hz
- Harmonic 2 (55 × 2) = 110 Hz
- Harmonic 3 (55 × 3) = 165 Hz
- Harmonic 4 (55 × 4) = 220 Hz
- Harmonic 5 (55 × 5) = 275 Hz
- Harmonic 6 (55 × 6) = 330 Hz
- Harmonic 7 (55 × 7) = 385 Hz
- Harmonic 8 (55 × 8) = 440 Hz
- etc.

As you see on the musical staff in Figure 2.12, harmonics are related to one another musically, although some frequencies differ from the common deviations used to create pitches in today's tuning system known as equal temperament. In synthesis, harmonics are often used to increase the strength of a sound's pitch and resonance. We also manipulate the number, and respective amplitudes, of the harmonics to control the tone quality, or *timbre*, of a sound.

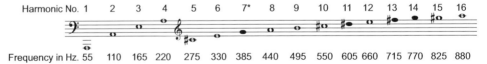

Figure 2.12
The harmonic series, beginning on A₂ (55 Hz) through the sixteenth harmonic. *The darkened notes represent substantial frequency deviation from that used in equal temperament.

> **TIP** *continued*
>
> *Important note:* every time you double a frequency, you raise the pitch by one octave, and every time you halve a frequency, you lower the pitch by one octave. For example, 110 Hz is one octave higher than 55 Hz, and one octave lower than 220 Hz. It is also important to note that each higher octave contains twice as many frequencies as the octave below.
>
> *Inharmonics* are noninteger multiples of the fundamental frequency (e.g., 55 Hz × 1.3 = 71.5 Hz; 55 Hz × 3.72463 = 204.85465 Hz). Because there are so many possible inharmonics, they are not numbered. Inharmonics are not usually related musically to the fundamental, and in synthesis the subtle dissonances they create are often used to add "bite" or "edge" to a sound.

Since they maintain a constant rate of change, sine waves produce only the fundamental frequency. The other wave types (triangle, sawtooth, and pulse), with their angularities, produce not only a strong fundamental but also a variety of overtones that make their timbre brighter and edgier than the sine wave. Because sine waves produce no overtones, many synthesizers do not include them on their oscillators—a mistake, in this humble writer's opinion. As we will see in the next chapter, you can actually create triangle, sawtooth, and pulse waves by combining multiple sine waves in certain combinations of frequency and amplitude.

Noise Oscillators

Most of us, when we think of noise, probably imagine the obnoxious sounds our kids or our roommates are making while we are trying to work. In the audio world, though, noise has a very specific meaning, referring to rapid and totally random fluctuations of frequency and amplitude in an oscillator waveform. The result is a sound that moves through the entire frequency spectrum so rapidly that any sense of discrete pitch or frequency is completely lost. Synthesizer oscillators sometimes have the option of producing noise instead of a fixed-frequency signal. We often use noise to add some "sizzle" or "splash" to a sound when creating things like snare and cymbal sounds, breaths, chiffs, bow noise, sibilance, etc. When mixed with a standard oscillator wave, especially at the beginning of the sound, noise can add a bit of realism to a sound or brighten the attack so the sound stands out better in the mix.

> **TIP** **Where'd All This Noise Come From?**
>
> Synthesizers capable of producing noise typically create it in one of two ways. Some instruments simply have a digitally recorded sample of noise that loops repeatedly when the noise oscillator is triggered. More sophisticated instruments use a special oscillator capable of randomly changing its frequency across the entire audi-

TIP	*continued*

ble spectrum thousands of times per second, thus producing the hiss sound we call noise. Since this type of noise, by definition, is the random occurrence of all frequencies, it does not make much sense for the keys on the synthesizer keyboard to have any effect. With a noise oscillator, then, no matter which key you press, you will usually hear the same "hissy" sound.

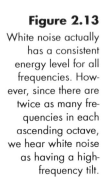

Demo 2.2

The Color of Noise

You may have heard of "white noise," or even "pink noise." Noise actually comes in a variety of "colors," and understanding these differences helps as you use them in your sounds. Most oscillators do not have all colors of noise, but it is common to see at least a couple of them available. To help you understand the colors of noise, remember that the color spectrum of visible light goes from reds at the low-frequency end to blues and violets at the high-frequency end. Likewise, when you see noise described with a color, it refers to the part of the audio frequency spectrum being emphasized.

White Noise

In the visible (light) frequency spectrum, if you combine all colors of light equally, you produce white light. Similarly, if you randomly combine all frequencies of the audio spectrum equally, you create white noise. White noise has the same amount of energy at every frequency. However, recall from our earlier discussion of harmonics that whenever you go up an octave, there are twice as many frequencies in every successive octave. For example, the octave from A_2 to A_3 has 55 integer (whole number) frequencies, while the next octave (A_3 to A_4) has 110, and the next (A_4 to A_5) has 220. Even though the energy level is the same for all the frequencies, there are twice as many frequencies in every successive octave. So we perceive white noise as having a high-frequency tilt. People often describe the sound of white noise as "hissing steam."

Figure 2.13

White noise actually has a consistent energy level for all frequencies. However, since there are twice as many frequencies in each ascending octave, we hear white noise as having a high-frequency tilt.

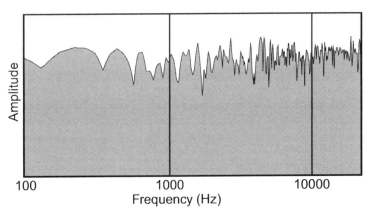

Red Noise

Red noise (sometimes called brown, or Brownian, noise) exhibits a substantial drop in energy level as the frequency ascends. Because the emphasis of this noise is at the low end of the frequency spectrum, it is named red, like the low end of the light spectrum. Some people call this type of noise brown noise, referring not to a color but to Robert Brown, the nineteenth century scientist who was the first to observe the apparent random drifting of particles suspended in a gas, which became known as Brownian motion. The frequencies in red noise follow the drift characteristics of Brownian motion. Red noise is often described as having a low "roar," like a distant waterfall. It comes in handy for things like "boomy" sound effects, bass drums, and other low-frequency sounds.

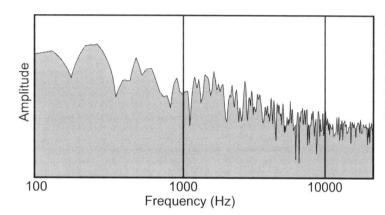

Figure 2.14
Red noise emphasizes the lower frequencies and rapidly drops in amplitude at the higher end of the frequency spectrum.

Pink Noise

Pink noise is noise that continuously reduces its energy level by half as you pass upward through each octave. Since there are twice as many frequencies in each successive octave, decreasing the energy level by half produces a noise that to our ear sounds at the same level in all octaves. This noise has the name "pink" because it is halfway between red and white noise. It sounds a bit like a heavy rainfall, and is commonly used by acousticians and studio engineers to measure the frequency response of an acoustic space.

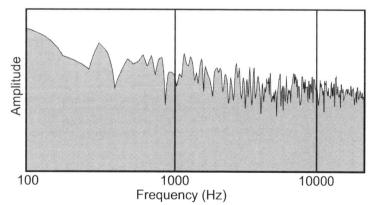

Figure 2.15
Pink noise also emphasizes lower frequencies, but the drop in amplitude at higher frequencies is not as extreme as red noise. Since every octave has twice as many frequencies as the octave below, and pink noise drops by half with every ascending octave, we hear it as having an equal energy level across the entire frequency spectrum.

Violet Noise

The opposite of red noise (low-frequency emphasis) is violet noise (high-frequency emphasis). This type of noise has an extremely high-frequency tilt, with little or no low-frequency content. Violet, sometimes called "purple," noise can be useful for creating sibilance, or "s" sounds, when judiciously applied to a sound.

Figure 2.16
Violet noise emphasizes the higher frequencies and rapidly drops in amplitude at the lower end of the spectrum.

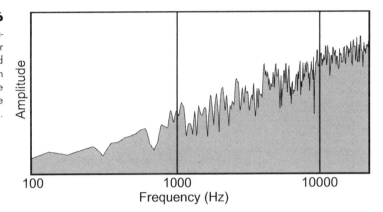

Blue Noise

Halfway between violet and white is blue noise, the opposite of pink noise. Here, the energy of each successive octave is doubled. Like violet noise, there is little low-frequency content and an upward-tilting emphasis, but not nearly as dramatic a tilt as with violet noise. Because blue noise provides a little bit of low-frequency content, with a lot of high-frequency emphasis, it can sometimes add "shimmer" and "sparkle" to things like cymbal sounds and reverberation.

Figure 2.17
Blue noise also emphasizes the higher frequencies, but the drop in amplitude at lower frequencies is not as extreme as violet noise.

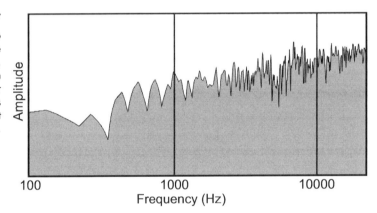

Crackle

Crackle noise is a special type of noise made up of randomly spaced bursts of noise at varying amplitudes. Think of a fireplace crackling, or the clicks and pops you get with an old vinyl LP record. That is the type of noise you get if your oscillator has a "crackle" (sometimes called "random") setting. As you might guess, it is often used to create a noisy, "analog" type of sound. In that same light, many synthesizers also include specific types of noise to create such sounds as tape hiss, amplifier noise, electrical hum, and so forth.

Table Lookup Oscillators

Digital synthesizers do not use the large, electrical oscillators we have been discussing to generate their waveforms. Instead, they use samples of sine, triangle, sawtooth, and pulse waves stored as tiny digital files loaded into a quickly accessible memory location called a lookup table. By simply changing the speed with which the instrument reads and loops through the table, it can synthesize digital representations of analog oscillators. For example, if you load a single cycle of a triangle wave into a lookup table, and then read through that table two hundred times a second, you create a 200 Hz triangle wave. Technically, this type of oscillator is known as a *table lookup oscillator*.[2] Most synthesizer manufacturers, however, simply call them oscillators or digital oscillators.

TIP **Setting the Table**

If you are not already familiar with a lookup table, you should still find its concept actually quite simple. Imagine a set of individual memory locations numbered 0 through 255. At each location is a single numeric value between 1 and −1. When the lookup table receives a number (between 0 and 255), instead of outputting the number it outputs the value (between 1 and −1) stored at that numbered location.

On most digital synthesizers, digitized sound waves have a value of 1 as their maximum compression and −1 as their maximum rarefaction. If you split a single cycle of a sound wave into 256 slices (remember, 0–255 is actually 256 units) and store the amplitude for each individual slice in the appropriately numbered memory slot, you make the wave cycle easily accessible. All the synthesizer has to do is count from 0 to 255 over and over.[3] The table sees the incoming number from the count and outputs the stored amplitude value from the numbered location.

This approach is incredibly efficient, as the wave needs to be generated (stored) only once. All the synthesizer has to do is keep counting at a steady rate. Want a new pitch? Simply read through the table at a different speed. Want another sound? Just load a new set of data values into the lookup table, and the counting numbers from the synthesizer will cause the table to output the new wave.

Many synthesizers have taken this idea a step further. If a table lookup oscillator can repeatedly loop through a table containing one cycle of a sampled sine wave, why can't it also loop through a table containing a much more complex wave, perhaps one that represents multiple wave cycles and is extracted from a harmonically rich, recorded sound? This is exactly how the oscillators on a number of digital synthesizers work today. The complex waves they produce are much richer-sounding than anything possible with one of the basic oscillator wave types.

As we discussed in the Digital Audio and Synthesis section of the previous chapter, the use of digitally sampled oscillators has the potential for creating aliasing. Some synthesizer programmers like to use aliasing in their sounds, and many digital synthesizers provide an option of using either an aliased or an anti-aliased version of their oscillator waves.

---

2 It's a bit confusing, but a *table lookup oscillator* reads through a *lookup table* to create the sound wave.

3 For the sake of this example, we are using 256 values for the lookup table. Although this was a common memory size for older lookup tables, most newer instruments use much larger tables capable of storing data in thousands of memory locations.

Wavetable Oscillators

In many ways, a wavetable oscillator is similar to a table lookup oscillator. It too reads through a lookup table containing a single cycle of a waveform in a continuous loop. However, in spite of the similarity in name, there is a difference in their operation. The true wavetable oscillator reads a user-generated array, or table, of *x-y* coordinates to *create* a wave cycle in real time, while the table lookup oscillator reads a prerecorded digital sample of a wave cycle.

Wavetable oscillators can generate complex waves that create the effect of combining multiple waveforms together. In the next chapter, we will discuss the concept of additive synthesis in detail, but for the moment, know that it is a process of adding multiple simple waveforms to create a much more complex waveform. Wavetable oscillators allow you to create a formula that represents multiple frequencies and amplitudes. When the output of that formula is plotted into a lookup table, the result is a single cycle of a complex waveform. By looping through the table at the desired rate, or frequency, a synthesizer wave is created with a much more complex and richer sound.

The actual formulae that create these tables can be quite complicated, so most synthesizers implement them in a much more user-friendly manner. The simplest wavetable synthesizers allow the user to select waveforms from some sort of menu and let the wavetable oscillator do all the work. Some synthesizers allow you to create the waves yourself by selecting certain frequencies (usually harmonics) to be added to the fundamental frequency, and setting the relative amplitude for each frequency. In Figure 2.18, one cycle of a complex waveform is created in a wavetable by adding the second, third, fifth, sixth, and seventh harmonics, at varying percentages of full amplitude, to the fundamental's wave cycle.

H1* @ 100 % + H2 @ 25 % + H3 @ 85 % + H4 @ 0 % + H5 @ 75 % + H6 @ 20 % + H7 @ 75 % =

Figure 2.18
A wavetable formula and its resulting plot. *In this example, H1 @ 100 % means that Harmonic no.1 (the fundamental) is at full (100 percent) amplitude. It is combined with additional harmonics (H2, H3, and so forth) at varying amplitudes to produce the complex waveform.

In the early days of digital synthesis, the available computational power in synthesizers was rather low. For the synthesizer to loop through something as complex as a digital wave, it needed to be loaded into the lookup table's memory in advance, a process that took a bit of time to complete. The wavetable, on the other hand, was designed to respond to a mathematical formula and generate its wave instantly. Since even very complex formulae rarely create anything as complicated as an actual sound wave, the instrument's limited computer power could handle this real-time waveform creation. As computational power increased over the years, the need for two different table types has all but disappeared. Today's synthesizers can usually load a complex digital wave instantaneously, and the desire to generate mathematically calculated waveforms has greatly diminished. Thus both functions are now usually done in the same table. Technically, the process is still using a table lookup oscillator, but most manufacturers refer to it as a wavetable oscillator.

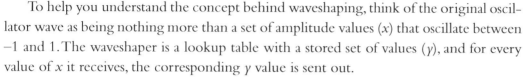

Demo 2.4

Waveshaping Oscillators

A waveshaping oscillator is actually not a different kind of oscillator at all. It is simply a basic wave-type oscillator whose output is manipulated by means of a lookup table. However, since a number of synthesizers use the term *waveshaping* as an oscillator type, it seems appropriate to include it here as a separate category. In addition to being used as a sound source, waveshaping is also quite common as a form of distortion in effects processing.

To help you understand the concept behind waveshaping, think of the original oscillator wave as being nothing more than a set of amplitude values (x) that oscillate between −1 and 1. The waveshaper is a lookup table with a stored set of values (y), and for every value of x it receives, the corresponding y value is sent out.

Waveshaping offers the advantage of needing only a single basic oscillator and a lookup table to create rich sonic textures. The lookup table can be something as simple as a basic mathematical formula like $y = x^n$ (x raised to the power of n), or $y = |x|$ (the absolute value of x). Other formulas might restrict the amplitude of the wave to a certain range—or even reflect or fold it back in the opposite direction—if the wave attempts to exceed a predetermined value. Perhaps the most popular formula uses a set of mathematical expressions called polynomials, developed by the nineteenth-century Russian mathematician Pafnuty Chebyshev (1821–1894). The *Chebyshev polynomials*, as they are known, produce a set of pure harmonics from a single sine wave. Much as we did with the wavetable, by adjusting the amplitude of those harmonics we can create numerous complex waves. In addition to using formulae to create the y values in their table, some waveshapers can also load an audio sample. They then analyze the amplitude values of the waveform and use those data to create their y values.

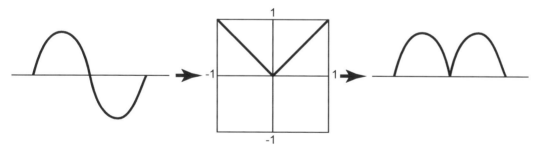

Figure 2.19

A sine wave passing through a waveshaper using the formula $y = |x|$ converts all the negative values of the original wave to positive values. The net result is a wave an octave higher since it now has two peaks per period of the original wave. Because of the quick change in direction between the peaks, it also has a slightly brighter timbre than the original sine wave.

TIP   **Disambiguation**

With similar names, and even similar sounds, it is easy to confuse the terms *lookup table*, *table lookup oscillator*, *wavetable*, and *waveshaper*. As mentioned previously, the distinction between lookup table, table lookup oscillator, and wavetable has blurred, and most people now use the term *wavetable* for all three types.

TIP continued

1. *Lookup table*: loads a set of values (*y*) at individual memory locations (*x*). When it receives a number that matches one of its memory locations, the lookup table outputs the value stored at that memory location.

2. *Table lookup oscillator*: the part of the synthesizer that reads through the lookup table hundreds of times per second, creating a sound wave based on the values in the table.

3. *Wavetable*: generates a set of *x-y* values for a lookup table based on a mathematical formula. As with the table lookup oscillator, the wavetable oscillator repeatedly reads through its table to generate the sound wave.

4. *Waveshaper*: passes a basic oscillator wave through a lookup table, changing the incoming *x* values of the wave to the *y* values from the table. The table data can be derived from either a formula or a digital audio sample.

Hybrid Oscillators

From the beginning, synthesizers have been quite good at making unusual and exotic "electronic" sounds with their oscillators. As synthesizers became more popular in the 1980s, though, users also wanted the ability to make "natural" acoustic instrumental sounds as well. In addition to the many wonderful oscillator–created colors available, they wanted to emulate the sounds of flutes, clarinets, trumpets, violins, and other acoustic instruments.

It is possible to create a decent representation of the middle, or sustain, portion of many of these instruments' sounds using only oscillators, especially wavetable oscillators. However, they still do not sound very realistic. It has been known for some time that the first few milliseconds (abbreviated ms) of a sound's attack is critical to our perception and recognition of the sound. With this idea in mind, some synthesizer manufacturers began experimenting with a system that first played a very short sample of a sound's attack and then smoothly transitioned into an oscillator waveform. This hybrid oscillator approach, sometimes called Sample+Synthesis (or S+S), did a nice job of using limited memory capacity for maximum effectiveness, while still relying on a basic oscillator to produce the majority of the sound. Perhaps the most popular application of this technique came with the line of Linear Arithmetic (LA) synthesizers produced by Roland in the 1980s and still found on stages and in recording studios today.

Figure 2.20
The Roland D-50 Linear Arithmetic Synthesizer was famous for its complex sounds produced by combining short attack samples with oscillator waveforms. (photo printed with permission of Roland Corp.)

Sample-Playback Sources

As good as the hybrid oscillators were at improving the "realism" of sounds, their reliance on oscillator waveforms for the bulk of the sound still presented problems for users wanting to recreate authentic acoustic instrument sounds. By the late 1980s, the idea of recording, storing, and editing audio as a digital file was quite common. As computer memory became cheaper and its storage capacity much greater, synthesizer manufacturers took advantage of this technological growth to increase the capacity for storing digital audio files in their instruments. They were no longer limited to the small single-cycle wave files needed before but could store numerous sound files of several seconds each. It did not require too much of a leap to realize that if you wanted to make a synthesizer that sounded like a clarinet, you could just record a clarinet sound as a digital audio file, and have the instrument play the sound back when triggered.

Technically, these instruments are no longer using "oscillators" but are instead using sample-playback devices. Some manufacturers acknowledged this difference and began calling the internal sample-playback device something like a "source" or a "sound source." Other companies, though, continued to use the name oscillator. Creating even further confusion for many synthesizer users, manufacturers would sometimes call this approach to using samples "wavetable synthesis." As we have already seen, though, wavetable synthesis is actually a completely different process.

With the use of digital audio files, or *samples*, as their source material, a whole new breed of devices sprang up generally referred to as "samplers." Technically, the word applies only to devices that can record their own samples. Instruments that can load and play prerecorded samples are more correctly known as "sample players" or "ROMplers" (referring to read-only memory, the portion of the instrument's internal memory where the digital audio files are stored). Although some instruments simply play the recorded samples when triggered, others treat the samples as the same type of raw material as that created by an oscillator, manipulating them with the same synthesis processing they would use on an oscillator wave. For the sake of this text, we refer to these instruments as sample-based synthesizers. There are numerous sources of information on the recording and editing of samples, so I will not deal with that here. Instead, let's examine the sample-playback sources in the same manner with which we have been looking at the oscillators.

TIP **Disambiguation**

In digital audio and synthesis, the word *sample* can have three meanings. All three relate to digital recording of audio, but the word's specific meaning comes from its context, and it generally refers to the length or type of usage of the audio file.

1. In digital recording, a sample usually means one single measurement of a sound wave as calculated by the analog-to-digital converter (ADC). These are usually either sixteen or twenty-four bits in data size and represent one 44,100th or less of a second.

TIP *continued*

2. With synthesizers, a sample usually refers to a short recording of a sound that is meant for playback when triggered by the instrument. The length of these recordings varies according to the amount of storage memory available on the instrument as well as the sustain length of the sound being recorded. For example, a cymbal crash sample would need to be much longer than a woodblock sample because of the long decay of the cymbal's sound.

3. In the composition and production world, a sample often refers to a prerecorded section of a piece of music that is used as a compositional element. These samples might be things such as a particular guitar riff, a drum groove, or a vocal chorus.

Obviously, there is some overlap among the three uses of the word, but it is helpful for the synthesizer user to be aware of these subtle differences.

Just as you need multiple oscillators to play multiple notes, you need multiple sample-playback sources and audio files to play multiple notes. Since the earliest sample players had very little storage memory, the designers of these instruments looked for ways to conserve it. The first solution—quickly abandoned—was to use lower-quality samples that needed less storage space. These samples sounded inferior to what people expected and, as soon as more memory became available, were replaced with samples of the same audio quality as that found on a compact disc.

Another space-saving method was to assign one sample to a range of four or five notes, instead of recording a sample for every possible note. The samples were then transposed up or down as needed by simply playing the file faster or slower. With an oscillator, you can easily change the frequency (pitch) by either speeding up or slowing down the rate of the oscillator wave. With samples, though, you can change the speed by only a small amount before the timbre of the sample begins to change dramatically, and the difference in sample length becomes obvious.

Since it is impossible to predict how long a user will want to sustain a sample, the concept of sample looping was implemented. Within each sample, a specific loop zone is identified that represents the middle, or sustain, portion of a note. When the user presses the key, the sample begins. If the key is still being pressed when playback reaches the end of the loop zone, the player jumps back to the beginning of the loop zone and keeps repeating that section until the key is released, telling the playback source to go to the final release portion of the sample. In addition to allowing samples to be unlimited in their playback length, looping also helps with storage memory as the samples can all be rather short, so long as they have a good loop section identified. Of course, sounds such as piano notes and cymbal crashes that have a continuous decay as they sustain will not work in this scenario, and they are usually reduced in volume as they loop, or actually sampled for the entire duration of their sound.

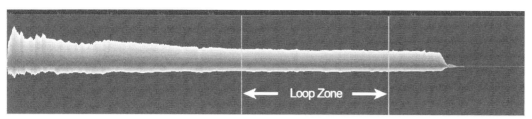

Figure 2.21
A trumpet sample with a loop zone identified.

51

Listen carefully to a good musician playing an instrument and you will notice numerous, subtle variations in timbre, articulation, vibrato, pitch, loudness, and so on. When the musician plays a loud note and then a soft note—even on the same pitch—is there a difference in more than just loudness? On most instruments, changing the loudness of notes also changes the attack and release to the notes, the timbre of the notes, and even the length of the notes. Put that into the context of the music being played—a rock tune, a jazz waltz, a march, or a symphony—and those differences are modified further. In other words, when musicians sing or play their instruments, they make thousands of subtle changes to their sound according to the context in which the particular sound is happening. Since samples are digital recordings, they do not have as much flexibility for adjustment and morphing as oscillators do. You need dozens of sets of samples to produce all the various articulations, dynamics, timbres, phrasings, and so forth that musicians can produce naturally.

The early sample-based synthesizers generally had only one set of samples for every recorded sound, and no matter how you played the synthesizer you always got the same quality of sound. On listening, you quickly found it obvious that the sound was a sample and not an acoustic instrument due to the lack of subtlety expected from an acoustic instrument's sound.

As sample-based synthesizers gained more memory, and especially as they moved onto the personal computer, many of the memory restrictions of the older hardware instruments began to vanish. With increased memory came the ability to load multiple sets of samples to help recreate the many articulations and sounds that acoustic instruments produce. Most sample-based synthesizers also added a number of tools and controls to let the player instantly switch, or morph, between these samples, allowing a much more realistic performance of the sound. It is well beyond our scope to explain all the various techniques of working with layered samples, but the user of a sample-based synthesizer is likely to encounter some of the following terminology when working with sample-playback sources, so I include brief definitions here:

- *Multisampling*: recording more than one sample per note of an instrument. These might be different articulations or timbres, or even multiple recordings of the same note and articulation, to provide some variety.
- *Keymap*: assigning various samples to specific keys on the controller (usually a MIDI keyboard).
- *Velocity map*: assigning multiple samples recorded at different dynamic levels to a single key. As you strike the key harder, not only does the sound grow louder but the playback source switches to a sample that has a "louder" tone quality to it.

- *Key switch*: assigning a set of keys on the MIDI keyboard (usually the very low-est octave) to switch between types of samples. This is often used to change between articulations, as with legato and staccato, for example.
- *Control switch*: similar to key switch, but using some sort of MIDI controller like the Modulation Wheel or Sustain Pedal to switch between types of samples.
- *Round-robin*: the ability of a sample-playback synthesizer to switch between multiple versions of the same sample so that repeated notes do not all sound alike.

Figure 2.22

A piano sample keymap with eight velocity samples for every key. Each box represents one loaded sample with velocity range progressing from softest at the bottom to loudest at the top.

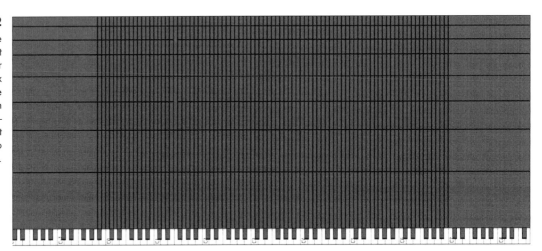

Grain Sources

Demo 2.5

No, this section is not about where to buy wheat or barley, but about Granular Synthesis, one of the newest trends in synthesizer sound creation. The secret to this approach is the use of tiny fragments of digital sound recordings (usually less than 50 ms in length) known as grains. Each grain is so short that when heard individually it often sounds like a click or a short hiss. Combine it with hundreds of other grains at the same time, and you can create a wonderful, swirling "cloud" of sound.

To help create a mental picture of granular synthesis, imagine attending a sporting event in a huge stadium. If you listen to the sound of the crowd, you often hear a sustained roar that tends to rise and fall in loudness and even pitch. However, if you think about it, that roar is actually the result of thousands of individual voices, each saying or shouting something different from all the other voices in the stadium. Similarly, granular synthesis creates a composite sound by randomly combining hundreds, even thousands, of microscopic grains of sound. Think of each grain as an individual voice, and the granular sound as the roar of the crowd.

Depending on the structure of the granular synthesizer, sound grains may be extracted from a single section of a sound file, from multiple locations in the same sound file, or even from locations in completely different sound files. Once the selection boundaries have been chosen, you are usually presented with a number of options for defining the creation of the grains. Because the intent is to create a somewhat random sound, these options are usually in the form of ranges rather than specific values. For example, you might select a range for a grain duration of 10–20 ms. In this case, the grain source would randomly select tiny snippets of sound varying between 10 and 20 milliseconds in length from your preselected region. Other ranges include values such as transposition amount, loudness, density, and spatial placement of the grains. As each grain is created, a quick fade-in and fade-out is applied to prevent clicks as the grain starts and stops.

With so many variables for creating grains, the sound constantly morphs. When played slowly, the grains tend to produce an atmospheric cloud of sound that evolves over time, and when played quickly they tend to produce pitched notes with exotic timbres. If the boundaries from which the grains are chosen are repositioned, the timbre of the grains also changes according to the frequency content in the new section of audio. One popular technique in granular synthesis is to slowly move the section window around while the grains are playing, to produce these sonic changes.

Of course, creating and making all these changes to hundreds of grains in real time requires a large amount of computing power. Even though the concept of granular synthesis has been around for a long time, it was not practical until recently. Because of the need for computing speed and power, most granular synthesizers are available only as computer applications, not as hardware devices.

Figure 2.23
A granular synthesizer such as Granite from New Sonic Arts allows the user to select a portion of a sound wave and extract hundreds of tiny "grains" of sound that are then manipulated and combined to create a rich, and evolving, sonic texture.

Throughout this chapter, we have looked at common methods of sound creation for synthesizers. As we have seen, there are a variety of ways to create these sonic raw materials, and many synthesizer manufacturers provide multiple ways of doing so. Regardless of the method, these raw materials still need to be refined and forged into the incredibly rich sonic textures we have come to expect from synthesizers. We will start that refining process in the next chapter, when we begin mixing our raw materials to create exotic compounds of sound. For now, though, it's your turn to explore and experiment with the concepts we have discussed in this chapter.

Your Turn

Working with Crystal

In Chapter 1 you explored the preset sounds that came with Crystal. Now you will begin working with Crystal to create your own sounds. With the Modulation tab chosen, click the Browse button in the Patches pane and choose **RefiningSound.fxb** from the Banks menu. Click the Patches menu and you will see that the first item in the list is called **default** and all the other slots are labeled **unused**. Selecting the default patch sets Crystal to a basic sine wave oscillator with all other effects disabled. You will use the default patch as a starting point throughout this book as you create new sounds and store them in the unused slots of the RefiningSound.fxb bank.

Figure 2.24
Select the "default" patch from the RefiningSound.fxb bank of patches.

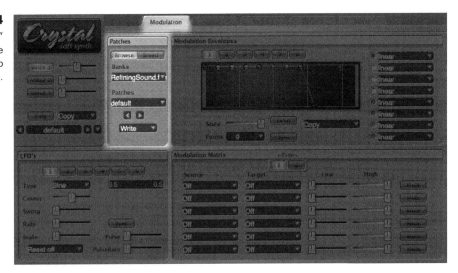

After selecting the default patch, click the Voice 1 tab. As with many newer synthesizers, rather than using a single oscillator to create a sound Crystal uses a set of oscillators to create a single "voice" in the synthesized sound. Crystal has three such voices, all identical in function. In this chapter, we focus on voice 1 and ignore the two large panes in the window labeled Filters and Amplitude. We will work with those in coming chapters.

Locate the voice mixer, polyphony (Poly) button, and control value display directly beneath the Crystal logo as shown in Figure 2.25. This pane will always be available regardless of the selected tab. The default patch turns the volume down in the voice mixer for voices 2 and 3 so that you hear only voice 1. We will add the other two voices in the next chapter.

The polyphony button is set to twelve-note polyphony in the default patch. Click the polyphony button once to give Crystal twenty-four-note polyphony, and click again to turn polyphony off, putting Crystal in monophonic mode. With some sounds it is best to leave a synthesizer in monophonic mode, while others need to be polyphonic. Although it is not usually a problem on newer computers with large amounts of RAM, increasing the polyphony of a software synthesizer can put greater demands on a computer's operating system and available memory. For our purposes here, leave the polyphony button set to **Poly 12**. Now that Crystal is configured, let's start exploring its oscillators.

Voice 1 tab

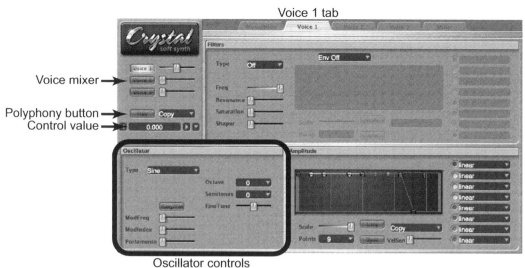

Voice mixer →

Polyphony button →
Control value →

Oscillator controls

Figure 2.25
Location of the
various oscillator
control functions for
voice 1.

55

Oscillator Type

On all three voice tabs, the oscillator controls are located directly beneath the control value display. The first control allows you to choose the type of oscillator sound. Clicking the Type menu reveals three submenus (Synthesized, Sampled, Sound fonts), each with its own menu of sounds. The default patch loads **Synthesized:Sine**, and if you play some notes you will hear the dark tones of sine wave oscillators.[4]

The Sampled submenu produces a number of complex sounds that are actual recordings of other synthesizers' finished sounds. The Sound fonts submenu provides access to a number of instrumental samples that can be used to represent a variety of acoustic instruments. Sound fonts are a special type of sample file initially developed for the Emu line of samplers and sample playback instruments. These files usually contain multiple layers and keymaps of acoustic instrument samples to create a greater degree of realism as the sound is distributed across the keyboard. Of course, feel free to listen to all these sounds, but since our purpose here is *creation* of sound, we will mostly concern ourselves with the first submenu.

Highlight the Synthesized submenu to reveal its list of synthesizer wave types. Notice that when you select some sounds from the menu three additional controls appear: Mogrify, PulseMix, and PulseWidth. We will look at the Mogrify control in Chapter 3 when we discuss oscillator sync, but the other two controls will be important for us here as we examine the types of oscillator sounds in Crystal.

- *SawSquare* produces a sawtooth wave when the PulseMix slider is all the way to the left and a pulse wave when pushed all the way to the right. Positioning the slider somewhere in the middle produces a mix of both wave types. The PulseWidth slider adjusts the width of the pulse wave (see Figure 2.10). Placing the slider at the far left produces a square wave, while moving it to the right changes the pulse width to produce varying degrees of negative and positive pulse waves.
- *Sine* produces a basic sinusoidal waveform.

---

4 In this text, I will use the convention of **Synthesized:Sine** to identify an oscillator type. Interpret this as selecting **Sine** from the **Synthesized** subdirectory of oscillator types.

- *Noise* produces white noise.
- *Triangle* produces a triangle-shaped waveform.
- *Clang* is similar to SawSquare, but with a large number of inharmonic partials to create a more "metallic" sound.
- *WarmSaw* is also similar to SawSquare, but with a "warmer," "analog" sound.

Select each oscillator type and play both single notes and chords. Be sure to play in a number of registers of your keyboard, as many sounds differ when played up high versus down low. With the SawSquare, Clang, and WarmSaw waves, experiment with the Pulse-Mix and PulseWidth controls as well. To hear a sawtooth wave, select SawSquare and position the PulseMix and control all the way to the left. To hear a square wave, position the PulseMix control all the way to the right and the PulseWidth control all the way to the left.

Oscillator Tuning

To the right of the oscillator type dropdown menu are three controls for adjusting the tuning of the oscillator. Octave allows you to raise and lower the pitch of the oscillator ±2 octaves, while Semitones raises and lowers the oscillator ±11 semitones. The Fine-Tune slider raises and lowers the oscillator frequency within a single semitone. These controls will be quite important when we begin combining oscillators in the next chapter.

Portamento

Beneath the oscillator type menu and controls are several controls for ring modulation and FM synthesis that we will examine in coming chapters. For now, look at the slider labeled Portamento. In musical terms, *portamento* is a slide between pitches as when a violinist keeps a left-hand finger pressed down on a string while sliding to a new note. On a synthesizer, the portamento control—often called the *glide* control—is used to create such a glide between notes. It is typically used in monophonic mode. When you play a new note, instead of the new pitch sounding instantly the note starts with the previous pitch and glides to the new pitch. On Crystal, moving the slider all the way to the left turns portamento off, while moving the control to the right increases the effect.

Granularization

Although it is not a granular synthesizer in the strictest sense, Crystal does have the ability to create grains of sound from its sampled and sound font oscillator types. To hear the granular effect, select an oscillator type such as **Sampled:Cymbal**. You will notice that two new sliders, labeled Granular and WaveDens, appear beneath the oscillator type menu. With both sliders all the way to the left, first listen to the Cymbal sound with no granularization. Next, move the Granular slider to the middle and notice that the cymbal sound begins to break up into short, changing snippets of sound rather than a continuous sound. The further the slider is moved to the right, the more pronounced the effect becomes.

With the Granular slider in the middle, move the WaveDens slider to the middle as well. This slider adjusts the boundaries of the grains, causing them to overlap one another. The further you move the slider, the greater the amount of overlap, producing a more continuous quality to the sound. Even small changes in one or both of the granular sliders can have a large impact on the granularization of the sound. Like all the other oscillator types, this granular sound can be used as one of the voices in the composite sound.

Using Your Own Synthesizer(s)

Now that you have a sense of the basic oscillators in Crystal, take a look at other synthesizers you own or to which you have access.

1. What are the oscillators called?
2. How many oscillators does the synthesizer have?
3. Are the oscillators (or sources) all the same type, or are there different kinds?
4. Set your synthesizer to its Basic preset as described in the Introduction of this book to make sure that all modulators, filters, envelopes, effects, etc. are turned off, allowing you to focus just on the oscillator sounds.
5. Isolate a single oscillator by turning the others off (usually by turning their volume all the way down).
   A. Listen to the types of waveforms and sounds the oscillator can make.
   B. Experiment with the various controls that may be available, such as Coarse and Fine Tuning, Pulse Width, Phase, etc.
6. Repeat no. 5 with each type of oscillator you have on your synthesizer until you have heard all the various oscillator sounds your instrument is capable of making.

Remember that oscillators are the raw materials of the synthesis process. As such, it is extremely important that you have a strong sense of how they work and sound. We will build on this foundation in the coming chapters, so spend some time getting familiar with your oscillators and their sounds.

3

Oscillator Combinations

Creating Exotic Compounds *from Your Raw Materials*

Online materials for this chapter:

http://www.oup.com/refiningsound/Chapter3.html

In the previous chapter, we examined the oscillators, or raw material resources, of a synthesizer. Although raw materials in the physical world can be quite valuable on their own, their true worth often comes from being combined with other raw materials to create complex and exotic compounds. Likewise, the complex and exotic sounds created by synthesizers usually come from combining the raw materials of synthesis: the oscillators. Oscillator combinations typically occur with one of two basic methods. The first involves simply adding or mixing the oscillator outputs together to create a more complex sonority. The second method uses one oscillator to control, or manipulate, another oscillator. In this chapter, we examine both methods and the most common applications of each.

Figure 3.1
The two basic methods for combining oscillators: mixing their audio outputs (left) and using the output of one oscillator to control another oscillator (right).

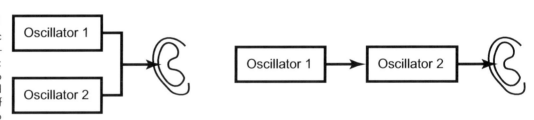

Combining Sound Waves

Demo 3.1

Before we can effectively discuss combining oscillators, we need to spend a bit of time talking about combining sound waves. Anyone who has ever used an audio mixer is familiar with the idea of combining sounds to create a "mix" of the individual sounds. Let's say you mix the sound of a trumpet, a guitar, and a snare drum together. Does the loudspeaker, or your eardrum for that matter, vibrate separately for each of the three sounds? No, it vibrates with the composite oscillations created by adding the energy of the three sounds together.

TIP Get in Line! (or Not)

Acousticians, audio engineers, and synthesizer designers often describe the behavior of complex sound waves with the terms *linear* and *nonlinear*. A linear system is one in which the input and output remain proportional. In other words, for every change in input, there is a proportional change in output. A nonlinear system does not maintain the proportional relationship between input and output.

With sound waves, the term *linear* is used to describe the natural interaction of sound wave energy where the composite sound is simply the sum of all the individual sounds. In the purest sense, the parallel combination of oscillators on the left in Figure 3.1 produces a linear sound response.

Nonlinear sound refers to sound waves that are combined in such a way that the output sound is quite different from the input. Nonlinear sound usually contains a number of frequencies that are not part of the original waves. This is the concept behind the oscillator combination on the right in Figure 3.1.

It should be noted that the human ear is also nonlinear in responding to sound. When sound energy consisting of combined frequencies strikes our eardrum, especially at high amplitudes, we frequently hear so-called *combination* or *Tartini* tones as a result of the nonlinear distortion produced in our ears. Named after the eighteenth-century Italian violinist Giuseppe Tartini, who is often credited with being the first to notice these additional frequencies, Tartini tones are a psychoacoustic phenomenon that varies greatly from person to person and is also highly dependent on the amplitudes and frequencies of the original sounds being produced. Although some composers and electronic musicians have attempted to create music that produces such additional frequencies, the result tends to be rather unpredictable, since it depends on the listener.

For our purposes, let's confine our study to the types of combination tones that are produced acoustically, by natural sound wave interactions (linear combinations), and through deliberate manipulations of sound waves that force the creation of new frequencies (nonlinear combinations).

From our discussion in Chapter 1, recall that sound energy consists of two phases, called compression and rarefaction. When two sound waves are at the same point in their compression or rarefaction phase, we describe them as being *in phase* with one another. When this happens, their two energy levels complement each other and are added together (linear combination) to create a larger amplitude of compression or rarefaction. By contrast, when one wave is in its compression phase while the other is in its rarefaction phase, we refer to the waves as being *out of phase* with each other, and the positive energy from one wave cancels the negative energy of the other wave. In fact, if you combine equal amounts of positive and negative energy—as can happen when a sound wave is combined with a 180° out-of-phase copy of itself—the two waves completely cancel each other out, and you have total silence, as shown in Figure 3.2.

As you combine more sound waves together, the process of adding and subtracting energy levels continues. In Figure 3.3, note the frequency and amplitude of the three

Figure 3.2

Equal amounts of positive and negative energy cancel each other out.

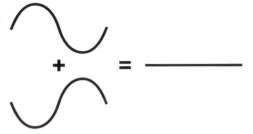

source waves and how they add together to create the composite wave at the bottom. If you look vertically down the diagram, you will see that when all of the waves are in a positive phase (1), the composite wave is also positive, and its amplitude is quite large, being the sum of the three source waves. Similarly, when the three source waves are all in a negative phase (2), you see a large negative trough in the composite wave. Where things get really interesting is when some waves are in a positive phase while others are in a negative phase (3). When this happens, some of the energy is canceled out, just as happens in mathematics when you add positive and negative numbers together.

Figure 3.3

Natural sound wave energy is added together (linear combination) to create a more complex composite wave.

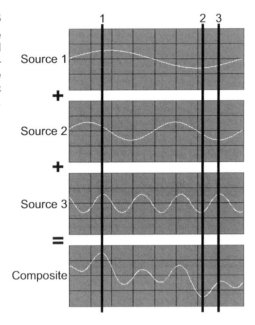

In Figure 3.3, we combined only three simple sine waves. As you might imagine, if you mix numerous sound waves together, all of their myriad interactions with one another can create an incredibly complex composite wave, like that shown in Figure 3.4.

Figure 3.4

A complex composite wave created by mixing hundreds of sound waves together.

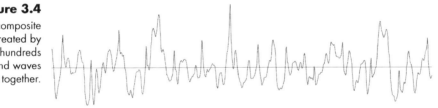

Demo 3.2

Beat and Combination Frequencies

In the complex acoustic world, all the frequencies we hear add together in such a way that the sums and differences of their various amplitudes can appear random in the composite wave. However, if we limit the sound source to a small number of steady frequencies, as often happens with electronic instruments, or even two acoustic musicians playing together, the rising and falling amplitudes in the composite wave can occur at a steady, recurring rate that begins to take on a life of its own.

We know that when two waves are in phase with each other, their amplitudes add together to create even greater amplitude. When the waves are out of phase with each other, their amplitudes cancel each other out to produce low amplitude, even silence. If two sound sources are close to each other in frequency, their waves might begin in phase. As time passes, though, they will gradually drift out of phase as the higher-frequency wave moves ahead, until their amplitudes begin to cancel each other. As time passes, they will eventually drift back in phase with each other. They will repeat this in-and-out-of-phase cycle as long as the two frequencies continue to sound.

Remember from Chapter 1 that frequency is a by-product of changing amplitude. The faster a sound wave rises and falls, the higher we perceive it to be in frequency. In our scenario above, we have a pair of sound waves whose rising and falling amplitudes create the frequencies of the two waves. We also have an additional rising and falling amplitude as a result of the linear interaction between the two waves producing a *combination tone*. If the resultant rising and falling amplitude of the combination tone occurs more than twenty to thirty times a second, we sometimes hear a new frequency. On the other hand, if the combination tone produces a rising and falling amplitude fewer than twenty times a second, we usually hear a pulsing or throbbing in the overall amplitude of the two original sound waves, known as *beats*.

Although there are actually several combination tones produced, if we can hear them at all, we generally hear only the one that occurs at the mathematical difference of the two original frequencies, known as the *difference frequency*. Calculating difference (and beat) frequencies is quite simple: subtract one frequency from the other; $f_{diff} = (f_1 - f_2)$. Remember that there is no such thing as a negative frequency, so even if the formula produces a negative number, we always use the absolute value of the difference. Thus, 1,000 Hz − 800 Hz = 200 Hz, and 800 Hz − 1,000 Hz = |−200| or 200 Hz.

If one tone (f_1) has a frequency of 201 Hz, and the other tone (f_2) a frequency of 200 Hz, the difference is less than 20 Hz, so instead of a combination tone we hear a beat once per second, or at 1 Hz (201 Hz − 200 Hz = 1 Hz). If the first tone is raised to 206 Hz, we hear beating at 6 Hz. These beat frequencies occur whenever there are two similar tones at a close frequency interval; just like the difference frequency, they can always be calculated with the formula $f_{beat} = f_1 - f_2$. Beat frequencies are one way musicians tune to each other. If you listen to two instrumentalists tuning, you will notice that they both play the same note, and if they are not perfectly in tune a beat frequency occurs. Usually, one player (the principal) will hold steady while the other player slowly adjusts the tuning on their instrument until the beats disappear. At that point, they are perfectly in tune.

If you listen very carefully to the two frequencies that are producing a beat frequency, you may also notice that it sounds as if the pitch has shifted just a bit to fall between the two original frequencies. This is, again, a by-product of our nonlinear hearing. When two tones are quite close in frequency, rather than hearing the two distinct frequencies we tend to hear the *average frequency* of the two original frequencies, $f_{avg} = \frac{1}{2}(f_1 + f_2)$. As the two original frequencies move farther apart, we hear the sound change from the average frequency to a rather "fuzzy" and hard-to-identify frequency, and eventually we hear the sound separate into the two original tones once they are far enough apart.

For the sake of making this explanation as clear as possible, we have been assuming the use of basic sine waves to illustrate combination and beat frequencies. As you may recall from Chapter 2, sine waves produce only a fundamental frequency with no overtones. Thus if we combine sounds that are much more complex, each with a number of audible overtones, not only will we create combination tones from the fundamental frequencies, we will also create them between all the corresponding overtones, and even between the stronger combination tones themselves. The resulting sonic richness is a key to synthesis and, as we will see throughout this chapter, plays a fundamental role in the creation of sound on a synthesizer.

Mixing Oscillator Sounds

On the earliest hardware synthesizers, the oscillators were individual pieces of equipment. In order to mix them together, they were all connected to an audio mixer with cables, and the controls on the mixer were used to combine the oscillators and set their individual levels. Although many synthesizers still have an oscillator mixer in their design, others assume that the individual oscillators need to be mixed, and rather than having a separate mixer they combine the oscillators but provide separate volume, or level, controls on each oscillator. To mix two oscillators together, you simply turn both of their level controls up until you have the desired sound.

Figure 3.5
Rather than having an oscillator mixer, the oscillators in Avid's Hybrid synthesizer all have their own level controls, allowing them to be easily combined.

Oscillator Stacking

The most basic approach to mixing oscillators is combining timbres to create a blended sound. In much the same way an orchestrator might combine the sound of a clarinet, a horn, and a viola to create a different timbre, oscillators with contrasting waveforms may be mixed together, or stacked, to produce new and interesting sounds. In Chapter 4 we explore using envelope generators to cross-fade between these different sounds, creating evolving timbres, but for the sake of our current discussion, we will consider all sounds to occur simultaneously. Although the concept of stacking oscillators together is one of the oldest and most basic approaches in synthesis, there are several other ways of mixing oscillators, including two of the newest synthesis techniques: granular synthesis and physical modeling synthesis.

Granular Synthesis

In Chapter 2, we discussed grain sources and the manipulations a grain can undergo to create an evolving sound. In practice, though, there are usually multiple grains sounding at any one time. The same types of manipulations—both random and controlled—that were applied to the individual grains can also be used on a larger scale to govern things such as the location and boundaries of the area (or areas) from which the grains are selected, the number of grains sounding simultaneously, and even cross-fades between multiple selection areas. The sounds of all the grains are mixed together in such a randomly changing way that the composite creates the constantly morphing and evolving sound for which granular synthesis is known.

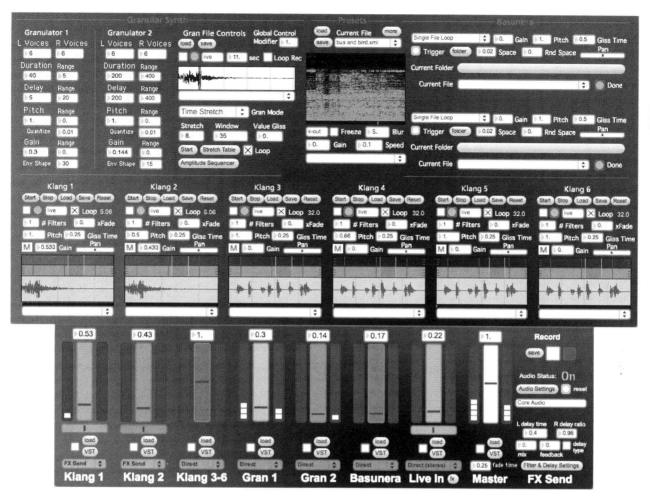

Figure 3.6

A full-featured granular synthesizer such as Kenaxis allows users to create rich sonic textures by manipulating and combining grains from multiple grain sources.

TIP

Graintable Synthesis

For a number of years, the Swedish software company Propellerhead has touted a process they call Graintable Synthesis in their Malström synthesizer. This synthesizer has become so popular that a brief clarification of the term *graintable* is warranted here. As an elision of the words grain and wavetable, it implies a hybrid between granular synthesis and wavetable synthesis. The company's own literature describes the process as "neither granular nor wavetable synthesis but a combination of the best of both methods."[1] Although they are rather coy in their description of the process, it is built on a number of complex, pre-programmed samples (they call them wavetables) to which the user is able to apply many of the various granular processes described above.

1 "Propellerhead—Reason—Malström Graintable Synthesizer," http://www.propellerheads.se/products/reason/index.cfm?fuseaction=get_article&article=devices_malstrom (accessed Aug. 21, 2012).

Physical Modeling Synthesis

You probably know that the sound of an acoustic musical instrument is made up of multiple complex vibrations. The sound of a trumpet, for example, consists of numerous sonic elements: buzzing lips on the mouthpiece, air vibrations radiating through the cylindrical brass tube, air interactions with the valves, physical vibrations of the bell, air vibrations coming out of the bell, and even the type of room in which the trumpet is sounding. The acoustic behavior of each of these sonic elements can be described by complex mathematical formulae. What if a synthesizer could do all of the calculations necessary to recreate each sonic element in a wavetable, and combine them all together in the proper order and relationship? Theoretically, then, the synthesizer could accurately "create" the sound of an acoustic musical instrument. Such is the idea behind physical modeling synthesis.

Physical modeling synthesizers attempt to accurately reproduce and combine all of the acoustical elements that go into a sound. The instrument typically allows the user to select items such as bow placement, mouthpiece type, reed type, tube length, instrument shape, instrument material, etc., and build a sound by combining these various elements. Although these synthesizers frequently allow users to create some "new" instruments, they are usually focused on creating, as realistically as possible, existing acoustic instruments. The final output of the physical modeling synthesizer, then, is a mix of the sounds created by multiple wavetables driven by various mathematical formulae. In theory, although not always in practice, these synthesizers combine their elements into a fairly *realistic* representation of an acoustic instrument.

As you might suspect, physical modeling requires a large amount of computational power for the many calculations and wavetables. This means it is usually available only in a computer software application. Additionally, because of the complexity in creating the formulae that go into physically modeling an acoustic instrument, these synthesizers tend to focus on a particular type or category of instrument, such as woodwinds, brass, pianos, drums, or strings.

Figure 3.7
Pianoteq, a physical modeling piano synthesizer by Modartt, allows the user to shape and control nearly every aspect of a piano's sound.

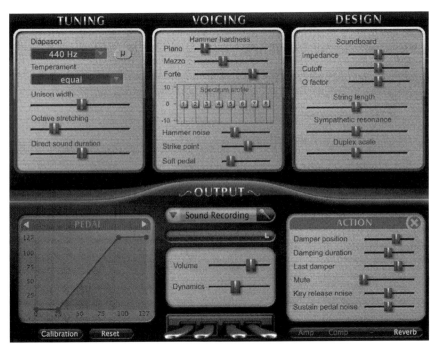

Multiwave Oscillators

In the previous sections we discussed the idea of combining contrasting oscillator sounds to produce a complex, layered sound. What happens, though, when we combine similar, or even identical, oscillator sounds, but at slightly different frequencies? Remember from Demo 3.2 that when you combine two sine wave oscillators that are close together in frequency, a strong beat frequency is created. However, when you switch the oscillator type to sawtooth, the intensity of the beating diminishes while the richness of the combined sound dramatically increases. Remember also that when two oscillators are close enough together in frequency to produce a beat frequency, our ear tends to hear the *average* frequency rather than the two original frequencies. With multiwave oscillators, we use both of these concepts to generate an extremely rich oscillator sound.

The multiwave oscillator is usually created with a minimum of three oscillators, all typically producing the same type of complex wave, such as a sawtooth or pulse wave. The second oscillator is tuned a few cents higher than the first oscillator, and the third oscillator is tuned the same number of cents lower than the first oscillator. The result of this detuning, a bit of "fighting" between the harmonics of the three oscillators, creates a wonderfully rich timbre, while the average frequency of the two outer oscillators coincides with the frequency of the original oscillator to create a stable pitch. For even more richness, add two additional oscillators. Tune one of them a different number of cents higher than the original oscillator, and tune the other the same number of cents lower than the original. Again, these two new outer oscillators should be equidistant in cents from the original. The more you add to the mix, the richer the sound becomes.

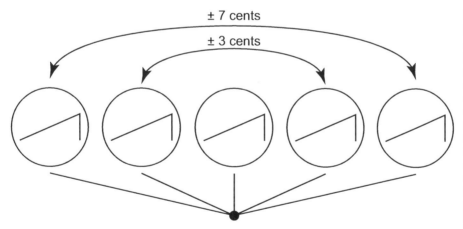

Figure 3.8
In this example, detuning two sawtooth oscillators ± 3 cents from the central sawtooth oscillator, and two additional sawtooth oscillators ± 7 cents from the central oscillator, creates a multiwave oscillator when they are all mixed back together. Since each pair of detuned oscillators is equidistant from the central one, their *average* frequency is the same as the frequency of the central oscillator, creating a stable pitch, but with a wonderfully rich sound.

Changing the detuning amounts of all the outer oscillators, or even making the detunings asymmetrical, can create numerous interesting variations of the multiwave oscillator. You can also change the levels of the individual oscillators to adjust the timbre of all the harmonics created by this technique. Try mixing both sawtooth *and* pulse wave oscillators for an edgier timber from your multiwave oscillator.

Additive Synthesis

As we just saw, combining similar oscillator sounds can create some wonderfully interesting results. Another type of multi-oscillator combination takes a rather different approach, though. Instead of mixing a few complex oscillator waves, here we combine numerous—often dozens, or even several hundred—basic sine waves at differing frequencies and amplitudes to create a complex harmonic spectrum; this is the core of the process known as *additive synthesis*. Technically, any of the methods described in the paragraphs above could be considered additive synthesis, but the term is usually reserved for this concept of adding multiple sine waves to create a harmonic spectrum.

Additive synthesis combines multiple basic oscillators so that their summed outputs create more complex colors and timbres. In the quest to create more interesting synthesizer sounds, additive synthesis was one of the earliest approaches and was the process behind Cahill's Telharmonium. Unfortunately, since it required a large number of individual oscillators—and oscillators in the early days of synthesizer development were large and costly—additive synthesis was mostly abandoned in favor of another technique known as subtractive synthesis. With the advent of wavetable synthesis and the amount of processing power available in modern computers, though, additive synthesis is staging a bit of a comeback.

TIP

Addition or Subtraction?

- *Additive synthesis* is the process of combining the basic waves of multiple oscillators to produce a complex sound.
- *Subtractive synthesis* is the process of using audio filters to remove frequencies from an already complex sound. We will explore subtractive synthesis at length in Chapter 5 when we discuss audio filters.

These two common approaches to synthesis are somewhat analogous to the two basic approaches to sculpture. Think of additive synthesis as the sculptor who builds up clay until it takes on the desired shape. Subtractive synthesis, on the other hand, is like the sculptor who begins with a large block of stone and then carves away until it takes on the desired shape.

In the early nineteenth century, the French mathematician Joseph Fourier (1768–1830) posited the idea that any complex, periodic wave can be deconstructed into the sum of a series of simple sine waves. This series of waves became known as the Fourier series, and has become the foundation of additive synthesis as well as harmonic spectral analysis.

Demo 3.3

Once we accept the idea that a complex sound can be deconstructed into basic sine wave components, we must also accept the reverse: basic sine waves can be combined so as to construct a complex sound. Not only can complex sound waves be constructed this way, but as described in the following paragraphs—and as you will experience in Demo 3.3—even the other basic oscillator waveforms (triangle, sawtooth, and pulse) can be created from a Fourier series of harmonically related sine waves.

To create sounds with additive synthesis, begin with a single oscillator producing a fundamental frequency. Then add multiple oscillators with their own amplitude controls, each tuned to a fixed ratio of the fundamental oscillator's frequency. By using ratios to tune the other oscillators, the timbre of the sound remains constant as you raise and lower the pitch of the fundamental, say with a MIDI keyboard.

Using additive synthesis to create the other basic waveforms from sine waves is relatively easy. Set the fundamental oscillator's frequency. Add more oscillators, with each tuned to a successively higher harmonic of the fundamental frequency (twice the fundamental, three times, four times, etc.). For example, if the fundamental frequency is 80 Hz, the successive harmonics will be 160 Hz (2×80 Hz), 240 Hz (3×80 Hz), 320 Hz (4×80 Hz), and so on. As you add the harmonics, you will begin to hear an "organlike" sound develop.

Next, adjust the level of each harmonic so that its amplitude is the inverse of its harmonic number (e.g., harmonic no. 2 is at one-half amplitude, harmonic no. 3 is one-third amplitude, harmonic no. 4 is one-fourth amplitude, etc.), and you will see, and hear, that the composite wave begins to turn into a sawtooth wave. Now, turn off all of the even-numbered harmonics, leaving only the odd-numbered ones, and you begin to create a square wave.

Creating a triangle wave is only bit more complicated. Like the square wave, it is also built from odd-numbered harmonics, but with two major changes. The harmonic's amplitudes are set to the inverse square of their harmonic number (e.g., harmonic 3 is at one-ninth amplitude, harmonic 5 is one twenty-fifth amplitude, harmonic 7 is one forty-ninth amplitude, etc.). Second, the phase of every other odd-numbered harmonic (3, 7, 11, 15, etc.) is inverted, turning those waves upside down. With these modifications to a series of basic sine waves, you begin to produce a triangle wave. Adding more and more oscillators with the same types of ratios and amplitudes will move the rendered waveforms closer and closer to their ideal models, but it would require an infinite number of oscillators to attain the perfect shapes.

Since oscillators capable of producing the basic waveforms already exist, using additive synthesis to do so is generally unnecessary. However, this little exercise does help us understand how complex waves can be created from simple, harmonically related sine waves. Additive synthesis is best, though, when used to combine both harmonics *and* inharmonics. When you tune some oscillators to non-integer ratios (3.2, 4.73, 13.2, etc.), the additive synthesis process begins to produce wonderfully rich and exotic sounds.

As simple as the concept of additive synthesis is, as mentioned already there is one major drawback. In order to produce all the frequencies needed, a synthesizer requires a huge number of oscillators. Given the cost and computational inefficiency of large numbers of oscillators, additive synthesis today is almost always done with a wavetable approach, as discussed in Chapter 2. Wavetables allow the composite shape of multiple oscillator waveforms to be stored in a table, thus creating the effect of dozens of oscillators but with a single source. There are, however, a small number of synthesizers such as the Cube from VirSyn that take advantage of the processing power in modern computers to do actual additive synthesis, combining hundreds of sine wave oscillators to create incredibly rich and exotic sounds.

Figure 3.9

The Cube synthesizer by VirSyn uses additive synthesis with as many as 512 individual sine wave partials to create its sounds.

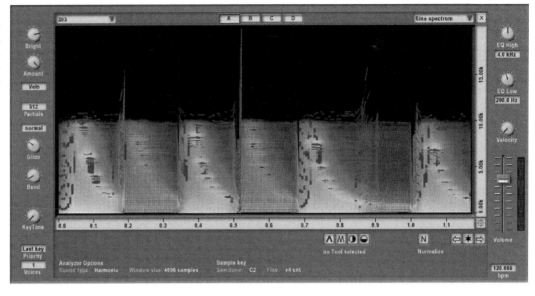

Controlling One Oscillator with Another Oscillator

Up to now, the methods of combining oscillators we have discussed all involve mixing the outputs of oscillators together in a linear fashion. In other words, all of them are sounding, and we hear the result of their combined outputs. The other common method of combining oscillators is to have one (or more) oscillator(s) manipulate, or control, another oscillator. With this approach, we usually do not hear the controlling oscillators, but only the sound of the controlled oscillators after being manipulated. Several popular approaches for controlling one oscillator with another have been used over the years. The beauty of these approaches is that wonderfully rich, fascinating sounds can be created with only a small number of oscillators thanks to their nonlinear response, whereas to create equally exotic sounds with a linear approach such as additive synthesis would require a huge number of oscillators.

In addition to its wave type, the typical oscillator has three primary characteristics that may be easily controlled: wave phase position, wave amplitude, and wave frequency. All three have been manipulated as a synthesis technique to create complex sounds.

Demo 3.4

Oscillator Sync Synthesis

Thus far, the starting phase position of an oscillator wave has been of little more than academic concern to us. Since oscillator waves repeat over and over, the "beginning" point of the wave matters little to our ear. In fact, an oscillator running by itself can start anywhere in its phase, and we most likely will never hear the difference. However, as we saw earlier, in combining oscillators, the phase position can be quite important to the sound.

Unless otherwise indicated, oscillators start their waves at the 0° position and proceed through the entire wave cycle. Many oscillators in contemporary synthesizers, though, have a phase control that allows the user to change the starting position. If an oscillator is forced to abruptly change its phase position in the middle of a cycle, a tiny "ripping" occurs in the oscillator's sound that produces a number of sonic anomalies.

Recall from Chapter 2 that the 0° position of a sine wave is the point where the wave begins the compression phase from the *zero crossing* (see Figure 2.11). The same is true for the pulse, or square, wave. When working with sawtooth and triangle waves, we typically move the 0° starting position to the very beginning of the upward ramp, rather than starting in the middle of a ramp. So when a sawtooth or triangle oscillator is instructed to restart, or retrigger its wave, it immediately jumps to the bottom of the ramp and begins ascending, no matter where it is in the cycle.

The concept behind oscillator synchronization—oscillator sync, as it is normally called—is that a controlling "master" oscillator forces a controlled "slave" oscillator to restart its wave, thus shifting the phase position. When synchronizing two oscillators, we connect them so that the master oscillator's output is not actually heard but forces

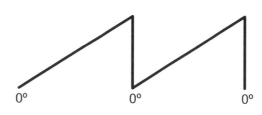

Figure 3.10
The "conventional" 0° position of a sawtooth wave is at the beginning of the ramp segment.

the slave oscillator to retrigger the wave from the 0° phase position every time the master oscillator begins its own wave.

Although the slave oscillator may be set to produce any type of waveform, the sawtooth and pulse waves tend to produce the most interesting results, with the sawtooth being the most popular by far. Since we do not actually hear the master oscillator, its wave type is relatively unimportant, but usually either a pulse or sawtooth wave is used as both waveforms have an instantaneous directional change that makes a good trigger for the slave oscillator.

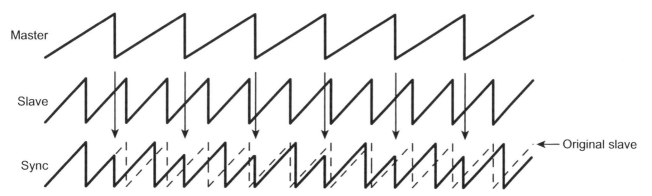

Figure 3.11
The master oscillator forces the slave to restart its wave every time the master starts its own wave. The resulting output of the oscillator sync is shown at bottom, along with the trajectory of the original slave oscillator wave.

Setting the master oscillator at a higher frequency than the slave oscillator simply causes the slave to output the same frequency as the master. In other words, if you set the frequency of the master oscillator to 400 Hz, and set the slave oscillator to 300 Hz, you will just hear a 400 Hz wave as the slave oscillator is forced to restart four hundred times a second.

However, if you set the frequency of the master oscillator *lower* than that of the slave oscillator, say at 200 Hz, an interesting thing happens. You continue to hear the 200 Hz frequency of the master oscillator, but you also hear a strong, secondary frequency of the slave oscillator (300 Hz in our example), as well as multiple additional frequencies that are created by the nonlinear interaction of the two oscillators. Remember that with oscillator sync you do not hear the master oscillator directly. Instead, you hear its frequency superimposed onto the slave oscillator. What is exciting, though, is the timbre of the sound changing dramatically according to the amplitudes and ratios of all the other frequencies generated. Those secondary frequencies—and thus the overall timbre of the sound—will vary, depending on the frequency relationship between the two oscillators.

In common practice, the slave oscillator is tuned not to a specific frequency but to a set percentage or ratio above the frequency of the master oscillator. Thus, you might set the slave oscillator to 150 percent of (or 1.5 times) the frequency of the master oscillator. Then, if the master oscillator is tuned to 200 Hz, the slave oscillator will be at 300 Hz as in the example above. By using a ratio rather than a set frequency, the relationship between the two frequencies remains constant, and the sonic color created by the oscillator sync is maintained no matter the frequency of the master oscillator. Thus, as you play notes on a MIDI keyboard, the pitch changes, but the timbre remains the same.

Raise and lower the slave oscillator ratio, and you will hear an interesting "swoosh" sound as a result of the changing ratios and amplitudes of all the secondary frequencies. In fact, one popular technique with oscillator sync is to use a low-frequency oscillator (more about LFOs in Chapter 6) to slowly sweep the slave oscillator ratio up and down, producing a repeating phase shift effect. Oscillator sync remains an extremely popular technique, and many of the "blistering" synthesizer sounds you hear are created with synced sawtooth oscillators.

TIP   **Hard or Soft?**

The oscillator sync process we have been describing—where the slave oscillator is forced to restart every time the master oscillator restarts—is often referred to as *hard sync*. Some synthesizers also offer an oscillator sync function called *soft sync*. Unfortunately, there are about as many versions of what gets called soft sync as there are manufacturers using the term. In general, soft sync refers to a process that is not quite as rigid in forcing the slave oscillator to restart. For example, it may force the slave oscillator to restart only when the master oscillator is within a certain amplitude range, or when it is in a specific positive or negative phase. However it works, the idea is to make the effect of the sync a bit gentler, or softer. If your synthesizer offers soft sync, be sure to consult the owner's manual for a specific explanation of how it is implemented on that instrument.

Although the origins of oscillator sync required two separate oscillators, most synthesizers today have combined the two into a single process. You no longer have to actually synchronize two oscillators. You simply choose something like saw sync or square sync as a wave type for the oscillator and then adjust the timbre of the sound. The timbre control is actually adjusting the ratio between the slave oscillator and an unseen master oscillator. In reality, though, many synthesizers do not even use actual oscillators for oscillator sync. Instead, they use either a wavetable that creates a representation of the synced oscillators, or recorded samples of actual synced oscillators to simulate this wonderful effect.

Amplitude Modulation (AM) Synthesis

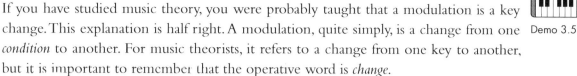

Demo 3.5

If you have studied music theory, you were probably taught that a modulation is a key change. This explanation is half right. A modulation, quite simply, is a change from one *condition* to another. For music theorists, it refers to a change from one key to another, but it is important to remember that the operative word is *change*.

In the audio and synthesis worlds, modulation is used in a number of contexts, but always referring to something changing. At the most basic synthesis level, an oscillator produces a modulating—or changing—voltage that rises and falls and is perceived as a sound wave. The final two oscillator combinations we examine in this chapter involve one oscillator (known, appropriately enough, as the *modulator*) changing the output of another oscillator (known as the *carrier*).

As the words suggest, *amplitude modulation* refers to changing the *amplitude* of a sound. If you turn the volume knob up and down several times per second on an amplifier, you create an amplitude modulation known as tremolo, where you can actually hear the amplitude rising and falling.

The concept of AM synthesis is the same as creating a tremolo, except at a much faster rate. The modulator in this case is in the audio-rate range (greater than 20 Hz). When the amplitude of the carrier's oscillator signal rises and falls that quickly, we no longer hear a tremolo. Instead, we hear a new set of frequencies on either side of the original carrier frequency, known as *sidebands*, that are a result of the peaks and valleys produced by the modulated amplitude.

With AM synthesis, the carrier oscillator usually produces a wave at a fixed frequency that is considerably higher than the modulator's highest frequency. The modulator, in turn, modulates, superimposing its shape onto the amplitude of the carrier wave. As it does so, sideband frequencies are produced on either side of the carrier frequency that are the sum of the carrier and modulator frequencies $(f_c + f_m)$ and the difference of the carrier and modulator frequencies $(f_c - f_m)$. For example, if the carrier is 1,000 Hz and the modulator 700 Hz, then in addition to the carrier frequency (the modulator is not heard) you will hear sidebands at 1,700 Hz $(1,000 + 700)$ and 300 Hz $(1,000 - 700)$. Remember that in practice the modulator frequency is continuously changing, so the sidebands constantly shift as well.

Figure 3.12

In AM Synthesis, the modulator wave controls the *amplitude* of the fixed-frequency carrier wave.

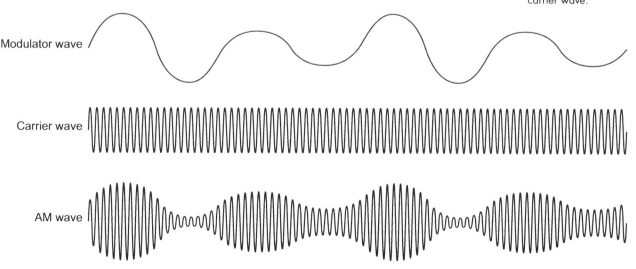

Modulator wave

Carrier wave

AM wave

In reality, because of the limited number of sideband frequencies created, few modern synthesizers implement amplitude modulation as a sound-making technique. With the exception of a specific form of AM synthesis known as *ring modulation*, which we will examine when we discuss effect processes in Chapter 8, most synthesizers have abandoned AM synthesis in favor of a more exotic form of audio-rate modulation called frequency modulation, or FM, synthesis.

Frequency Modulation (FM) Synthesis

In the previous section, we examined a process whereby a modulator oscillator controls the *amplitude* of a carrier oscillator. As the name suggests, *frequency modulation* synthesis uses a modulator oscillator to control the *frequency* of a carrier oscillator.

> **TIP** **What's in a Name?**
> Professor John Chowning of Stanford University first developed FM Synthesis in the 1960s. In the 1970s, it was licensed to the Yamaha Corporation, which subsequently became one of the biggest proponents of FM synthesis in commercial synthesizers. Even though Yamaha called their approach Frequency Modulation synthesis, it was actually a subtle variant known as Pulse Modulation synthesis. In the mid-1980s, the Casio Corporation produced a line of synthesizers using yet another FM variant that they called Phase Distortion synthesis. Although you will occasionally see references to these individual variants, all three approaches are quite similar in both technique and sound, and the subtle differences among them are beyond the scope of this text. For our purposes, we will simply refer to them all as FM synthesis.

Play a note on a synthesizer keyboard as you rapidly move the pitch bend wheel up and down, and you will create frequency modulation. In fact, almost all of us use a subtle amount of frequency modulation—typically at a rate of about 2–5 Hz—when we sing or play an acoustic instrument. We just call it *vibrato*. With frequency modulation synthesis, we use the modulator oscillator to rapidly raise and lower the frequency of the carrier oscillator, and just as in AM synthesis, the modulator is operating in the audio-rate range (greater than 20 Hz).

Demo 3.6

With FM synthesis, as you raise the level of the modulator's amplitude, the frequency of the carrier goes up. As the modulator amplitude goes down, so does the carrier's frequency. The more extreme the changes in modulator amplitude, the more extreme are the changes in the carrier's frequency. Note that in pure FM synthesis, the amplitude of the carrier wave remains constant; only its frequency changes.

Oscillator or Operator?

In Chowning's treatise on FM Synthesis for Yamaha, he made a clear distinction between analog oscillators that produce a varying electrical voltage and their digital counterparts, to which he assigned the name *operators*.[2] As Yamaha brought their line of FM synthesizers to market, they continued to use Chowning's terminology, referring to their digital oscillators as operators. Thanks to the immense popularity of instruments like the DX7 and the TX81Z, when writers at the time wrote about FM synthesis they were usually talking about Yamaha products. Consequently, in numerous articles, texts, and manuals, you will see the word *operator* instead of *oscillator*. Please understand that for all practical purposes they are one and the same.

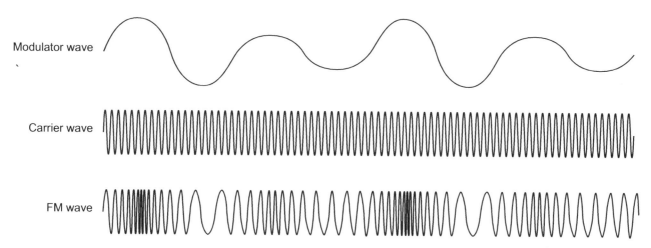

Modulator wave

Carrier wave

FM wave

Figure 3.13

In FM Synthesis, the modulator wave controls the *frequency* of the carrier wave while the carrier's amplitude remains constant.

In FM synthesis, as the modulator forces the carrier wave to rapidly speed up and slow down, a complex set of sideband frequencies is created.[3] Depending on the amplitude of the modulator, some of these sidebands can be quite strong and even mask the original carrier wave frequency (again, the modulator is not heard).

As with oscillator sync, the modulator and carrier are usually set at a fixed ratio to each other.[4] If their ratio is a harmonic one (e.g., an octave, a perfect fifth, a perfect

---

2 John Chowning and David Bristow, *FM Theory & Applications by Musicians for Musicians* (Tokyo: Yamaha Music Foundation, 1986), 38.

3 FM sidebands are considerably more complicated than AM sidebands. In addition to the sum and difference of the frequencies between the carrier and the modulator, there are also sidebands at the sum and difference of the frequencies between the carrier and all integer multiples of the modulator. Thus, in addition to the carrier frequency (f_c), sidebands are produced at $f_c + f_m$, $f_c - f_m$, $f_c + 2f_m$, $f_c - 2f_m$, $f_c + 3f_m$, $f_c - 3f_m$, etc. Remember that negative frequencies do not exist, so any negative frequency values become positive values, but the frequency's phase is inverted.

4 Many early writers on FM synthesis, among them Chowning, describe the harmonic ratio between the two frequencies as the carrier frequency divided by the modulator frequency (f_c/f_m). We are using the *harmonicity ratio* described by F. Richard Moore in his *Elements of Computer Music* (f_m/f_c). Both methods create a usable ratio between the two frequencies, but Moore's method has the advantage that whenever the ratio is represented by an integer (whole number), the produced tone tends to be strongly harmonic with the carrier frequency (f_c) as its fundamental.

fourth, etc.), the carrier produces a strongly pitched sound. However, if the modulator is tuned to some inharmonic ratio, the carrier tends to produce a noisy, clangorous type of sound. It is this latter category that has been particularly attractive to synthesizer users as these tones work wonderfully for things like bells, metallic sounds, basses, electronic pianos, and all manner of special effects.

The two primary controls in FM synthesis are the *harmonicity ratio*, the ratio of the modulator's frequency to that of the carrier (f_m/f_c), and the so-called *modulation index*, the ratio of the modulator's amplitude to its frequency (a_m/f_m).[5] Consider again our earlier example of using the pitch bend wheel to create frequency modulation. Think of the speed with which you move the wheel up and down as analogous to the harmonicity ratio, while the distance you move the wheel up and down, away from its center point, is like the modulation index.

Creating sounds with FM synthesis can be rather mercurial, as the tiniest amount of change to either the harmonicity ratio or the modulation index can have enormous impact on the sound. Consequently, a great deal of working with FM synthesis uses more of a trial–and–error approach rather than a predesigned one. With FM synthesis, we frequently start with an existing sound and start making small adjustments to the harmonicity ratio and modulation index rather than trying to start a sound from scratch.

To make the process even more interesting, most FM synthesizers allow users to modulate the modulators. These synthesizers often have a set of building blocks called *algorithms* that allow you to configure multiple oscillators in a number of ways affecting each other. You might have one modulator affecting another modulator, with that output affecting yet another modulator, which is then controlling a carrier. Some instruments even let you loop a modulator's signal back into itself to create a feedback modulation. In terms of the sonic output, things can get quite complex and interesting, not to mention completely unpredictable, with so many variables in FM synthesis.

---

5 The *modulation index* describes how far in frequency the carrier is modulated away from its original frequency. Think of the modulation index as a percentage of the modulator frequency (f_m). If the modulator frequency is 500 Hz and the modulation index is 1.0, then the carrier will modulate $\pm$ 500 Hz ($\pm$ 100 percent of f_m) from its original frequency. If the modulation index is 4.0, the carrier will modulate $\pm$ 2,000 Hz ($\pm$ 400 percent of f_m); remember that "negative" frequencies are folded back up above 0. If the modulation index is 0.1, then the carrier will modulate $\pm$ 50 Hz ($\pm$ 10 percent of f_m) from its original frequency. From a practical perspective, changing the modulation index on a synthesizer changes the amplitude of the modulator causing the carrier frequency to modulate by greater or lesser amounts. As the modulation index increases, so do the number and the strength of the audible sidebands, creating a brighter timbre to the sound.

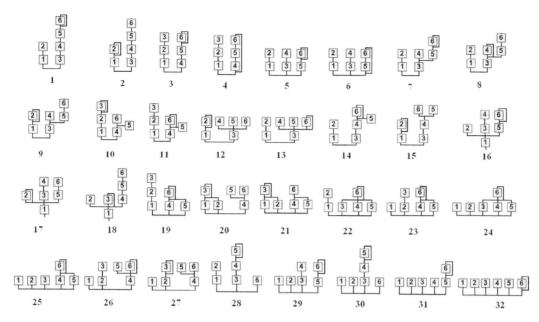

Figure 3.14
The thirty-two available algorithms of the six operators on the Yamaha DX7 synthesizer. Operators on the bottom row of each diagram are carriers, while all others are modulators. Some operators also have feedback circuits. The Yamaha DX7 made FM synthesis a household name, at least for those who had synthesizers in their households in the 1980s.

Both AM and FM synthesis are types of audio-rate modulation synthesis, and on some instruments they are actually labeled as such rather than as AM or FM. Since the use of AM synthesis as a sound source is rather rare, you often see the oscillator designation RM (ring modulation) used instead. In most cases, the ring modulation oscillator will have a control for the intensity, or depth, of the effect. Moving the control to its lowest setting usually produces AM synthesis, while moving the control higher produces ring modulation. Also, as we mentioned earlier, some manufacturers use the designation phase distortion, phase modulation, or even pulse modulation instead of frequency modulation.[6] Although there are subtle differences between these approaches, for practical purposes you can consider them all as FM synthesis.

TIP ### Am I on the Radio?

No, but AM and FM synthesis do use the same audio-rate modulation concept as AM and FM radio. Both the synthesis and radio versions of this approach use a modulator oscillator to control a carrier oscillator. The differences are primarily in what happens to the modulated carrier wave. In synthesis, the carrier wave is an audible signal that you hear after it has been modulated, while you do not hear the original modulator signal. In AM and FM radio, the carrier is an extremely high-frequency electromagnetic wave well above the audible level, but below the frequencies of visible light, that is used only to "carry" the modulator signal to its destination. Once the radio wave energy reaches the receiver, the modulated energy is separated from the carrier and only the original modulator signal (the music or the DJ) is heard.

---

6 Although the initial form of frequency modulation synthesis was known as pulse modulation synthesis, the latter term is rarely used, perhaps to avoid confusion with the common synthesizer term *pulse width modulation*, which we will explore in Chapter 6.

Figure 3.15

The FM8 software synthesizer by Native Instruments extends the DX7's six-operator FM synthesis process, adding a number of new tools, including the ability to create your own operator configurations.

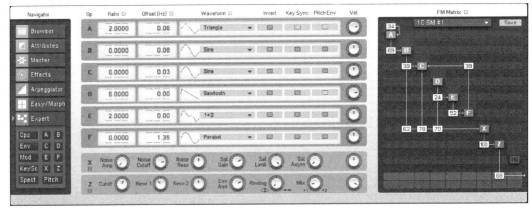

As wonderful as all the oscillator sounds are by themselves, the true power of a synthesizer comes from combining these raw material resources into new and exotic sounds. As we have seen, synthesizers offer a variety of methods for combining their oscillators, and indeed most offer multiple ways of doing so. Now that we have a grasp of the various approaches to mixing and combining oscillators to create our complex sounds, we will begin shaping those sounds with envelope generators in the next chapter. For now, though, it's your turn to put some of these oscillator combination techniques into practice.

Your Turn

Working with Crystal

In Chapter 2 you looked at and listened to the types of oscillator waves available in Crystal. Now you will combine those oscillator sounds to create new timbres. As you did in the Your Turn section of the previous chapter, select the RefiningSound.fxb bank and the default patch.

Oscillator Stack

In the last chapter, all of the examples were done with only voice 1 (oscillator 1); voices 2 and 3 were turned off in the voice mixer directly beneath the Crystal logo. To create an oscillator stack, you will use all three voices and need to turn them all up in the voice mixer. The default patch also has output for all three voices turned up in the Mixer tab. You will work more with the mixer in later chapters, but for now confirm that the three voices are turned up in the Mixer tab.

Mixer tab

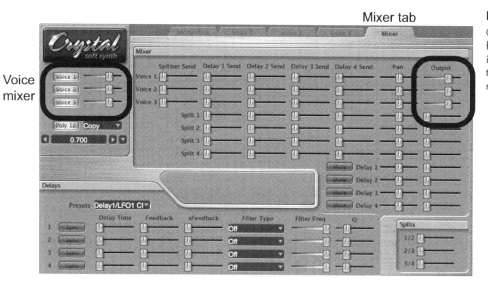

Voice mixer

Figure 3.16
Confirm that the level for all three voices is turned up in both the voice mixer and mixer tab.

For this oscillator stack, you will select three oscillator sounds and layer them together.

- Voice 1: choose **Synthesized:SawSquare** as the oscillator type and push the PulseMix slider all the way to the left.
- Voice 2: choose **Synthesized:Clang** as the oscillator type. Push the PulseMix slider all the way to the right and set the PulseWidth to the left (0.000 in the control value display).
- Voice 3: choose **Sampled:EPiano** as the oscillator type and leave all the controls at zero.

With all three voices sounding, play some notes to hear the stack of oscillators. Using the voice mixer, isolate each individual voice by turning the other two off, and note what the individual oscillator contributes to the sound of the oscillator stack. In voice 2, try raising the octave tuning by **+1**. Notice how this adds a "glistening" sound to the mix. Experiment with different levels for the individual voices by adjusting their sliders in the voice mixer. This is one of the simplest approaches to oscillator combinations, and there are numerous possibilities for stacking oscillator sounds to create rich sonic textures.

TIP

Naming and Storing a New Patch in Crystal

Before moving on to the next type of oscillator combination, reset the oscillator stack as described above with voice 2 raised an octave (**+1**). Once all three voices have been reset, select the Modulation tab and click on the control value display to bring up a text edit field. Type the name *OscStack* in the field and click the Write menu at the bottom of the Patches pane to show a list of all available patch slots. Select one of the unused slots, and Crystal will store the name and characteristics of your oscillator stack sound at that location. In Chapter 4, we will use envelope generators to dynamically alter the balance between the voices in this stack to make them morph between sounds.

Multiwave Oscillator

A multiwave oscillator is built much like an oscillator stack, except the wave types are usually similar, if not identical, to one another. Some synthesizers have a multiwave oscillator option that automatically creates these types of sounds within one voice, but with Crystal we build it manually. Since you will use all three voices layered together, make sure that all three are turned on and that their levels are turned up by the same amount in the voice mixer.

In voice 1, choose **Synthesized:SawSquare** as the oscillator type and set the PulseMix slider in the middle (0.500) and the PulseWidth slider to the left (0.000). You are going to do the same thing for both voices 2 and 3, but Crystal provides an easier way to accomplish this task than by manually configuring each voice. After configuring voice 1, click the dropdown menu next to the polyphonic button and select **Copy Voice1**. Next, select **Paste to Voice2** and **Paste to Voice3** to copy all the settings from voice 1 onto the other two voices.

Now that all three voices are configured identically, you will slightly detune voices 2 and 3 to create the rich sound of the multiwave oscillator.

- Voice 1: leave all the tuning controls at zero.
- Voice 2: move the FineTune slider a tiny amount to the left (−0.08).
- Voice 3: move the FineTune slider a tiny amount to the right (0.08).

Notice the "shimmering" quality that is now produced as well as the slight pulsing resulting from the beat frequencies between the oscillators. Try different amounts of detuning between the oscillators. What happens if the amount of detuning is not symmetrical (e.g., −0.12 and 0.08)? You should also experiment with modifications to the PulseMix and PulseWidth controls for the oscillators and even with other oscillator types. Although multiwave oscillators are frequently built with identical oscillators, they may also be built from slightly different oscillators to heighten the intensity of the sound.

Oscillator Sync

Like many current digital synthesizers, Crystal does not have a way to manually synchronize one oscillator with another. Instead, these instruments usually provide an oscillator sync function as one of their oscillator types. With Crystal, oscillator sync is accomplished with the Mogrify slider that appears when certain oscillator types such as **SawSquare** and **WarmSaw** are chosen.

Turn voices 2 and 3 off in the voice mixer, and select **Synthesized:SawSquare** for voice 1. Turn voice 1's oscillator into a pure sawtooth wave by moving the PulseMix slider all the way to the left. Play a note on the keyboard and notice the pitch that is produced. Move the Mogrify control a little to the right, and notice that in addition to the original pitch a high-frequency tone is also produced. As you move the Mogrify slider to various positions, the frequency of the secondary tone changes, but the fundamental pitch remains constant. Placing the Mogrify slider anywhere other than all the way to the left turns oscillator sync on, and changes the ratio of the slave oscillator frequency to the master oscillator.

Although sawtooth waves are usually used for oscillator sync, experiment with the Pulse wave as well as the settings for the PulseMix and PulseWidth controls.

AM Synthesis (Ring Modulation)

As mentioned earlier in the chapter, AM synthesis has mostly been abandoned in favor of FM synthesis. One particular version of AM, called Ring Modulation, is still found, although most synthesizers put it in their effects stage rather than the oscillator stage. You will recall that AM synthesis produces a tone at the carrier frequency (f_c) and two sideband tones at the sum ($f_c + f_m$) and difference ($f_c - f_m$) of the carrier and modulator frequencies. Ring Modulation outputs only the sideband frequencies, not the original carrier frequency. We will discuss this process in greater detail in Chapter 8, but since Crystal includes Ring Modulation at the oscillator stage, you can try it out now.

79

With voices 2 and 3 still turned off, select **Synthesized:Sine** as the oscillator type. Play the C an octave above middle C (C5) and notice the pitch that is produced.

- Click the Ring/FM button one time so that it illuminates the word **Ring**.
- Move the ModFreq slider a little to the right (0.100).
- Move the ModIndex slider all the way to the right.

Again, play the C an octave above middle C. Notice that you no longer hear the original pitch you were playing, but a higher and lower pitch instead. Changing the ModFreq slider adjusts the frequency of the modulator oscillator and thus the frequencies of the two sidebands that are heard. Note that at times, you may hear only one sideband, if either the sum or the difference frequency is pushed beyond the audible frequency range. Changing the ModIndex slider adjusts the amplitude of the modulator oscillator, thus changing the loudness balance between the carrier and the sideband tones. With the ModIndex all the way up, you hear only sidebands (ring modulation). With the ModIndex in the middle (around 0.500) you hear both carrier *and* sidebands (AM synthesis).

Ring modulation and AM synthesis typically use a sine wave for the carrier wave while the modulator is usually a more complex wave type. Crystal, however, allows you to use any type of oscillator wave as the carrier; I encourage you to experiment with the sounds the other oscillator types create.

FM Synthesis

Before you change to FM synthesis, reset the Ring Modulation so that the oscillator type is Sine, the ModFreq is at 0.100, and the ModIndex at 0.500. Play a note, and as described above you will hear AM synthesis producing tones at the carrier and both sideband frequencies. Now, click the Ring/FM button a second time to change the function to FM synthesis and replay the same note. Notice how much more complex the tone is, as a result of the many sidebands being produced.

In this implementation of FM synthesis, the ModFreq slider adjusts the frequency of the modulator in relation to the carrier frequency (e.g., a ModFreq of 0.500 tunes the modulator to half the frequency of the carrier). The ModIndex increases and decreases the intensity of the frequency modulation. As you move the two sliders, notice how dramatic and unpredictable the end result is. FM synthesis is capable of producing wonderfully exotic sounds, but it often requires a lot of trial-and-error to dial in the exact "right" sound.

As with AM synthesis, the carrier in FM synthesis is usually a sine wave oscillator being modulated by a much more complex wave type. Again, Crystal allows you to use other types of oscillators, and I strongly encourage you to experiment with the sounds those other oscillators produce.

Using Your Own Synthesizer(s)

1. What kinds of oscillator combinations does your synthesizer allow?
2. Does your synthesizer have a separate mixer for the oscillators, or does each oscillator have its own level control?
3. Does your synthesizer have granular or physical modeling capabilities?
4. Can you do additive synthesis, oscillator sync, or FM?
5. Set your synthesizer to its "basic" preset and experiment with oscillator combinations while all the other settings and effects are turned off.
6. Do certain oscillator combinations work best for different types of sounds?

Now that you have had a chance to combine oscillators to create complex sonorities, it's time to start shaping those sounds. In the next chapter, we will shape the amplitudes of these sounds to create a sound envelope that gives your synthesized sound a more musical and dynamic quality.

Amplitude Envelope Generators

Shaping *Your Sounds*

Online materials for this chapter:

http://www.oup.com/refiningsound/Chapter4.html

Sounds do not last forever. They start, they stop, and quite frequently they change in a number of ways between starting and stopping. The many changes that occur from the beginning of a sound until it completely dies away make up what is known as the sound's *envelope*. Within that envelope there will often be changes in elements such as amplitude, pitch, and timbre. Because these elements often change at different rates and intensities, it is usually more practical to consider separate envelopes for each element. Thus there might be envelopes for a sound's amplitude, pitch, timbre, or any other element that changes through the sound's duration.

Amplitude Envelopes

The most prominent of the various envelopes, though, is the amplitude envelope, which gives a sound its beginning, middle, and ending shape. The amplitude envelope is so prominent that most people, when using the phrase *sound* envelope, actually mean the *amplitude* envelope. In this chapter, we focus exclusively on amplitude envelopes and how to generate them as we shape our synthesizer's sounds. In Chapter 6, we will examine many other types of envelopes and ways to use them in further refinements of those sounds.

Since the nineteenth century, acousticians and musicians have traditionally identified three distinct sections of a musical tone's amplitude envelope: the attack (the section of time in which the tone is first heard), the steady state (the section of time in which the tone settles into a relatively consistent level), and the decay (the section of time in which the tone dies away). Most of those scholars also recognized that the attack section had two subsections: the initial, upward slope that usually leads to the peak amplitude of the sound, and a downward-sloping section that descends from that peak into the steady state.

Figure 4.1

The three traditional stages of a musical tone's amplitude envelope.

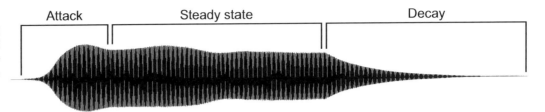

Attack | Steady state | Decay

Although this model works for many instrumental sounds, such as strings and woodwinds, it works less well for sounds such as brasses, pianos, and percussion instruments. Consider the three sound waveforms shown in Figure 4.2. The vertical displacement of each waveform indicates the changing amplitude of the sound over the passage of time from left to right. If we examine the general contour of these amplitude changes, we see that the downward-sloping section of the trumpet sound after the initial onset is almost as long as its steady-state section. In the piano envelope, the steady-state and decay sections seem to merge together, and on the kick drum there is no steady state at all, but an immediate transition from the peak of the attack into the decay of the sound. Hence, even though the three-stage amplitude envelope model is convenient for describing how a sound's amplitude evolves over time, not all sounds conform to the traditional model of the amplitude envelope.

Figure 4.2

Not all sounds conform to the traditional amplitude envelope model.

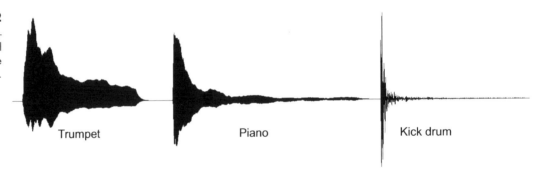

Trumpet | Piano | Kick drum

May I Have the Envelope (Generator), Please?

TIP Some MIDI sequencing programs still refer to the duration of a note as the note's *gate time*.

A common misconception about synthesizer oscillators is that they start and stop when a note is played. Actually, oscillators run continuously at full amplitude, but we hear them only when we trigger a note. On the earliest synthesizers, an electrical circuit called a *gate* allowed the oscillator's signal to pass when a key was depressed, and it stopped letting the signal pass when the key was released. The gate was simply an on-off controller. Consequently, the amplitude envelope of the gated oscillator looked like a rectangle as it was abruptly turned on, sustained at full amplitude, and then abruptly turned off, as shown in Figure 4.3. Since sounds in the natural world have contours to their amplitude envelopes, these gated sounds seemed unnatural and rather mechanical to most listeners.

In 1965, with the goal of creating sounds that behaved more like those in the natural world, Vladimir Ussachevsky, head of the Columbia-Princeton Electronic Music Center, asked pioneering synthesizer designer Bob Moog to build a device capable of generating an amplitude envelope for oscillator sounds. The envelope generator Moog designed used four stages, instead of the traditional three, to create its envelope. He separated the attack

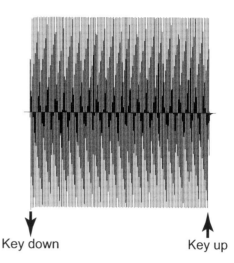

Key down   **Key up**

Figure 4.3

An oscillator wave shaped by an on-off gate produces a mechanical sound with an abrupt beginning and end to the sound envelope.

83

section into its two subsections, labeled *attack* and *decay*, and renamed the steady state and decay sections *sustain* and *release* respectively. Moog's device transmitted a control signal that regulated the output level, or amplitude, of an oscillator when a synthesizer key was pressed and released.

The amplitude envelope generator quickly became so popular that it was soon a must-have item on any synthesizer. In the techno-speak that often accompanies electronic device users, the envelope generator started to be known by the initials of its controls: ADSR (attack, decay, sustain, release). To this day, some synthesizer manufacturers still refer to their envelope generator section as the ADSR section, even though many of them have more stages than the four of Moog's original design.[1]

TIP   **Help, I Don't See an Amplitude Envelope Generator!**

As you have probably discovered already, there is a great deal of inconsistency between synthesizer manufacturers when it comes to labeling elements on their instruments. Amplitude envelope generators are no exception. They go by a number of names and abbreviations, among them EG, AmpEG, ADSR, VCA (voltage-controlled amplifier), and DCA (digitally controlled amplifier). You may have to do a bit of digging in your synthesizer's manual to find the particular instrument's nomenclature, but whatever the amplitude envelope generators are called, they shape the amplitude of the sound from the moment a key is pressed until it is released.

---

1 It is worth noting that when Moog released the more performance-oriented Minimoog in 1970, there were only three envelope controls for the player to manipulate: attack, decay, and sustain. The time value set with the decay knob was also applied to the final stage of the envelope, thus making it, in essence, an ADSD envelope generator.

Envelope Stages

Think of the amplitude envelope generator as a remote controller for an imaginary volume knob on an oscillator. When a synthesizer key is pressed, the envelope generator's control signal causes the "knob" to quickly turn up from zero to full amplitude (*attack*), and then down (*decay*) to a predetermined level (*sustain*) until the key is released. At that point, the control signal turns the knob down from the sustain level back to zero (*release*).

Figure 4.4

The four stages of an ADSR amplitude envelope generator.

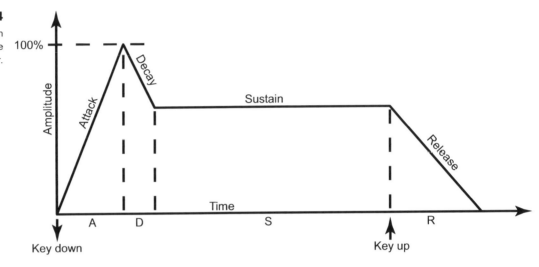

Figure 4.5

An oscillator wave shaped by an ADSR amplitude envelope generator produces a more natural sounding envelope.

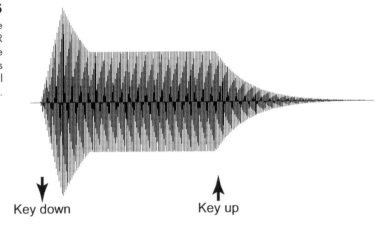

TIP

ADSR at a Glance
- *Attack*: the amount of time it takes for the sound to go from silence to full amplitude when the synthesizer key is pressed, usually expressed in milliseconds or seconds
- *Decay*: the amount of time it takes for the sound to transition from full amplitude to Sustain level amplitude, usually expressed in milliseconds or seconds
- *Sustain*: the level at which the sound maintains as long as the synthesizer key is held down, usually expressed as a percentage of full amplitude, or as an audio level in dB

 *continued*

> • *Release*: the amount of time it takes for the sound to completely die away after the synthesizer key is released, usually expressed in milliseconds or seconds
>
> Note that attack, decay, and release are all time values. Only sustain is an actual level.
>
> ## Where's My Sustain Control?
>
> On some instruments, you may not see a separate control for sustain. Instead, these synthesizers allow you to set a level for the end of the decay stage. It is assumed that once the envelope reaches the end of the decay, the amplitude will remain at that level until the key is released.

Envelope Times and Rates

As we have just learned, three of the four stages are time values (attack, decay, and release). Most envelope generators are *time-based*, using units of seconds and milliseconds to determine how quickly they transition through each stage. You will see some envelope generators, though, that are *rate-based*, using the rate of change between stages instead of time units. On time-based envelope generators, for example, if you have a sustain level at 65 percent and set the release time to 0.5 seconds, it will take half a second for the envelope to transition from sustain level to zero. If you change the sustain level to 35 percent, the release still takes a half second, meaning the actual transition speed is slower.

With rate-based envelope generators, you do not set a time value, but some sort of slope or rate-of-change value. Whereas time values are absolute, slope and rate change values are usually based on an arbitrary scale such as 0–100, or 0–127. A low value creates a slow rate of change, and a high value a fast rate of change. Consider our previous example of a release stage transitioning from a sustain level of 65 percent. If you set a release rate of 60, for example, you will create a moderately paced transition from the sustain level down to zero. If you change the sustain level to 35 percent, the release will still move at the same rate of change as before, but you will reach the level of zero in a shorter time.

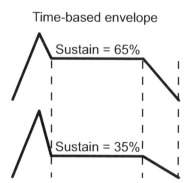
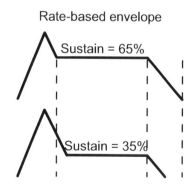

Figure 4.6
With time-based envelopes, the transition times for the stages remain the same, but the angles of the segment slopes change. With rate-based envelopes, the angles of the slopes change, but the transition times remain the same.

Shaping Sounds

The shape of the amplitude envelope creates the *articulation* of a sound. It determines whether a sound is short and percussive, long and legato, or anything in between. In

Demo 4.1

general, the shorter the times (or steeper the slopes), the more percussive and staccato a sound becomes. As you lengthen the time values (or flatten the slopes), the quality of the sound becomes more legato and sustained.

Look again at the three waveforms in Figure 4.2. Imagine creating ADSR envelopes that follow the contours of each of those sounds, and applying them to oscillator waves. Would the oscillator tones now sound like a trumpet, a piano, or a kick drum? At this point, none of them will, as we have not yet done anything with the timbre of the sounds. However, the sounds will now have articulations similar to those original models.

Figure 4.7

ADSR shapes for a "trumpet" envelope, a "piano" envelope, and a "kick drum" envelope.

Adding Extra Stages

Just as the original three-stage envelope is not adequate for describing all sounds, neither is Moog's four-stage envelope generator adequate for shaping all sounds. To give users greater control in shaping their sounds, many synthesizers have begun including additional stages in their envelope generators.

Some manufacturers have implemented one of the popular variations of ADSR: ADADSR, ADSHR, AHDSR, and DADSR (Figure 4.8). In the first example, a second attack and decay is added before the sustain segment. This design helps create the double-attack sound commonly associated with brass instruments as seen with the "trumpet" envelope in Figure 4.2. Other variations add another sustain segment known as *hold* (labeled *H*) to the envelope. Some envelope generators use this hold section to delay the release stage when the key comes up, and others put the hold between the attack and decay stages to create two sustained levels. The initial *D* on the DADSR envelope is a *delay* that offsets the beginning of the envelope by a specified time value after the key is pressed.

Figure 4.8

Common variations of the ADSR envelope generator.

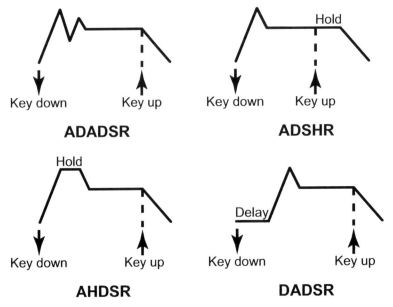

Instead of using one of these variations of ADSR, other synthesizers allow the creation of extra *breakpoints* in the four standard segments of the ADSR envelope generator. These additional breakpoints give the user even greater control over the amplitude envelope of a sound.

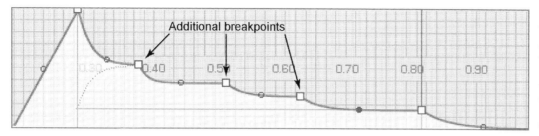

Figure 4.9

The amplitude envelope editor window in Native Instruments' FM8 allows the user to add multiple break-points to create custom-shaped sound envelopes.

87

Where Did I Put That Envelope?

The amplitude envelope generator on a synthesizer is usually found in one of two—or sometimes both—locations within a synthesizer's signal flow. Less sophisticated instruments with fewer features often have a single envelope generator that controls the amplitude of the combined oscillator sounds. In this scenario, you can combine the tones of your oscillators, but they are treated by the envelope generator as one articulated sound.

Synthesizers with more sophisticated features often have a separate envelope generator for each oscillator. Multiple envelope generators, especially ones capable of generating multistage envelopes with onset delays, allow wonderfully complex sound shaping, and they are particularly effective when working with additive synthesis where we use the delays and complex envelope shapes to cross-fade between partials, creating a richly evolving sound.

Demo 4.2

Finally, some instruments have separate envelope generators for the individual oscillators *and* another final envelope generator for the combined sound. As you would imagine, this feature provides the greatest amount of flexibility in creating complex sound articulations.

Segment Curves

The envelope shapes we have shown thus far all have straight-line segments. Many synthesizers today allow you to curve these segments. Most people, when making a musical transition like a crescendo, decrescendo, accelerando, or ritardando, do not make the change in a straight, linear fashion. We often begin with a greater rate of change at the beginning, and then lessen the rate of change as we approach the end of our transition. Using segment curves, instead of straight lines, we can apply a bit more of a human touch to our envelopes. On some instruments, the attack, decay, and release segments are curved by default, and on other instruments they can be individually curved by the user. Flat segments like sustain, hold, and delay usually remain flat and do not curve.[2]

Envelope segment curves come in two forms, known as *logarithmic* and *exponential* curves. Logarithmic curves have a greater rate of change when the input value is lower,

---

2 As we will see in Chapter 6, though, some of the newer envelope generators allow the user to create sustain segments that loop through a number of up and down curves.

while exponential curves change more when the input value is higher. Since our natural tendency is to make a greater amount of change at the beginning of a transition, we frequently select logarithmic curves when an envelope segment is rising, as it does in the attack segment. We often use exponential curves when the segment is falling, as it does in the decay and release stages. On some instruments, the curves are already defined, while other instruments allow you to control the type and depth of the curvature. Be aware, though, that many instruments do not show the actual curve in their display—the segments look straight—but the envelope generator is implementing the curve.

Figure 4.10
Logarithmic curves have a greater rate of change when the values are low and are commonly used for ascending stages in an envelope. In contrast, exponential curves have a greater rate of change when the values are high and are normally used for descending envelope stages.

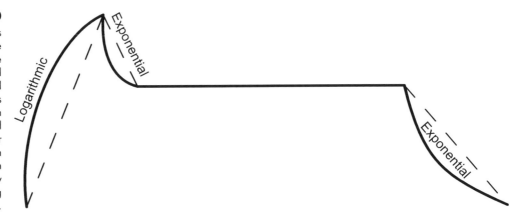

Inverted Envelopes

You may see on your synthesizer a setting that allows you to invert the envelope so that it is turned upside-down. Inverted envelopes assume a starting and stopping value of 100 percent. If you attempt to use such an envelope to shape the amplitude of a signal, your oscillator will sound continuously *except* during the period in which the envelope is being generated. Consequently, inverted envelopes are not terribly practical for sounding notes. However, as we will see in Chapter 6, they can be quite useful for some other functions.

Figure 4.11
The amplitude envelope generator section in Native Instruments' Absynth 5 allows you to assign an individual, multistage envelope with delay to every oscillator. You can also add breakpoints to create extra curves in the segments, and even invert the envelopes to generate crossfades between oscillator sounds (bottom envelope). In addition to the individual envelope generators, there is a "Master" envelope generator on the instrument that controls the final output of the combined oscillator sounds.

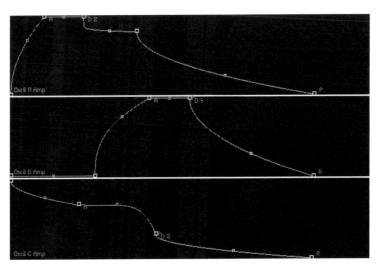

Envelope Generator Behavior Modes

Demo 4.3

Our discussion of envelope generators to this point has assumed that only one key is being pressed at any given time, and that the envelope is allowed to complete its full path. In actual synthesizer playing, though, we often have notes that are shorter than the times programmed into the envelope generator, and we frequently have overlapping notes where a new note begins before the previous envelope has finished. How an envelope generator behaves under these differing playing techniques is another important aspect of using envelope generators.

Free-Run Mode

Imagine you play a note so short that the key up happens before the envelope has reached the sustain stage, or even the decay stage. In that scenario, envelope generators behave in one of two ways. Many simply jump, when the key is released, to the release segment and fade the sound out. If an envelope generator is in *free-run* mode (sometimes called *one-shot*

Key up   Key up

mode), then the envelope always completes the full attack and decay stages before jumping to the release. Since attack and decay are so vital to our perception of a sound, having *free-run* mode helps maintain the sound quality even with extremely short notes.

Figure 4.12
When a synthesizer key is quickly struck and released with *free-run* mode off (left), the envelope generator jumps immediately to the release segment. When *free-run* mode is turned on (right) and a key is quickly struck and released, the envelope is forced to complete the full attack and decay segments before moving to the release segment.

Retrigger Mode vs. Multi-Trigger Mode

What if you release a note, but start a second note before the first note's release stage has finished? Or what happens if you play a note and then start a second note before you let the first one go (as happens when we play legato)? If your envelope generator is set to retrigger mode, then each new note will trigger a new envelope starting at zero amplitude, even if the old note is still sounding. If *multi-trigger* mode is on (this might be called *mono* mode or simply *retrigger-off* mode), then each new note's envelope begins wherever the previous envelope's level is when the new note is triggered.

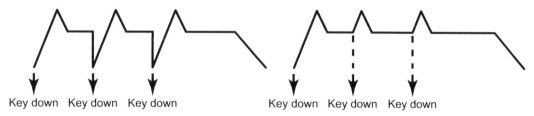

Key down   Key down   Key down   Key down   Key down   Key down

Figure 4.13
Retrigger mode (left) starts the next note's envelope at zero even if the previous note is still being held. *Multi-trigger*, or *mono*, mode (right) begins the next note's envelope wherever the previous envelope is when the new note is triggered.

Single-Trigger Mode

Sometimes you want to create a sound that, when played legato, produces no discernible attack for the subsequent notes. It sounds as if one note just morphs into another. To accommodate this smooth type of articulation, some synthesizers implement *single-trigger* mode (often called *legato* mode). With single-trigger mode, for as long as a note is held down, all subsequent notes begin at the sustain level of the held note and do not have

Figure 4.14

Single-trigger mode does not re-attack notes so long as other notes are still being held.

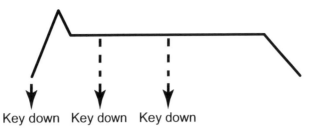

Key down   Key down   Key down

any attack or decay segments associated with them. Once all notes have been released, the next note played will get a full attack–decay segment to its envelope. Single-trigger mode, designed for smooth melodic lines, first came about on earlier monophonic synthesizers. It is generally impractical for polyphonic playing and is usually employed only on the newer, polyphonic synthesizers when the instrument is set to monophonic, or solo, mode.

TIP **Disambiguation**

There is some inconsistency in the use of the word *legato* to describe envelope generator modes. Some synthesizers use legato mode to describe the multi-trigger envelope, while others use it to describe single-trigger envelopes. If your synthesizer has a setting called legato mode, you will need to check the instrument's documentation to determine which version of legato mode is actually employed.

Dynamic Envelope Shapes

Demo 4.4

Listen carefully to good musicians playing their instruments and you will quickly notice that the articulations they use change quite a bit. Of course we expect articulations to change from staccato to marcato to legato. But notice that even on the same kinds of notes, musicians will produce subtly contrasting articulations when they play using different dynamic levels or registers. It is these changes in articulation that add so much of the "live" quality to musical performance.

Adding envelope generators to synthesizers went a long way toward reducing the mechanical nature of electronic music. Unfortunately, if an envelope generator uses the same shape for all sounds, it can still get monotonous and boring rather quickly. In an attempt to add a spark of life to their sounds, synthesizer designers have devised a couple of ways to manipulate the amplitude envelopes in real time while playing the instruments.

In Chapters 6 and 7, we will discuss in much greater detail the many real-time modulator controls available for synthesizers. However, two of these controls, *velocity scaling* and *key tracking*, have become such an integral part of envelope generators that we need to include them here.

If you have spent any time with a modern synthesizer, you are probably aware that on most instruments the harder you strike the key, the louder the sound gets. The force with which you strike the key is called *velocity*, and in the wonderful world of MIDI (Chapter 7) velocity has a range of data values from 0 to 127. Striking the key with very gentle force produces a low velocity, like 15 or 20. Striking the key with a great deal of force produces a high velocity, like 100 or 115. Incidentally, a key velocity of 0 is the same thing as turning a note off.

Key tracking simply refers to the physical location from lowest note to highest note on the synthesizer's keyboard. We commonly think of key tracking as controlling the pitch of the synthesizer. Every time we go up from one key to the next adjacent key, the pitch rises by one semitone. Like velocity, the notes on the MIDI keyboard are numbered from the lowest note of 0 to the highest note of 127. The beauty of both of these data types is that in addition to controlling loudness and pitch, we can also use them to control an envelope generator.

TIP The eighty-eight notes of the piano keyboard are equal to MIDI note numbers 21–108. Thus MIDI actually extends another octave and a half from each end of the piano keyboard.

Most modern synthesizers allow you to map the velocity data to the overall amplitude of the envelope generator. In so doing, the envelope actually becomes taller or shorter, depending on how hard the key is struck. Until now, we have assumed that the peak of the attack stage takes the oscillator's amplitude up to one hundred percent, and that the sustain stage is some fraction of that. When we assign velocity data to the envelope's amplitude, the overall height of the envelope changes with the velocity. So if we strike a key softly, the attack may go up to only about 50 percent, with all other levels scaled similarly. Strike the key with medium force and the entire envelope scales to, say, 75 percent. Strike the key as hard as you can and the envelope scales to the full 100 percent. In this scenario, not only does increasing velocity create a louder sound, it produces relevant changes in the amplitude envelope that make the articulations of the louder sounds more realistic. As the envelope becomes taller, the slopes are steeper, giving the sound slightly more percussive quality for the louder notes.

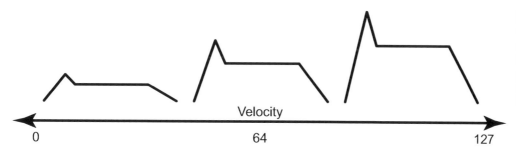

Velocity

0   64   127

Figure 4.15
With positive velocity scaling, the amplitude levels of the envelope generator increase as the key velocity increases.

In general, we expect higher velocities to produce taller and louder envelopes. However, many instruments also provide the capability of *inverse* scaling. In this case, the harder you strike the key, the quieter the sound gets. Such an effect can be quite handy when layering sounds. For example, you may have one sound that works best for soft notes and another sound for loud notes. You can create a normal envelope for the loud sound and an inverted envelope for the soft sound. Then, as you strike the key with more and more force, the soft sound fades into the background while the loud sound becomes more prominent.

Like many synthesizer controls, envelope scaling often uses an arbitrary set of values such as 0–100 to determine how much scaling occurs. In most cases, a value of zero means no velocity scaling. As you increase the scaling value, the effect becomes more pronounced. A value of 10, for instance, produces a subtle change in the envelope's amplitude depending on how hard the key is struck, while a value of 90 yields a substantial change in the amplitude of the envelope.

Instruments that allow inverse scaling often have controls that go from a negative number to a positive one, as with –100 to +100. In this case, a velocity scaling of zero still has no effect. A positive value causes the amplitude to increase the harder you strike the key, and a negative value lowers the amplitude of the envelope with higher key velocities.

Key velocity may also be used to adjust the time, or rate, values on many synthesizers. With most acoustic instruments, the louder you play them, the more percussive their attacks become. However, as happens on many instruments, the louder you play them, the longer their release becomes as well. For this reason, most synthesizers that allow velocity to affect envelope times let you set the value for the individual envelope stages. For example, you may want high key velocities to shorten the attack and decay times so that the sound grows more percussive. However, you might also want the release time to increase so the sound takes longer to die away. To accommodate this, you will find that the controls allowing you to manipulate envelope stage times usually have both positive and negative values.

As with velocity scaling, many synthesizers implement key tracking for their envelope generators as well. Just as you can use velocity data values to control an envelope's amplitude and times, you can use the data values of the MIDI note numbers to control the envelope.

Figure 4.16

Key tracking can also be used to manipulate the amplitude levels of an envelope generator.

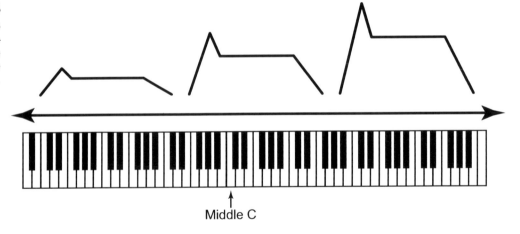

Middle C

Typically, when an instrument uses key tracking to manipulate an envelope, middle C is the center point. Notes above middle C increase the amplitude, and notes below decrease the amplitude of the envelope. As with velocity scaling, many instruments also allow you to invert the effect, so that lower notes produce greater amplitudes and higher notes, lower amplitudes.

But Wait, There's More!

This is, by no means, the end of our discussion of envelope generators. In Chapter 6, we will revisit them, looking at other uses, types, and further manipulations of envelope generators. At this point, though, we can use our amplitude envelope generators to create articulations and shape our synthesizer sounds into musical notes. In the next chapter, we will look at refining the timbre of those notes with frequency filters, but now it's time to put some of what we have learned about amplitude envelope generators into practice.

Your Turn

Working with Crystal

Immediately to the right of the oscillator controls pane, you will find the pane labeled Amplitude, which contains all of the controls for the sophisticated amplitude envelope generator that Crystal provides for each of its three voices. Before we begin using the envelope generator, we need to create an oscillator sound. For the following examples, we will use a warm sawtooth sync sound.

- Select the default patch from the RefiningSound.fxb bank.
- In voice 1, select **Synthesized:WarmSaw** as the oscillator type.
- Position the PulseMix slider at 0.000 and the Mogrify slider at 0.660.

Figure 4.17
The envelope generator in Avid's Hybrid synthesizer has controls for using velocity scaling to change the amplitude levels of the envelope (VEL), the time of the attack stage (ATT VEL), and the times of the decay and release stages (DEC VEL). The envelope's amplitude levels can also be changed with key tracking (KEY TRACK). All four control knobs have ranges from –100 percent (higher key velocities and pitches *decrease* the levels and times in the envelope) to +100 percent (higher key velocities and pitches *increase* the levels and times in the envelope).

93

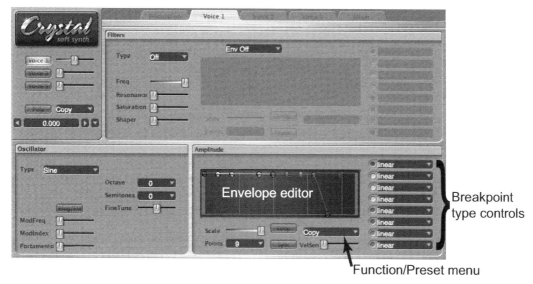

Figure 4.18
The amplitude envelope generator controls are located in the lower-right pane of the three Voice tabs.

Amplitude Envelope Controls

The amplitude envelopes in Crystal can have between four and nine breakpoints, indicated as colored balls in the envelope editor window. Here are the controls that may be used to create anything from a simple ADSR envelope to complex looping and tempo-synchronized envelopes.

- *Envelope editor:* use this window to manually position a breakpoint by dragging it with your mouse. (Note that the breakpoints remain in a specific left-to-right order in the window, so you cannot reorder them.) When a note is triggered, the envelope proceeds through all the breakpoints until it reaches the penultimate one. At that point, it will either sustain until the key is released, or loop back to the first breakpoint if the Loop button is illuminated. The final breakpoint will always have an amplitude value of zero.

- *Scale* adjusts the time scale of the envelope editor window. When the Sync button is off, the grid values are seconds and fractions of seconds. When the Sync button is on, the values are quarter notes and subdivisions of quarter notes.
- *Points* menu allows you to select the number of envelope breakpoints in the editor window. Envelopes may have as few as four breakpoints to as many as nine.
- *Loop* button causes the envelope to repeatedly loop from the penultimate breakpoint back to the beginning of the envelope as long as the key is held down.
- *Sync* button synchronizes the envelope to the tempo of the VST host application and changes the scale of the envelope editor window from seconds to quarter notes.
- *Function/Preset* menu allows you to copy and paste envelopes into different voices and select from a list of envelope presets.
- *VelSen* slider adjusts the sensitivity of the amplitude envelope to key velocity from your MIDI keyboard. With the slider all the way to the left, velocity has no effect on the envelope. The further the slider is moved to the right, the greater the impact of key velocity on the amplitudes of the envelope.
- *Breakpoint type* controls allow you to select a specific breakpoint type for each of the points in your editor.
    - *Linear* creates a straight line to the next breakpoint.
    - *Curve positive* creates a greater amount of change at the end of the transition between breakpoints.
    - *Curve negative* creates a greater amount of change at the beginning of the transition between breakpoints.
    - *Pulse (1.0, 0.9, 0.75, 0.5)* causes the amplitude to instantly jump to the numeric value and halfway between breakpoints to instantly jump to the next breakpoint value.
    - *Spike (1.0, 0.9, 0.75, 0.5)* is similar to the pulse option, but instead of staying at the numeric value it immediately begins a curve toward the value of the next breakpoint.
    - *Flat* remains at the breakpoint value until the next breakpoint and then instantly jumps to that value.
    - *Inverse pulse down* remains at the breakpoint value until halfway to the next breakpoint, where it drops to zero until jumping instantly to the next breakpoint value.
    - *Inverse pulse up* is similar to inverse pulse down except the value rises to maximum at the halfway point and then drops down to the next breakpoint value.

Creating a Simple ADSR Envelope

To create a traditional-*looking* ADSR envelope, select **Flat 4 pt** from the preset menu and increase the number of breakpoints to five from the points menu. Notice that all of the breakpoint types are set to "linear."

1. Drag the first breakpoint (blue) down to (0.00, 0.00 in the control value display).[3]
2. Drag the second breakpoint (yellow) a bit to the left (0.07, 1.00).
3. Drag the third breakpoint (green) to the left at half amplitude (0.14, 0.50).
4. Drag the fourth breakpoint (red) to the right and down so that it is the same amplitude as the green breakpoint (0.50, 0.50).
5. Drag the last breakpoint (blue) to the right (0.75, 0.00).

Play a note, and you will hear the simple four-stage ADSR envelope produced. In common practice, most instruments, including Crystal, create this traditional ADSR envelope with only four breakpoints. Since the third stage of this envelope is sustain, and the penultimate breakpoint (red) stops the progress of the envelope until the key is released, you do not need the third (green) breakpoint. Change the points menu back to four, and the red breakpoint will move to replace the green one. Now move the last breakpoint to the left so that its slope is the same as before (0.39, 0.00), and you will hear the same envelope sound as before. Although adding a separate breakpoint for sustain may be visually appealing, it is unnecessary for the actual envelope.

With this basic ADSR envelope, experiment with time and amplitude values for the breakpoints. Can you create envelopes similar to those in Figure 4.7?

Creating a Multistage Envelope

Select **Flat 9 pt** from the preset menu and set the breakpoint types and values from left to right as follows (remember that holding down the Shift key while moving a control puts it into fine resolution mode, so you should be able to set these exact values):

1. (Blue) 0.00, 1.00
2. (Yellow) 0.25, 0.30, **curve positive**
3. (Green) 0.50, 1.00
4. (Turquoise) 0.54, 1.00
5. (Purple) 0.54, 0.25
6. (Rose) 0.70, 0.25
7. (Brown) 0.70. 0.67
8. (Red) 0.85, 0.67
9. (Blue) 1.00, 0.00 (last breakpoint does not have a type)

You should now hear an envelope with a quick attack that drops and swoops up before stepping down and back up to the sustain level. As you will see in the next example, these step effects can be used to create rhythmic pulses.

Dynamic Oscillator Stack

In the previous chapter, you created an oscillator stack in Crystal by using different sounds in each of the three voices. In this example, you will use that same stack with

---

3 When editing breakpoints in Crystal, remember that the first data value is the amount of time in seconds (left-to-right) and the second value is the amplitude on a scale of 0 to 1 (bottom-to-top). Thus, a value pair such as 0.15, 0.50 means to position the breakpoint at 0.15 seconds with an amplitude of 0.50. If no breakpoint type (linear, curve positive, etc.) is specified, the breakpoint is a linear type.

separate envelope generators to morph between the sounds of the three voices. Select the Modulation tab and choose your stored **OscStack** from the Patches menu.

Set the amplitude envelopes for the three voices as follows:

VOICE 1:

1. Select **Flat 4 pt** from the preset menu and increase the number of breakpoints to five.
2. (Blue) 0.00, 0.00
3. (Yellow) 0.25, 0.60, **curve negative**
4. (Green) 0.50, 0.15, **curve positive**
5. (Red) 0.75, 0.40
6. (Blue) 1.00, 0.00

VOICE 2:

1. Select **Flat 4 pt** from the preset menu and increase the number of breakpoints to five.
2. (Blue) 0.00, 0.00
3. (Yellow) 0.25, 0.00, **curve positive**
4. (Green) 0.50, 0.11
5. (Red) 0.75, 0.06
6. (Blue) 1.00, 0.00

VOICE 3:

1. Select **Flat 4 pt** from the preset menu
2. (Blue) 0.00, 1.00
3. (Yellow) 0.25, 1.00, **curve negative**
4. (Red) 0.75, 0.30
5. (Blue) 1.00, 0.00

You should now hear that the sound begins with the electric piano voice and the other two voices fade in and out as the key is held. Currently, all the breakpoints are set to fall on quarters of a second. If you turn the Sync button on in all three voices, the breakpoints will fall on sixteenth notes. Change the tempo in the Crystal Player keyboard window to 40 bpm and the evolution between voices will be slower. Speed the tempo up to around 100 bpm and the envelopes begin to create a rhythmic pulse from the three voices.

Looping Rhythm Envelope

Use the settings you have just completed in the previous example, but select **Arpeggio** from the envelope preset menu in voice 1. You will notice that the envelope looks like a number of up-and-down amplitude steps of 0.00, 0.50, or 1.00. You will also see that each breakpoint falls on a grid line and that both the Loop and Sync buttons are illuminated.

The Loop button causes the envelope to keep repeating as long as the key is held. The Sync button changes the time values from seconds to beats and subbeats. In this example, the envelope is spread across two beats, with breakpoints falling at sixteenth-note intervals. Sustaining a note with this envelope creates a syncopated rhythm at the tempo of the VST host. In they Crystal Player keyboard window, select a slower or faster tempo (you may need to replay the note after changing tempo) and you will hear that the rhythm of the envelope changes to the new tempo.

With the VelSen slider all the way to the left, it does not matter how hard you strike the keys on your MIDI keyboard; the envelope always produces the same amplitudes. Move the slider to the middle and notice that the envelope changes its amplitudes according to how hard you strike the keys. The further the slider is moved to the right, the greater the effect of velocity will be on the envelope amplitudes.

Try creating your own rhythms by moving the various breakpoints to different amplitude and time positions. If you want to copy this envelope to another voice, choose **Copy** from the envelope's function/preset menu. Select the tab for the voice to which you want to apply the envelope and choose **Paste** from the function/preset menu of that voice's envelope generator.

As with all of the Your Turn examples in this book, these are merely starting points to show you the kinds of things that are possible. Take some time to familiarize yourself with the amplitude envelope generators. Not only do they create the sound's amplitude envelope, they can be used to create a number of rhythmic and timbral effects by morphing layers of sounds and synchronizing their breakpoints to a tempo.

In addition to amplitude envelope generators, Crystal has envelope generators specifically for the audio filters and another assignable set for a variety of modulation control purposes. We will explore their uses in detail in coming chapters. Fortunately, all the envelope generators in Crystal work the same way, so their functions will be easy to adapt to these other purposes.

Using Your Own Synthesizer(s)

1. How many amplitude envelope generators do you have? Note that they may be labeled something like EG, AmpEG, ADSR, VCA (voltage-controlled amplifier), or DCA (digitally controlled amplifier), as well as Envelope Generator.

2. Does your synthesizer have separate amplitude envelope generators for each oscillator, or is there a single master envelope generator that controls the composite sound? Do you have both individual and master envelope generators?

3. What are the adjustment units on your amplitude envelope generators? Do they use times or rates for the attack, decay, and release values? Is sustain a percentage or an actual audio level in decibels?

4. Do your amplitude envelope generators allow:
   A. Multiple stages?
   B. Onset delays?
   C. Curved segments?
   D. Inverted envelopes?

5. How does your synthesizer's amplitude envelope generator handle extremely short notes? Does it immediately jump to the release stage, or do you have a *free-run* (or *one-shot*) mode?

6. How does your synthesizer handle overlapping notes? Does it use *retrigger*, *multi-trigger*, or *single-trigger* envelopes when notes overlap?

7. Can you modulate your amplitude envelopes with velocity or key tracking? If so, can you do both positive and negative scaling?

Now that you have seen the power of amplitude envelope generators to control the shape of your sounds, it's time to control the tone color of your sounds. In the next chapter, we look at audio filters and their functions as they manipulate the timbre of sound through the popular synthesis approach known as subtractive synthesis.

5

Audio Filters

Refining the Color *of Your Sounds*

Online materials for this chapter:

http://www.oup.com/refiningsound/Chapter5.html

Can you tell the difference between the sound of a trumpet and the sound of a clarinet, even if they are both playing the same pitch at the same loudness? If so, you are basing that distinction on the difference in *timbre* (rhymes with *amber*) between the two instruments. Timbre is often defined as the tone quality, or tone color, of a sound, although it is sometimes described more by what it is not than what it is. Timbre has even been described as a "psychoacoustician's multidimensional waste-basket category for everything that cannot be labeled pitch or loudness" by one pair of authors.[1] Regardless of how we define it, a sound's timbre is primarily the result of the relative amplitudes of all the sounding partials, what acousticians call the *frequency spectrum*.

TIP

Disambiguation

The terms *frequency spectrum* and *harmonic spectrum* are sometimes used—incorrectly—as synonyms for each other.

- *Frequency spectrum* is the distribution and relative amplitudes of *all* sounding frequencies.
- *Harmonic spectrum* is the distribution and relative amplitudes of *only* the sounding harmonics (whole-number multiples) of a fundamental frequency.

As we saw in Chapters 2 and 3, different types and combinations of oscillator waves create a number of interesting frequency spectra, or timbres. As interesting as all those timbres may be, they still do not always produce the exact sound we are trying to create on a synthesizer. At some point, we usually need to use audio filters to modify the frequency spectrum, thus refining the timbre of our sound.

---

1 Stephen McAdams and Albert Bregman, "Hearing Musical Streams," *Computer Music Journal*, Vol. 3, No. 4 (December 1979): 26–43, 60.

Audio Filters

In the mechanical world, filters are used to remove impurities and other undesirable materials from a liquid or a gas. In other words, they stop the undesirable items from passing, while allowing the desired items to pass. Audio filters work on the frequency spectrum of a signal, and like their mechanical counterparts they stop the undesirable frequencies from passing while allowing the desired frequencies to pass.

The original audio filters were relatively simple electronic devices that consisted of only two components, a resistor and a capacitor. As simple as these basic RC (resistor-capacitor) circuits were, they were quite powerful and brought a wealth of new timbral possibilities to synthesizers. As filters continued to be developed, a number of new circuit combinations arose that greatly expanded the features and capabilities of these devices.

Figure 5.1
Because of the frequency-variable reactance of a capacitor, swapping its position with a resistor in an RC (resistor-capacitor) circuit creates either a lowpass filter (left) or a highpass filter (right).

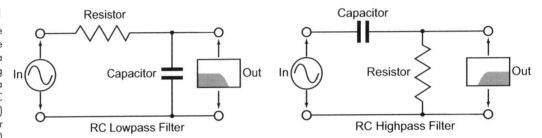

Today, most synthesizers use digital calculations to perform their audio filtering magic. In many ways, these digital filters behave much like their analog counterparts, and the controls we encounter are often designed to mimic those on an analog filter. It is important to mention, though, that some of the more interesting and desirable sonic characteristics of analog filters occur as a result of "flaws" and "imperfections" in their electronic components and circuit designs. Because of the "perfect" nature of digital filters, people often complain that they sound cold and sterile. To combat this problem, numerous digital filter designers have begun developing formulae that attempt to recreate the warmth of the analog filters by adding these flaws and imperfections back into their digital calculations.

It is safe to say that, other than some of the advanced effects processors, audio filters are the most complex elements of almost any synthesizer. This complexity is a double-edged sword, as it not only gives synthesizers amazing timbral sculpting capabilities but also can make them quite difficult to fully understand and use. In this chapter, we attempt to demystify the workings of audio filters, clarify their terminology (sometimes confusing or misused), and show how audio filters are used to refine the timbre of oscillator waves to produce the wonderfully rich sounds we have come to expect from a synthesizer.

A basic audio filter has a specified range of frequencies, called the *passband*, that are allowed to pass through unaffected, and a range of frequencies that it stops from passing, known as the *stopband*.[2] Because no audio filter can make a complete and abrupt change

2 Technically, all frequencies are affected to some degree or another, either by changing their phase relationship or by subtle changes in amplitude. For the purposes of our broad discussion here, though, we will assume that the passband allows all of its frequencies to pass at the same amplitude with which they entered the filter.

from passband to stopband, there is always a transition area between the two bands in which frequencies are allowed to pass, but with their amplitude gradually reduced, or *attenuated*, as the transition area approaches the stopband.

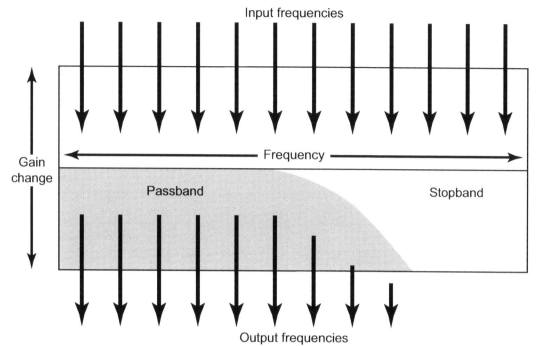

Figure 5.2
A lowpass filter allows frequencies in the passband (lower frequencies) to pass through, while frequencies in the stopband (higher frequencies) are stopped. Frequencies that occur at the transition area between the two bands are gradually attenuated as the transition area approaches the stopband.

Audio Filter Types

There are many types of filters available in a modern synthesizer, and with just a few exceptions the *type* classification for an audio filter is based on the location and function of the filter's passband. In general, a filter can be of only one type, but as we will see, it is quite common to *cascade* them to create a more complex type of filter. In this section, we examine a number of types of audio filters, but we begin with the four most commonly found on a synthesizer: the lowpass, highpass, bandpass, and bandreject filters.

Demo 5.1

TIP ### A Word About Filter Diagrams

Filter types are often displayed as an *xy* graph (see Figure 5.2) showing the passband and the stopband. Moving from left to right along the *x*-axis represents frequency from low to high, while moving up and down along the *y*-axis represents a gain change in the output amplitude of the frequencies. Passband values above the *x*-axis represent a boosting of frequencies, while values below the *x*-axis indicate an attenuation of frequencies. Most basic audio filters are designed so that the upper edge of the passband runs along the *x*-axis and drops away to infinity as it approaches the stopband. Generally, these types of diagrams are overly simplified approximations of the filter's response, as no audio filter is quite so "neat." In reality, filters have nu-

---

TIP *continued*

merous anomalies and wiggles along the boundary of the passband, so we should interpret these diagrams as indicating merely the "type" of filter, not its actual detailed response characteristics.

Lowpass

As its name implies, the lowpass filter allows lower frequencies to pass while stopping higher frequencies; it is probably the most common audio filter used in synthesis. The lowpass filter reduces and eliminates the higher harmonics and partials in a frequency spectrum, usually resulting in a darker, more "focused" timbre to a sound. Some people mistakenly assume that a lowpass filter lets only low frequencies pass. Depending on where the transition between the passband and stopband is set, you can actually allow some high frequencies to pass, but reduce those that are even higher.

Figure 5.3
A lowpass filter lets lower frequencies pass while stopping higher ones.

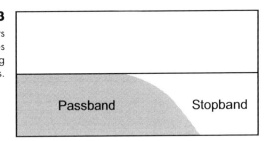

Highpass

The opposite of a lowpass filter is a highpass filter. This filter swaps the locations of the stopband and passband so that higher frequencies are allowed to pass while lower ones are stopped. The highpass filter is often used to remove the fundamental and lower harmonics from a sound to create a bright and edgy timbre.

Figure 5.4
A highpass filter lets higher frequencies pass while stopping lower ones.

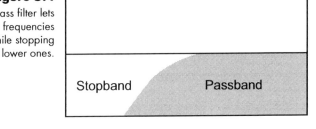

Bandpass (Peak)

Another of the common filter types is known as a bandpass filter. This filter, sometimes called a "peak" filter, has a passband in the middle with stopbands on either side. The bandpass filter is used to isolate a specific range of frequencies and reduce or eliminate all the others.

Figure 5.5
A bandpass filter lets frequencies pass that fall within a narrow range. All other frequencies are stopped.

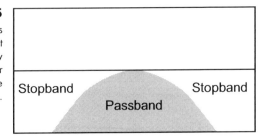

Bandreject (Notch)

The opposite of a bandpass filter is a bandreject filter. The bandreject, or "notch," filter allows all frequencies to pass, except for those in the stopband. Bandreject filters are used to remove a specific range of frequencies, and they are sometimes used to isolate and control unwanted noise in a signal.

Parametric (Peak/Notch)

The parametric filter, sometimes called a "peak/notch" filter, is a bit of a hybridization of the bandpass and bandreject filters. Like the bandreject filter, the parametric filter has a control to adjust the width of the stopband. However, it has an additional control that allows the user to adjust the amount of attenuation, or even boost, in the stopband. On these filters, the stopband is often referred to as the cutband when it is attenuating, or cutting, frequency amplitudes, or as the boostband when the amplitudes are being raised above their initial input levels. The parametric filter is the filter type commonly found in the equalization (EQ) stage of an audio mixer.

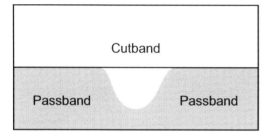 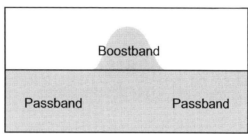

Figure 5.7
A parametric filter can either cut the frequencies or boost them in its active band, while all other frequencies pass unaffected.

Lowshelf

A lowshelf filter allows all frequencies to pass, but it applies a user-specified, and uniform, amount of attenuation or boost to the lower frequencies. Like its brother, the highshelf filter (below), the lowshelf is often used in place of a highpass or lowpass filter when you don't want to completely eliminate frequencies in the stopband.

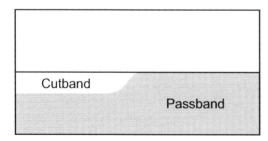 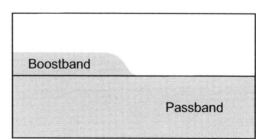

Figure 5.8
A lowshelf filter applies a uniform cut or boost to lower frequencies but leaves higher frequencies unaffected.

Highshelf

Opposite of the lowshelf filter, the highshelf filter allows all frequencies to pass but applies a user-specified and uniform amount of boost or attenuation to the higher frequencies. A highshelf filter is often used to exaggerate the higher harmonics and partials to add "sizzle" to a sound.

(Figure 5.6, top right)

Figure 5.6
A bandreject filter stops a narrow band of frequencies but allows all others to pass.

103

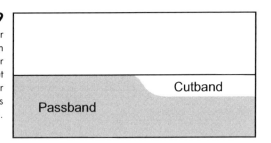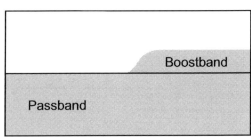

Figure 5.9
A highshelf filter applies a uniform cut or boost to higher frequencies but leaves lower frequencies unaffected.

Allpass

As its name suggests, the allpass filter allows all frequencies to pass at their original amplitudes. What this filter does, though, is invert the phase of the frequencies at some user-specified point in the frequency spectrum. When audio goes through an allpass filter, it begins perfectly in phase. As you move up through the frequency spectrum and approach the designated changeover point, the phase of the frequencies begins to shift until they are 180° out from their original position.

As we described in Chapter 3, our ears are not particularly sensitive to phase positions in a sound, and most people will not hear any difference in a sound processed by an allpass filter. In most audio devices, these filters are not used to alter the timbre of a sound, but to compensate for signals that have been shifted in phase by some other aspect of the audio process. However, if an allpass filtered audio signal is mixed back with the original, unfiltered signal, the point at which the phase is inverted creates a phase cancellation in the combined output, producing the equivalent of a lowpass filter.

With synthesizers, allpass filters are often used in pairs of identical allpass filters where the second filter flips the output of the first filter back into phase before mixing it with the original unfiltered signal. This produces a notch in the frequency response of the combined signals at the point where both allpass filters are changing phase. In common practice, the phase inversion point is moved back and forth to produce a "swish" in the sound as the band of phase-cancelled frequencies moves higher and lower. We will examine this process in much greater detail in Chapter 8 when we discuss a popular effect known as phaser.

The graph for this type of filter can be a bit confusing, as it no longer indicates the amplitude of frequencies, but rather the phase position of frequencies in relation to their original phase position. Remember that, like a compass, phase position is circular. Thus, the middle line on the allpass filter diagram usually indicates the 0° (or 360°) phase position while both the top and bottom edges of the graph show the 180° position. As a signal moves out of phase, the graph shows it descending from the middle line toward the bottom of the diagram. If the phase of the audio signal shifts past 180°, it starts moving back into phase. In this case, it will "reappear" at the top of the diagram and descend to the middle line.

Figure 5.10
An allpass filter allows all frequencies to pass but inverts the phase of the signal at a user-specified point. Synthesizers frequently use a pair of identical allpass filters to create a notch in the frequency response of a signal at the point where the two filters alternately flip the signal out of phase and then back into phase.

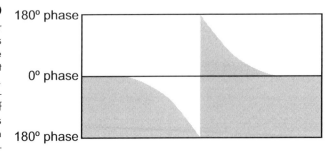

Comb Filter

Many synthesizers have a filter option called *comb filter*. This device is not a filter in the traditional sense, but an extremely short audio delay unit that creates an interesting metallic quality in the audio as a by-product. We will discuss the comb filter at length in Chapter 8.

Cascading Filters

As with audio mixers, most synthesizers have an equalization (or EQ) section that appears to be a multiband filter allowing the user to adjust the response of several frequency bands at the same time. In reality, these are a set of parametric filters connected in series, or *cascaded*, so that the second filter operates on the output of the first, the third filter on the output of the second, and so on. Since the filters are parametric, only frequencies at their particular cut or boost points are affected, and all other frequencies pass unaffected.

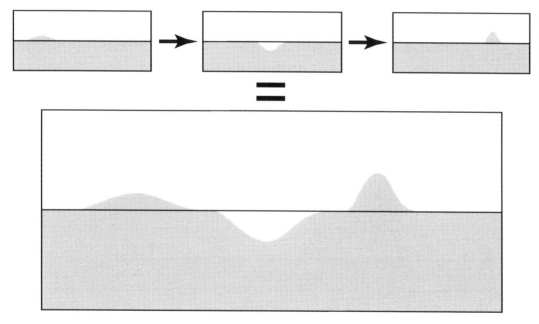

Figure 5.11
Multiband EQ filters are actually individual parametric filters cascaded together.

Parallel Filters

Cascading filters implies that they are arranged in a series: the output of filter 1 goes into filter 2, the output of filter 2 goes into filter 3, etc. Many synthesizers provide the option of arranging filters in a parallel configuration as well as in series. Since the outcomes of the two arrangements can be quite dissimilar, it is important to understand the difference between how cascaded and parallel filters operate.

Look at Figures 5.12 and 5.13 below. Both examples use a lowpass and a highpass filter, but in the first example they are arranged in series (cascaded), and in the second example in parallel. When filters are arranged in series, the output of the first filter is processed by the second to create a passband only where the two original filters' passbands overlap. When they are arranged in parallel, both passbands remain in the mixed signal, and only the spot where the stopbands overlap produces an effect.

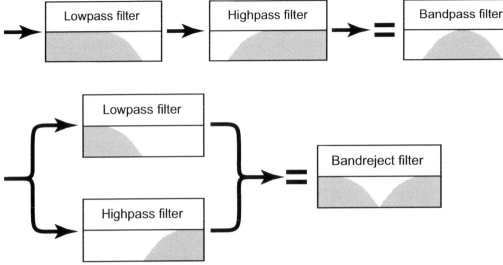

Figure 5.12
When combining filters in series (cascaded), the second filter operates on the output of the first. In this example, applying a highpass filter to the output of a lowpass creates a bandpass filter.

Figure 5.13
When combining filters in parallel, the outputs of the two filters are added together. In this example, a highpass and lowpass in parallel create a bandreject filter.

Although filter type is certainly important and is usually the first option you select when using a filter, it is by no means the only important control. Once you have selected the filter type, you then need to set the *cutoff* or *center frequency*, the *slope* (or "*Q*") of the filter, the amount of *resonance*, and any appropriate *gain*. We now examine each of these functions and controls in detail as we discuss their role in refining the timbre of your sounds with an audio filter.

Demo 5.2

Cutoff or Center Frequency

The cutoff frequency is used to indicate the frequency at which the filter transitions from its passband to its stopband, while the center frequency describes the center of a stopband or boostband. Even though these two functions differ, most audio filters use the same knob or controller for both cutoff and center frequency. The knob simply changes its function depending on the type of filter being used.

Look through the illustrations of the various filter types above, and you will notice that some of them (lowpass, highpass, lowshelf, highshelf) have two bands and only *one* transition, while the others (bandpass, bandreject, parametric, allpass) have three bands and *two* transitions. When a filter has one transition, the frequency at which the filter changes from the passband into the stopband (or boostband/cutband) is called the *cutoff frequency*. When a filter has two transitions, the frequency that falls at the center of the peak or notch is used instead and is called the *center frequency*.

The location of the center frequency is fairly obvious and easy to describe; it's at the center of the peak or notch in the filter. The cutoff frequency, in contrast, is a bit more problematic. Since single-transition filters gradually change from passband to stopband, it is impossible to identify one frequency as the transition point. Thus, a semi-arbitrary decision was made years ago to designate the point at which the frequencies are attenuated by 3 dB as the cutoff frequency. As you can see on the left side of Figure 5.14, the filter has already begun attenuating by the time it gets to the actual cutoff frequency. Regardless of whether a filter uses a cutoff frequency or a center frequency, the value will always be indicated in Hertz or kilohertz.

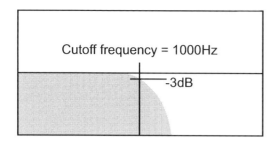

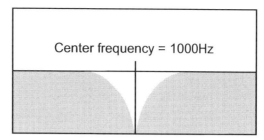

Although the diagram of a single allpass filter looks much like that of a lowpass filter, remember that the diagram is indicating phase relation, not amplitude, of frequencies. Consequently, the cutoff frequency (often called the *corner frequency* on allpass filters) is the point at which the phase shift passes through 90°.

Slope, Bandwidth, and Q

Perhaps no function of an audio filter creates more confusion than controlling and describing the steepness of the transition slope between the passband and the stopband. The problem is not that the concept itself is difficult, but that there are a number of methods for describing and controlling a filter's slope. Adding to the confusion is the fact that a filter with one slope controls steepness differently from a filter with two slopes even though, for GUI space-saving reasons, it is often done with the same control knob. It also does not help that filter designers do not all use the same method, and some synthesizers are inconsistent in their use of the terms, occasionally even using them incorrectly. In this section, we attempt to sort out all the methods you are likely to encounter and, where possible, relate them to one another. We begin with filters having a single slope.

First, it is important to understand that the slope of a filter is not a straight line, but a curve like those shown in all the figures above. Many synthesizer manuals show the filter's slope as if it is a straight, diagonal line going from the passband to the stopband. Although this might make it easier for the manual reader to comprehend the transition, it also creates confusion by implying that the rate of change is consistent throughout the entire transition. It is not. Look at the transitions in Figure 5.14, and notice that the rate of change accelerates as the curve approaches the bottom of the graph (it is logarithmic).

Because the rate of change is not constant, it is difficult to easily and accurately describe the slope of an audio filter. Consequently, a variety of methods for doing so have been used over the years. Depending on the design of your audio filters, you will probably have one or more of these values to control the slope of your audio filter.

dB/octave

The original RC-circuit audio filter tends to attenuate frequencies at a rate of about 20 dB/decade. A *decade* in audio frequencies is a change by a factor of ten. In other words, from 100 Hz to 1,000 Hz is a decade, as is 2,000 Hz to 20,000 Hz. Even though dB/decade was the measurement unit for designing filters, it was felt that so large a number was a bit cumbersome for users. Thus the decade was divided up into octaves.

Consider the decade 100 Hz to 1,000 Hz. If you begin at 100 Hz and go up an octave, you double the frequency to 200 Hz. Go up another octave and you are at 400 Hz.

The next octave is 800 Hz, and so on. Thus, the decade 100 Hz to 1,000 Hz has about 3.25 octaves in it. Divide 20 dB by 3.25, and you get slightly more than 6 dB per octave. Many filter designers, then, began using the dB/octave measurement rather than the larger decade unit. Again, remember that at the beginning of the transition, the rate of change will be less than 6 dB/octave, and by the end of the transition, it will be greater than 6 dB/octave. However, it all averages out to around 6 dB/octave, which is the value many filter designers use.

With early electronic audio filters, the steepness of the slope was fixed and could not be adjusted. You could make the slope steeper by cascading filters, but you could not make it shallower. If you connect two lowpass filters—with both having the same cutoff frequency—in series, then the second filter will steepen the slope by an additional 6 dB/octave, for a total of around 12 dB/octave. Add a third filter and you have an 18 dB/octave slope, a 24 dB/octave slope with a fourth filter, and so on. Although some filters provide a continuous control change for dB/octave, most have a switch that allows the user to choose only among 6, 12, 18, and 24 dB/octave.

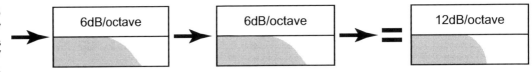

Figure 5.15
Cascading two 6 dB/octave lowpass filters produces a 12 dB/octave lowpass filter.

Order

In practice, designers did not use separate filters but simply increased the number of components within the filter's circuit. They also created a switching mechanism that allowed the user to choose how many components through which the signal would pass. The basic filter, with one set of components, was known as a *first-order* filter. Adding another set of components produced a *second-order* filter and the third set, a *third-order* filter. Since the basic filter was fixed at a 6 dB/octave slope, the term *first-order* filter became synonymous with a 6 dB/octave slope. A *second-order* filter meant a 12 dB/octave slope, a *third-order* filter an 18 dB/octave slope, and so forth.

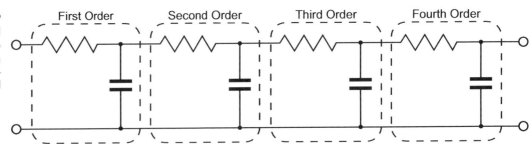

Figure 5.16
Second-, third-, and fourth-order filters are created by adding extra sets of RC circuits into the signal path.

Pole

Somewhere along the way, mathematicians and engineers began analyzing the outputs of their audio filters with a complex mathematical calculation known as a *Laplace transform*. When the output of a first-order filter (6 dB/octave) is rendered on a Laplace transform surface plot, it looks as though a large pole has been pushed up into a flat sheet of rubber. A second-order filter looks like two poles, and a third-order filter, three poles. Engineers looking at these surface plots began describing the response of audio filters with the term *poles*, and so a first-order filter also became known as a *one-pole* filter, a second-order filter as a *two-pole* filter, and so on.

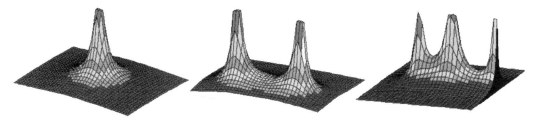

Figure 5.17
Laplace transform surface plots of one- (left), two- (center), and three-pole (right) filters look like tent poles being pushed up into a sheet of rubber.

109

TIP **Clarification**

Decibels per octave, order, and pole are all used to describe the slope of a filter's transition band. However, the terms are not quite synonymous.

- *dB/octave* describes an average of the actual rate of transition in the slope.
- *Order* describes the number of components used to create the rate of transition in the slope.
- *Pole* describes a visual representation of the rate of transition in the slope.

One describes the slope itself, the second describes how the slope is made, and the third describes how the slope is viewed. Although some real, albeit subtle, differences exist between the three methods of describing a filter's slope, the general usage and understanding of these terms is 6 dB/octave = first order = 1 pole. For each additional order or pole, the steepness of the slope increases by an additional 6 dB/octave.

Bandwidth

As mentioned earlier, filters that have two slopes use a completely different method for describing and controlling the steepness of their transitions. Instead of attempting to describe the actual rate of attenuation, as is done with single-slope filters, these filters measure the distance between the two slopes with a calculation known as *bandwidth*. As with the calculation of the cutoff frequency on single-slope filters, bandwidth is measured from the point on each side of the peak or notch where the frequencies have been attenuated (or boosted) by 3 dB. Although bandwidth is occasionally indicated as the actual difference in frequencies between the two points (f_2–f_1), it is most commonly measured in octaves and fractions of octaves. Thus a narrow bandwidth value might be 0.25 (one-fourth of an octave), while a very wide band might have a bandwidth value of 3.0 (three octaves). The larger the bandwidth value, the wider the band is, and the shallower the slopes of the two sides are. Small bandwidth values produce a narrow band with steep slopes on both sides.

Figure 5.18

A large bandwidth value produces shallow slopes, while a small bandwidth value produces steep slopes.

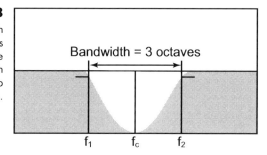
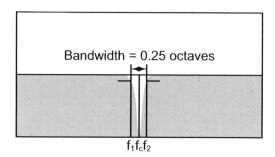

Q

As if all these ways of calculating the slope of a filter are not confusing enough, we now arrive at "*Q*" or *Quality* factor. A number of audio filters use a control labeled Q to control the steepness of the slope. Q is a mathematical and engineering term that describes how far a function deviates, or oscillates, from the center, or perfect, position. Functions with a high Q value have little deviation (high quality), and those with a low Q value have a wide deviation (low quality). In terms of an audio filter, a stopband with a high Q value is narrow with steep sides, while one with a low Q value is wide with shallow sides.

Q is calculated by dividing the center frequency (f_c) into the difference of the two side frequencies (f_c/f_2-f_1).[3] The Q value is a decimal point number that gets larger as the Q increases. Consider the two examples in Figure 5.18 above. If we use Q instead of bandwidth (Figure 5.19), we see that the large bandwidth example on the left has a low Q value of 0.4, while the small bandwidth example has a high Q value of 5.76. Remember, then, that bandwidth and Q measurements go in opposite directions. When you increase the bandwidth, you decrease Q, and vice versa.

Figure 5.19

A low Q value produces shallow slopes, while a high Q value produces steep slopes.

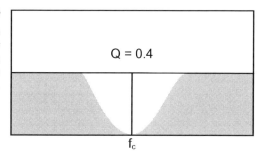
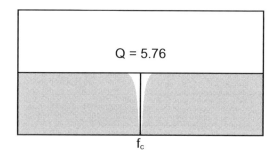

TIP **Reality Check!**

Although you will commonly see references to slope, order, pole, bandwidth, and Q, you will almost never need to calculate their values. Most audio filters these days include a visual display that shows how steep the slope is as you adjust the control knob, making it quite easy to find the right slope. Be aware, though, that for space-saving reasons most GUI designers for audio filters include only a single control knob to adjust the slope in the filter. The knob is often labeled simply as Q, but the

---

3 You can also calculate Q from just the bandwidth, but the formula is a bit more complex. Where N = bandwidth in octaves: $Q = \dfrac{\sqrt{2^N}}{2^N - 1}$

111

> **TIP** *continued*
>
> function actually changes with the type of filter being used. This GUI space-saving "feature" has most likely contributed to much of the confusion surrounding the terminology and functions for controlling the slope of a filter.

Resonance

We often think of acoustic spaces as being resonant when the dimensions of the room coincide with the wavelengths of a sound. Electronic devices can also develop resonance between components on a circuit board under certain signal conditions. Usually this is something designers try to avoid, but in the case of audio filters it has come to be a highly desired "feature." Some of the early RC analog filters added a small coil of wire known as an inductor to their circuit designs. When paired with the capacitor, the inductance coil had the effect of creating a pronounced, resonant oscillation right at the filter's cutoff frequency. By then allowing some of the filter's output to feed back to its input, the resonance can be further exaggerated, and these so-called *resonant* filters soon start producing sounds that were not part of the original input signal. The extra sonic possibilities created by resonant filters have made them extremely popular with synthesizer programmers. Many digital filters also provide resonance, although the process is created mathematically rather than by components interacting with each other.

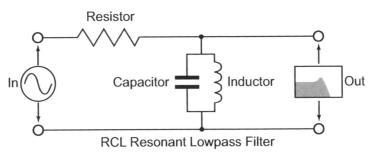

Figure 5.20

Pairing an inductor coil (usually labeled *L* in circuit diagrams) with a capacitor turns a basic lowpass filter into a resonant lowpass filter.

> **TIP** Since filter type and function can change the quality of the resonance peak, some filters include the resonance control as part of the continuum of the slope, or Q control.

Resonant filters on synthesizers usually have a control labeled, appropriately enough, *resonance*. This is one of those controls that tend to have an arbitrary range of values assigned to it on the order of 0–10, 0–100, or 0–127. The numbers themselves are meaningless except that as you increase them, you boost the amplitude of the resonant frequencies and steepen the slope of the transition band.

Filters that provide a graphical display often show the rising resonance peak and corresponding increase of slope steepness as you adjust the controls. For some reason, what they often do not show is that as the resonance increases, the amplitudes of the other frequencies in the passband are slightly lowered.

Figure 5.21
A lowpass filter with no resonance (left), low resonance (center), and high resonance (right).

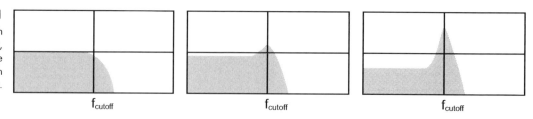

Moving a lowpass filter's cutoff frequency up and down has been a popular synthesizer effect for years. However, until the development of resonant filters, the effect tended to be rather subtle, owing to the shallowness of the filter's slope. By boosting the amplitude of the frequencies right around the cutoff frequency, it makes the use of a moving cutoff frequency much more obvious and more effective. Resonant filters can also help tighten the passband or stopband of bandpass and bandreject filters.

Users soon discovered another interesting "feature" of resonant filters: if the resonance is increased by a large amount, the filter starts to feed back and begins oscillating on its own, producing a sine tone at the cutoff frequency. This effect, known as *self-oscillation*, produces the high-frequency whistles and chirps that have become standard in many synthesizer sounds over the years. If resonance is pushed even higher, the amount of feedback overwhelms the filter, causing it to overload, or "blow up." When that happens, the filter typically stops working until it is deactivated and then reactivated. To deal with this overload, many resonant filters have a reset button to clear the filter's contents without having to actually deactivate it. However, if the resonance amount, or the input level, is not lowered then it will just blow up again. Other resonant filters avoid the problem altogether by automatically regulating the amount of feedback to prevent it from going too high. Raising the resonance to a point just below filter overload, however, creates a number of wonderfully unusual sounds that can be quite useful and interesting, as long as the filter is not pushed any further.

Gain

Depending on the type of filter being used, there may also be a gain control. We generally think of a filter as not changing the amplitude of frequencies in the passband. However, a gain control is needed to raise and lower the amplitudes in the boostbands and cutbands of both shelf and parametric filters.

Many audio filters also have a gain control that allows the user to raise or lower the amplitude of the entire filter output. Remember that a large increase in resonance actually lowers the amplitude of the passband, so a gain control could be used to make up the difference. Of course, boosting the passband has the added effect of further increasing the amplitude of the resonance peak, so be careful!

Dynamic Filters

Demo 5.3

As with amplitude envelope generators, the use of secondary controls, or modulators, to adjust the filter in real time has become such a common and important part of using filters that we need to include it in this discussion. Although it is possible to modulate nearly all the functions of an audio filter, raising and lowering the cutoff or center frequency, and the resonance amount, are by far the most popular. Depending on the amount the cutoff or center frequency is raised and lowered, one can create everything from subtle "swish" effects to the characteristic "wah-wah" sounds heard on so many synthesizers. Raising and lowering the resonance amount creates a shifting "focus" around the cutoff frequency that can be interesting on its own, but it can also be quite good at drawing our attention to the shifting cutoff or center frequency effect.

You will recall from Chapter 4 that velocity scaling and key tracking can be used to dynamically modulate an envelope. They can also be used to modulate filters. For example, you might have a sound that you want to make brighter when you play it louder. This effect is easily accomplished by mapping key velocity to the cutoff frequency of a lowpass filter, especially one with resonance boosted. As you strike the key harder, the cutoff frequency is raised higher, brightening the timbre of the sound. Take this idea a step further, though. In addition to assigning the output of your amplitude envelope to oscillator amplitude, assign it to the cutoff or center frequency of your filter as well. This causes the filter's cutoff or center frequency to follow the contour of your amplitude envelope, including any velocity modulation you have applied to the envelope generator.

Another use of velocity scaling is to have it affect the resonance amount. This can often be in addition to using it to control the cutoff or center frequency as described above. Harder key strikes push the resonance amount even higher, creating a stronger focus on the cutoff or center frequency. If you set the resonance amount quite high, strong velocities can push the filter into brief self-oscillation, creating interesting chirps on the loud notes.

Key tracking is often used to keep a filter focused on the note being played. Set the cutoff frequency of a highly resonant lowpass filter to track the note you are playing. As you move up and down the keyboard, the cutoff frequency shifts to that note, creating a nice timbral focus to your pitch. Similarly, key tracking can be used to emphasize certain harmonics and partials. Instead of setting the cutoff to track the note you play, set the cutoff at some interval above the note being played, such as two octaves plus a perfect fifth (that is, thirty-one half steps). Now your resonant frequency will emphasize the sixth harmonic of the note you are playing. For a nice added effect, set a small "glide time" of around 200 ms. This causes the cutoff frequency to glide to the target frequency over a fifth of a second, creating an interesting swoop in the sound.

These are only a few basic filter modulation techniques. Other means of modulating an audio filter might be with aftertouch, with the modulation wheel, or with a low-frequency oscillator (LFO). We will explore these and other modulators in much greater detail in coming chapters. Now, though, it is time to put audio filters to their most popular use on a synthesizer, refining the timbre of complex oscillator sounds in a process known as subtractive synthesis.

113

Subtractive Synthesis

In Chapter 3, we briefly mentioned the synthesis approach known as *subtractive synthesis*. You may recall that additive synthesis involves layering multiple oscillator sources to create a complex waveform. Subtractive synthesis works in the opposite way. It begins with an already complex waveform and applies selective audio filtering to remove some of the frequencies, thus refining the timbre of the original sound into the desired waveform. The original complex sound can come from any of the oscillator and oscillator combinations we examined in Chapters 2 and 3. Even instruments that used such techniques as FM or wavetable synthesis ultimately treated their sound to the subtractive process.

Because of the computational efficiency—and much lower cost—of using audio filters rather than multiple oscillators, subtractive synthesizers have become quite popular and were the first instruments to produce the classic synth sounds for which these instruments are now famous. The original Moog synthesizers were subtractive, as were many of their competitors. They produced a complex wave from their oscillators, often combinations of oscillators, and processed the wave with audio filters that were dynamically modulated. Even as synthesizers became digital instruments, they frequently modeled their structure on subtractive designs. Although the newest generation of software synthesizers offers a number of sound-making possibilities, the subtractive process is still a big part of the design for nearly all of them.

Figure 5.22

Although many contemporary synthesizers use a subtractive process, it is the core of Propellerhead's popular synthesizer Subtractor. (photo © copyright 2012 Propellerhead Software AB, used with permission)

Demo 5.4

As mentioned earlier, nearly all synthesizers these days implement some level of subtractive synthesis. It might not be their primary focus, but they all allow the user to sculpt the output of the oscillators and sound sources with audio filters. Because the subtractive process is so integral to synthesis, it seems appropriate at this point to illustrate a few examples of how sounds may be sculpted and refined through subtractive synthesis. The examples given here are certainly not the only kinds of things you can do with subtractive synthesis, but I hope they will give you some ideas for creating your own sounds. For all of these examples, use Demo 5.4: Subtractive Synthesis from the companion website.

Subtractive synthesis typically begins with a complex waveform that has a large proportion of upper partials in its frequency spectrum. The wave can be a basic oscillator wave like a sawtooth or square wave—triangle waves, and especially sine waves, generally do not work very well as they do not create enough upper partials—or a combination of sawtooth and square waves. Other types of sound sources that are frequently used in subtractive synthesis are noise, FM oscillators, and complex sample and wavetable sources. The critical element with any of these sound sources is that it must contain a rich, complex frequency spectrum. Once the complex source is created, the subtractive fun begins. In the examples given here, be sure to try them with both the Multi-Wave Oscillator and White Noise sound sources.

Focusing the Timbre

The most common form of subtractive synthesis uses a lowpass (usually a resonant low-pass) filter to reduce upper partials and create a warmer, more focused tone. In Demo 5.4, first listen to the Multi-Wave Oscillator option with the filter off. As you will hear, this oscillator combination produces a bright, edgy timbre with a great deal of high-frequency content.

Next, turn the filter on and set the cutoff frequency at the very top of its range (10 kHz). As you sustain a note on your MIDI keyboard, gradually lower the cutoff frequency until the sound completely disappears. When this happens, you have positioned the cutoff frequency so that it is lower than the note you are playing, and the synthesizer stops making a sound.

> **TIP** Having the cutoff frequency set too low is a common synthesizer mistake. I've lost track of the number of times a student has said his or her synthesizer is not making any sound, only to find that the cutoff frequency of the lowpass filter was turned all the way down.

Continue sustaining the note as you raise the cutoff up to around 5 kHz. Now, move the resonance control up and down. Notice that the frequency content above the cutoff remains attenuated, but raising the resonance value creates a strong focus to the frequencies around the cutoff frequency. It is subtle, but if you listen carefully, you may also be able to hear that the frequencies below the cutoff frequency are being attenuated as you raise the resonance amount. Begin by changing the resonance by large values to make the changes obvious. Once your ear has identified that sound, try making subtler changes and see if you can still hear the results.

Raise the resonance amount to around 60, and slowly move the cutoff frequency up and down again. You should now notice that the earlier frequency shifts you heard are much more obvious. For comparison, lower the resonance back to zero and repeat the frequency shifts. Try repeating this example with both the Multi-Wave Oscillator and White Noise as your sound source. As you have just experienced, a single resonant low-pass filter can have a remarkable effect on the timbre of a sound.

Filter Self-Oscillation

As described earlier, many resonant filters can be forced into self-oscillation so that they begin producing their own frequencies as a result of feedback. In the Lowpass Filter pane of Demo 5.4, select Relative Cutoff and set the Cutoff frequency to +48 (four octaves higher than the note being played). Turn both the Resonance and Velocity knobs up to

100. When you play a note, you should hear a high-frequency whistling or chirping sound in addition to the note you are playing. This is a result of feedback inside the filter causing it to oscillate at the resonant frequency, and thus its own tone is produced. Turn the filter off as you continue to play notes, and you will still hear the chirps until the feedback level drops low enough that the filter stops oscillating. Even without input from a sound source, a highly resonant filter can create its own oscillations just from the feedback present. The filter in this demo will only go into uncontrolled feedback with extreme settings. If it does blow up, press the Clear Filter button to reset it.

In the next chapter, we will look at a number of internal modulation sources on a synthesizer that can be used to control the instrument's components, including the filters. For now, though, spend a little time experimenting with the various filter options in Crystal and on your own synthesizer(s).

Your Turn

Working with Crystal

Like most contemporary synthesizers, Crystal offers a variety of audio filter types to manipulate the timbre of your sounds. Before using the filters, load the default patch and configure the oscillator and amplitude envelope in voice 1 as follows (voices 2 and 3 turned off):

OSCILLATOR SETTINGS
1. Type: **Synthesized:SawSquare**
2. PulseMix: 0.300
3. PulseWidth: 0.000
4. Ring/FM: off
5. ModFreq, ModIndex, Portamento, Mogrify: 0.000
6. Octave, Semitones, FineTune: 0

AMPLITUDE ENVELOPE SETTINGS
Four points
1. (Blue) 0.00, 0.00
2. (Yellow) 0.02, 1.00
3. (Red) 0.08, 0.45
4. (Blue) 0.25, 0.00
VelSen: 0.740

Filter Controls

The filters in Crystal are similar to those found on many synthesizers, but with a few extra features. There are the typical controls for selecting the filter type, setting the filter's cutoff or center frequency, and the resonance or Q of the filter. There is also a dedicated envelope generator that modulates the cutoff or center frequency. In addition to these standard filter controls, there are two extra control sliders, labeled Saturation and Shaper. We will look at these functions more in Chapter 8 when we talk about amplitude distortion effects. For now, know that Saturation applies a "tubelike" distortion to the filter's output, while Shaper creates a small distortion in the audio signal before it enters the filter.

The filter types in Crystal are the commonly found lowpass, highpass, bandpass, and notch filters with both resonant and nonresonant versions of the lowpass (ResLoPass, Low Pass) and highpass (ResHiPass, High Pass) filters. There is also an extra version of the resonant lowpass filter (XResLoPass) that has a richer sound than the ResLoPass filter.

Like most synthesizers, there is only one control, a slider labeled Freq, for the cutoff or center frequency; it adjusts between 50 Hz and 17.1 kHz. Whether it is the cutoff or the center frequency depends on the type of filter being used. When the filter's envelope is turned on, the frequency slider changes into two sliders, labeled LoFreq and HiFreq, that set the upper and lower boundaries for the cutoff or center frequency as it is modulated by the envelope generator.

The Resonance/Q slider changes its name and function depending on the filter type. For resonant filters, the slider controls the amount of resonance. For nonresonant filters, the Q slider narrows the width of the transition band.[4]

Focusing the Timbre

With the filter envelope off and the saturation and shaper sliders turned all the way down, select **Low Pass** as the filter type and push the cutoff frequency all the way to the right and the Q slider all the way to the left. While sustaining a note on your keyboard, gradually lower the cutoff frequency until the sound completely disappears. When that happens, the filter's transition slope is entirely below the frequency of the note you are playing.

Move the cutoff frequency up to around 5 kHz and notice that the sound is still rather dark, with only a little high-frequency content.[5] Since the Q slider is all the way to the left, the slope of the filter's transition band is rather steep, thus eliminating most of the high frequencies. Begin moving the Q slider to the right—decreasing the steepness of the slope—and the sound begins to brighten as more high frequencies are allowed to pass.

Position the Q slider in the middle and play a note while moving the frequency slider back and forth. Notice the sweeping timbral shift as the cutoff frequency moves higher and lower. Now switch to the ResLoPass filter type and, again, sweep the frequency slider. For comparison, try the same thing with the XResLoPass filter type. With both the ResLoPass and XResLoPass filters, the increased resonance adds a lot more focus to the sweeping of the cutoff frequency. Do you prefer the sound of the ResLo-Pass or the XResLoPass filter when you sweep its cutoff? What is the difference between the two?

---

4 With single-slope filters such as Low Pass and High Pass, Crystal's transition band functions like the lower (Low Pass) or upper (High Pass) half of a notch filter. Thus, raising the Q value narrows the width of the transition and brings the cutoff frequency closer to the "center" of the imaginary notch.

5 Even in fine resolution mode, setting a slider to an exact frequency can be difficult in Crystal. Consequently, the filter frequencies given in these examples are approximations. You do not need to set the exact frequency, just something close to the given value.

Modulating the Cutoff

Select the **ResLoPass** filter type and turn the filter envelope on. Set the LoFreq slider to around 250 Hz and the HiFreq slider to around 15 kHz. From the filter envelope preset menu, select **UpFastDnSlow** for the envelope shape, and position the Resonance slider at 0.500. Now when you play and sustain a note you will hear the cutoff frequency begin quite high and gradually drop down to 250 Hz as the sound continues. What happens if you increase or decrease the amount of resonance?

Sequenced Filter

Leaving resonance at 0.500, change the filter type to **XResLoPass** and choose **Arpeggio** from the filter envelope's preset menu. In the next chapter, we will look at step sequencers and low frequency oscillators to create rhythmic effects in a filter, but Crystal allows you to do this right in the filter's envelope generator. With the Arpeggio envelope selected, the filter creates a pulsing timbral shift at the speed of the sixteenth note. Change the tempo in the keyboard window of the Crystal Player and note that the speed of the sixteenth-note pulsing stays synchronized to the new tempo.

Amplitude = Filter

With all the previous settings still in place, select **Copy** from the function/preset menu of the *amplitude* envelope generator and then select **Paste** from the function/preset menu of the *filter* envelope generator. This changes the filter envelope to be identical to the amplitude envelope. Since the attack and decay stages of this envelope are so short, the envelope creates a bit of a wow at the beginning of the sound.

Laser Blasts

Move the resonance slider all the way to the right, and the wow of the previous example becomes a high-frequency squeal as a result of self-oscillation in the filter. You can change the frequency of the "laser blasts" by raising and lowering the HiFreq slider. Temporarily pushing a resonant filter into self-oscillation is a popular way to add the chirps one so frequently hears in synthesized sounds. As you did in Chapter 3, use the copy voice and paste voice functions to create a detuned multiwave oscillator with the same filter settings on all three voices.

These are but a few samples of what can be accomplished with audio filters. Here, we used only the most common type of filter for subtractive synthesis, the resonant low-pass filter, but dramatic effects can be created with any of them. Be sure to try out all the other filter types as you manipulate their controls in a similar manner to what you were doing in the examples above.

Using Your Own Synthesizer(s)

1. Where is the filter stage of your synthesizer(s)?
2. Is there a global filter for the composite sound, or are there separate filters for all of the oscillators or voices?
3. What types of filters do you have?
4. Do you have both resonant and nonresonant filters?
5. How is the transition slope of the filter measured: dB/octave, order, pole, Q, or something else?

6. For filters that have two transitions, is the slope measured with bandwidth, Q, or something else?
7. Do the filters have their own envelope generator, or do you need to assign an envelope generator to them?
8. Can you push your filters into self-oscillation?

Creating a sound with oscillators, shaping its amplitude, and manipulating the sound's timbre are the basic elements of the synthesis process. Now it's time to start modulating those elements with both internal and external controllers to bring a whole new level of dynamic control and musical quality to your synthesized sounds.

Internal Modulation Sources

Dynamic Shaping *of Your Sounds*

Online materials for this chapter:

http://www.oup.com/refiningsound/Chapter6.html

mod·*u·late* | ˈmäjəˌlāt| verb [trans.]: exert a modifying or controlling influence on

Derivatives: *mod·u·la·tion* | ˌmäjəˈlā sʜ ən| noun; *mod·u·la·tor* | ˈmäjəˌlātər| noun

In the acoustic music world, notes are usually not static, but constantly evolving. Musicians make subtle adjustments in pitch, tone, loudness, and so on to give life to their notes. An oboist, or violinist, sustaining a note may add a bit of vibrato; a trumpeter might brighten the timbre during a note; and a percussionist might strike the drum in slightly different locations. In each case, the performer is modulating the sound to produce one that is dynamic and not static.

At several points already in this text, we have used the words *modulation* and *modulator* in describing a synthesis element that controls another synthesis element. In Chapter 3, we discussed AM and FM synthesis, where one oscillator modulates the amplitude or the frequency of another oscillator, and in Chapters 4 and 5 we talked about modulating amplitude envelopes and audio filters. Those brief sections were a foreshadowing of the many modulation tools available to dynamically shape a sound as it is being played.

Nearly everything we do on a synthesizer involves some type of modulation. For example, when you press a particular key on the synthesizer's keyboard, you modulate the frequency of the oscillator to produce the desired pitch. Likewise, striking the key harder and softer modulates the amplitude of the oscillator to produce louder and quieter sounds. However, a synthesizer that merely turns oscillator sounds on and off will quickly begin to sound static and lifeless. In addition to the basic forms of modulation, most instruments therefore include a number of functions and controllers that are used to dynamically modify and control nearly every aspect of the synthesis process. These special functions and controllers are generically referred to as *modulators*, and they are often found in a separate window or screen of the synthesizer called the Modulator Section.

Very simply, a modulator on a synthesizer creates a signal that rises and falls. Nearly every function on a synthesizer involves a control that can be raised or lowered, and so the uses for modulators are almost unlimited. You might modulate frequency, phase, pulse width, amplitude, filter cutoff, resonance, envelope time, and even many of the elements of the modulators themselves.

The signals of modulators, such as low frequency oscillators, continuously rise and fall in repeating patterns, while envelope generator signals rise and fall as keys are pressed and released. Some modulators create time-based or rhythm-based signals, and others create their rising and falling signal by mathematically calculating the outputs of other functions. Also, many modulators are controlled directly by the performer, as with the modulation and pitch-bend wheels. With all of these types of modulators, synthesizers provide a wealth of possibilities for dynamically shaping your sounds while you play them.

Today, nearly all synthesizers have a wide assortment of modulators available for the user. These modulators are frequently capable of modulating multiple synthesizer elements and, as we will see shortly, being modulated themselves by other modulators. In this chapter, we focus on modulators that are internal to the synthesizer itself. We will examine methods and sources of external modulation in the next chapter. With so many modulator options, it is impossible to describe them all without this book becoming unwieldy. Therefore, we limit our examination to the common modulators found on most synthesizers and give a few examples of how they might be used. As we do so, though, feel free to experiment with them beyond the ways described below.

Modulation Matrix

Because the modern synthesizer usually has so many modulation sources as well as elements capable of being modulated, modulators are frequently not automatically connected to their destinations. The user needs to designate which modulators affect which elements and determine how much of an effect (*depth*) the modulator actually has on the destination element. This process of connecting modulators to synthesizer elements and adjusting their depth occurs in what is called the synthesizer's *modulation matrix*.

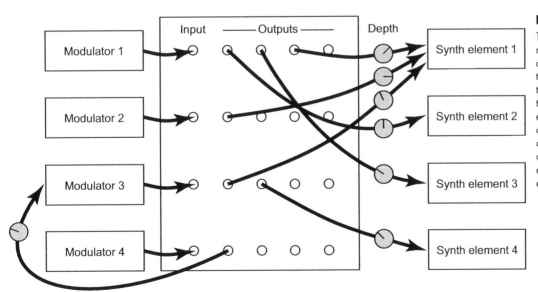

Figure 6.1
The modulation matrix allows you to connect the outputs of the various modulators to the inputs of the many synthesis elements, including other modulators, and control the depth of the modulation effect on each element.

Think of the modulation matrix as a big patch bay where the outputs of all the modulators can be routed to the inputs of the various synthesis elements, each with an individual depth control. In early modular synthesizers like the Moog and others, the modulation matrix was literally a patch bay with numerous cables connecting the modulators to their destinations. These days, it is usually done with on-screen menus or grids, although a few synthesizers still provide "virtual" patch cables that help make the matrix connections quite obvious.

Figure 6.2

Three approaches to the modulation matrix: Avid's Hybrid (top left) has drop-down menus in the various synthesis elements that allow you to choose the modulator, as well as horizontal sliders to control the depth of modulator effect. Arturia's Modular V (top right) uses virtual patch cables to connect modulators and elements. In an unusual GUI approach, depth is adjusted by "turning" the modulator cable input jack on the synthesis element. Propellerhead's Thor (bottom) uses a grid to assign modulators (SOURCE) to the various synthesis elements (DEST) and adjust the depth (AMOUNT) of the modulator effect.

Regardless of the connection method, once the user assigns the output of a modulator to the input of a synthesizer element she must also adjust the depth of the modulator. Modulator depth determines how much of an effect the modulator has on the selected synthesis element destination. A modulator with a depth of zero has no effect. As the depth increases, the modulator has a greater and greater effect on the synthesizer element.

As we discuss them, remember that a modulator is simply creating a rising and falling signal, and that the signal may be applied to nearly any control that accepts a rising and falling input value. Therefore, though we may describe a specific use of a modulator with a particular synthesizer element, in reality nearly any modulator may be used with almost any synthesizer element.

Low Frequency Oscillators (LFOs)

Demo 6.1

The oscillators we discussed at great length in Chapters 2 and 3 produced oscillating voltages in the audible range (greater than 20 Hz). As the name *low frequency oscillator* suggests, these oscillators produce changes in voltage well below the audible range, often between 0.25 Hz and 5 Hz. LFOs are not intended to be heard. Rather, the slowly rising and falling waveform is used to modulate some other synthesis element in a constantly repeating manner.

Imagine assigning an LFO with a 4–5 Hz oscillation to the pitch control of an audible oscillator. With a low depth setting, this LFO would cause the pitch of the oscillator to slightly rise and fall four or five times a second. In the acoustic world, this is known as vibrato. Similarly, the LFO could be assigned to the amplitude of the audible oscillator, thus creating a tremolo effect. As we will see, LFOs have numerous applications in the synthesis process and are some of the most popular internal modulators found on any synthesizer.

Like their audible counterparts, LFOs usually allow the user to select the LFO waveform as well as set the frequency, although the frequency control is usually limited at the top end to around 20–30 Hz. LFO waveforms typically consist of the basic oscillator waveforms: sine, triangle, sawtooth, and pulse (square), but they may feature several other LFO-specific waveform options as well.[1] The "shape" of the desired modulator effect determines which waveform is used.

LFO Shapes

Sine

A sine wave LFO is used to produce a smooth, symmetrical, and continuous oscillation effect. This type of wave is nice for things like pitch modulation, to create vibrato. Because the rate of change in a sine wave remains constant, this type of LFO wave can sound as if it has momentarily stopped moving when it gets to the top of the compression peak and the bottom of the rarefaction trough. Consequently, using a sine wave LFO on subtle effects such as filter resonance and amplitude change is often unsatisfactory to our ears. It is best used for more obvious effects such as a change in frequency or pitch.

Triangle

Like the sine wave, the triangle wave LFO produces a symmetrical oscillation. Because of the abrupt directional change, though, this wave is frequently used instead of the sine wave when working with subtler effects. The triangle LFO is also a good one for controlling a sound that needs to pan back and forth between the left and right channels.

Sawtooth

As opposed to the sine and triangle waves, the sawtooth LFO produces a unidirectional ramp with an abrupt jump back to the beginning of the ramp. Traditionally, the ramp is an upward slope, but many sawtooth LFOs allow selection of a downward ramp as well. The sawtooth LFO is frequently used to produce a "whoop . . . whoop . . . whoop" effect.

Pulse

Like the audible pulse or square wave oscillator, the pulse wave LFO produces an abrupt, binary switch between two opposite poles. Usually, the oscillation is symmetrical, producing a square wave, but some pulse wave LFOs allow adjustment of the pulse width to create asymmetrical oscillations. A pulse wave LFO can be very effective in giving a "throbbing" timbre to a sound when assigned to the cutoff frequency of an audio filter. It is also frequently used to create a trill by assigning the output to an oscillator's frequency and setting the depth so that it alternates between two pitches.

Sample-and-Hold

Whereas the previous four waveforms (sine, triangle, sawtooth, pulse) are commonly found on both LFOs and audio-rate oscillators, the sample-and-hold wave is exclusively an LFO type. Technically, it is not a "wave" type at all, but a low-frequency sampling of another sound wave.

---

1 See Chapter 2, "Oscillators," for a review of the basic oscillator waveforms.

The true sample-and-hold LFO has an input for an audio signal to enter. The LFO then samples the audio input at the very slow rate of the LFO's frequency. As it calculates each sample, the LFO outputs a steady (held) voltage equal to the most recent sample measurement. As the next sample is measured, the voltage abruptly jumps to, and holds, that level and so on. The net effect is a pulse type of wave, but with varying levels of voltage and polarity. Since the idea is to create a bit of a random-sounding pulse wave, noise is often used as the input to be measured, but nearly any varying audio signal may be used. Like the pulse-wave LFO, the sample-and-hold LFO is often used to create a rhythmic throbbing sound, but with varying degrees of intensity.

Figure 6.3
A random signal such as noise, when sampled at regular time intervals, produces a stepped sample-and-hold LFO "wave" at the frequency of the sampling interval.

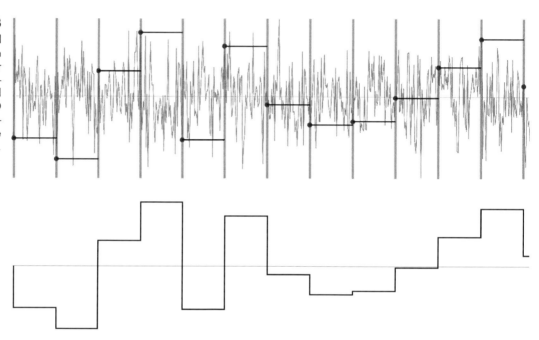

Not all sample-and-hold LFOs actually sample another wave these days. Many modern LFOs simply generate a pulse wave, but with randomly varying amplitudes. The result is nearly identical to actually sampling a sound wave and greatly simplifies the process for most users.

Random

A number of LFOs have a random setting in addition to the basic waveforms described above. The actual function of the random setting varies from manufacturer to manufacturer, but it is frequently a smooth (sinus-like) oscillation where the amplitude varies randomly. On some synthesizers, though, the random setting produces a stepped output like that of a sample-and-hold LFO, so be sure to consult your synthesizer's manual for the actual LFO behavior if it has a random setting.

Drift

We generally think of an oscillator as swinging back and forth between its opposite poles, but the drift LFO slowly fluctuates only a small, random distance from the zero-crossing line. Like sample-and-hold, drift is exclusively found as a modulator, not a sound source.

The earliest analog synthesizers used vacuum tubes to control their many functions. One of the quirks of vacuum tubes is that, as they continue to operate and heat up, they experience small fluctuations in performance. These fluctuations mean that whatever they are controlling (frequency, amplitude, filter cutoff, etc.) will fluctuate as well. In general, these subtle fluctuations contribute to the uniquely *analog* sound that so many modern digital synthesizers try to emulate.

The drift LFO is one way in which digital synthesizers can impart some of the random fluctuation inherent in vacuum tubes. Consequently, a drift LFO is often connected to the frequency of an oscillator, or the cutoff frequency of a filter, to create a bit of "imperfection" in the sound. Drift LFOs are also useful for creating slight fluctuations in a sound, such as what happens when a drummer strikes a ride cymbal in slightly differing locations, or a guitarist plucks the string with varying amounts of energy. On instruments without a drift LFO option, it is often possible to create this effect by using a random LFO with both the rate and LFO depth set extremely low.

Figure 6.4
A drift LFO produces gentle fluctuations that might be used to emulate the performance of vacuum tubes, or to create slightly fluctuating changes in the timbre of a sound.

Wavetable and Lookup-Table LFOs

A few of the more sophisticated synthesizers have the ability to create a custom LFO shape either with a wavetable or by loading in an actual wave sample. Although a sample-based LFO can be a bit unpredictable, a wavetable LFO with evenly spaced peaks can be quite effective when synchronized with a tempo. Rhythmic effects can be achieved with a wavetable LFO, but they are often more easily created with a step sequencer, as we will see a little later in this chapter.

Figure 6.5
A wavetable sawtooth LFO wave with symmetrically spaced subpeaks can be quite effective when synchronized with the tempo of a sequence. In this case, synchronizing the overall LFO wave with the quarter note will produce pulsed subdivisions at the rate of the sixteenth note.

LFO Rate

Low frequency oscillators, as mentioned earlier, also have a frequency setting, albeit one considerably lower than that of audible oscillators. Typically, an LFO rate is from just a few Hertz on down to a fraction of a Hertz. For example, you might set the LFO rate to 0.5 Hz, causing it to take two seconds to complete a single cycle. A smaller fraction like 0.25 Hz would take four seconds to complete a cycle.

Because we often want an LFO to work musically, many LFOs have the option of setting the rate to a tempo or note value. Most of these LFOs even let you slave them to the tempo of a MIDI sequencer. Therefore you could create an LFO that you want to cycle every measure of your 4/4 piece of music by slaving the LFO to the sequence tempo and setting the cycle to the whole note. This way, even if the sequence changes tempo, your LFO still completes its cycle in one measure. When slaving to a tempo and note value, LFOs often use an abbreviation for note durations that can be confusing at first. A *1* (or *1/1*) equals a whole note, a *1/2* a half note, a *1/4* a quarter note, and so on. Where the confusion often comes is when you see something like *1/4t* or *1/8d*, which represent a quarter-note triplet and a dotted eighth note respectively.

Even if your LFO does not allow direct synchronization of its rate to tempo and note durations, you can still accomplish the effect by using a little bit of math to calculate the desired LFO rate.[2]

LFO Trigger

In addition to controls for the waveform and frequency, most LFOs have additional controls to determine when the LFO wave is triggered, to set the starting phase position of the LFO wave, and to create an offset delay for when the LFO begins to oscillate.

When an LFO is triggered can be as important as the type and frequency of the LFO wave. On many basic synthesizers, the LFO operates continuously and is said to be in *free-running* mode. As notes are triggered, they "catch" the LFO wave at whatever position the LFO happens to be in during its oscillation. More sophisticated instruments will often have a control to determine when the LFO is triggered.

- *Trigger* (sometimes called *first-note*) mode begins the LFO wave when the first synthesizer key is pressed and runs continuously until all notes are released. Thus, if you play a note before releasing the previous note, the LFO does not start over. This mode works best with polyphonic sounds and sustained notes.
- *Retrigger* (sometimes called *each-note*) mode restarts the LFO wave with the attack of every new note. This mode is particularly effective with a monophonic melody voice as each new note retriggers the LFO wave. Retrigger mode is also necessary in order to modulate an LFO with an envelope control of some type.

> ### TIP Monophonic vs. Polyphonic LFOs
> Many synthesizers describe their LFOs as being either monophonic or polyphonic. Since we typically think of monophonic and polyphonic as referring to the number of notes being played, using these terms with LFOs can be a little confusing.
>
> - A *monophonic* LFO produces only one LFO wave and applies the wave to all the sounding notes of a particular sound.

2 To calculate the LFO rate from a tempo and note value, divide the tempo in bpm (beats per minute) by 240, and multiply the value by the number (n) of your chosen note values in a 4/4 measure. For example, say you want to set an LFO to the quarter-note triplet at a tempo of 108 bpm. Divide 108 by 240 for a value of 0.45, then multiply 0.45 by 6 (the number of quarter-note triplets in a 4/4 measure), and you arrive at an LFO rate of 2.7 Hz.

> **TIP** *continued*
>
> • A *polyphonic* LFO, on the other hand, creates a separate (retriggered) LFO wave for each of the individual notes of a particular sound.
>
> Monophonic LFOs are generally best for things like vibrato and tremolo as they create the same amount of modulation for all sounding notes. A polyphonic LFO can be quite nice for legato melodies and for simple contrapuntal lines. However, using a polyphonic LFO with multiple simultaneous notes can create a rather "jittery" sound since it is extremely unlikely the different LFO waves will be in phase with each other.

Some sophisticated LFOs allow users to synchronize the LFO trigger to both the note and the tempo of a sequence. In this scenario, the LFO often has two trigger settings. One option is to start the LFO wave when the note is pressed, but the LFO rate is synced to a tempo or note value. This can cause odd rhythmic effects with tempo-synced LFOs if a note begins in the middle of a beat. The other option always keeps the LFO synchronized with the beat, but it starts the LFO effect when the note is pressed. This second option is usually better for tempo-based LFO effects.

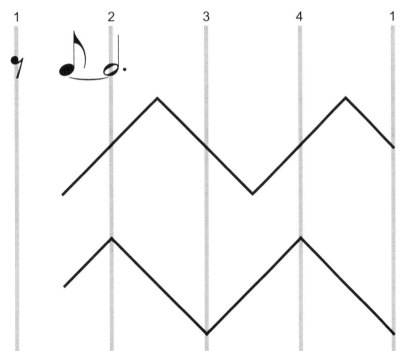

Figure 6.7
When an LFO is synchronized to a tempo or note value such as a half note, having the LFO wave set to trigger when the note is played can cause odd rhythmic anomalies if a note begins between beats (upper triangle LFO wave). Setting the LFO to always stay synced to the beat causes it to maintain metrical integrity, but only take effect when a note is played (lower LFO wave).

LFO Phase

The phase control allows you to choose where in the wave's cycle the LFO begins when it is triggered. It is usually measured in degrees, with 0° being the very beginning of the compression phase. Be aware, though, that some LFOs put the 0° position at other locations in the wave, so make certain to confirm where the 0° phase position is on your synthesizer. Fortunately, most software synthesizers now include a graphic display that shows exactly where the wave will begin.

Since we are meant to hear the effect of the LFO modulation, the starting phase position can be extremely important as this is where the wave will begin every time the LFO is triggered. For example, you might want to create a whoop . . . whoop . . . whoop . . . effect by modulating a lowpass filter's cutoff frequency with a sawtooth wave LFO. In this scenario, it would be critical to set the phase position of the sawtooth wave so that every time you trigger the LFO it begins at the very bottom of the upward ramp and not somewhere in the middle.

LFO Delay

Listen carefully to an oboist, or violinist, playing a long sustained note and you will probably hear that the note begins with a straight tone, and after about a half-second or so the player begins to add vibrato. This delay in the onset of an effect is the purpose of the LFO delay control. Set the delay to 500 ms and the LFO will begin to oscillate a half-second after the note begins. If the note happens to finish before 500 ms, there will be no LFO effect. Since acoustic musicians usually apply vibrato and tremolo only to longer notes, having no LFO effect on short notes and a delayed LFO effect on long notes is often desirable.

Using an LFO

A low frequency oscillator can modulate any synthesizer element that accepts a rising and falling input control signal. However, some uses are much more common than others. Perhaps the three most popular applications of an LFO are to modulate the amplitude of an oscillator, or bank of oscillators, producing a tremolo; to modulate the frequency of an oscillator, or bank of oscillators, producing a vibrato; and to modulate the cutoff or center frequency of an audio filter, producing a rhythmic pulsing of a sound's timbre. Although these three are the most common, they are by no means the only ways to use an LFO.

Other popular uses of an LFO include modulating the width of a pulse, or triangle, wave; modulating the resonance amount, or Q, of an audio filter; modulating the phase of an oscillator wave; and modulating the frequency width of additive synthesis oscillators. Remember, if a synthesis element accepts a rising and falling control input, it can probably be modulated with an LFO, so feel free to experiment with various combinations and depth settings as you discover all of the possibilities LFOs present.

Demo 6.2

Audio-Rate Oscillators

Just as an LFO creates a repeating modulator wave in the subsonic range (less than 20 Hz), an audio-rate oscillator creates a repeating modulator wave in the audible range (greater than 20 Hz). Even though the audio-rate oscillator's signal is in the audible range, it is not heard, but used to modulate something else. We have already experienced audio-rate oscillators controlling the amplitude and frequency of another oscillator in AM and FM synthesis.[3] Technically, the rising and falling signal of an audio-rate oscillator can be used to modulate anything, but the speed of the oscillations makes it impractical for most ap-

---

3 See Chapter 3, "Oscillator Combinations," for more on AM and FM synthesis.

plications. Consequently, other than for AM and FM synthesis, the most common use of an audio-rate oscillator is to modulate the cutoff or center frequency of an audio filter, and it is in this role that the audio-rate oscillator has become quite popular. Other uses you might occasionally encounter are for modulating the pulse width of a pulse wave or the phase position of an oscillator. These latter two uses are also quite similar to FM synthesis. Our focus here is on modulating an audio filter.

Applying an audio-rate oscillator to the cutoff or center frequency of a filter instead of directly to the frequency of an oscillator creates a kind of FM "lite" effect. Since the frequency modulation sidebands are created in the filter and not in the oscillator, the sidebands are not as strong and are added alongside the original oscillator sound. The result contains some of the wonderfully clangorous sounds for which FM synthesis is famous, but with the original oscillator sound remaining prominent in the mix.

Some synthesizers have separate audio-rate oscillators for modulators, while others simply allow you to designate one or more of the standard audio oscillators as a modulator by assigning its output to some synthesis function. Since they are modulating so rapidly, audio-rate oscillators tend to output only basic waveforms like sine, triangle, sawtooth, and pulse waves. Like their low-frequency counterparts, when audio-rate oscillators are used to modulate a filter's cutoff or center frequency, they are usually in a monophonic mode and often set to a fixed oscillation frequency. By contrast, when audio-rate oscillators are used in FM synthesis they are usually polyphonic and their oscillation frequency changes with the harmonicity ratio between the modulator and carrier oscillators.

Modulation Envelope Generators

We discussed envelope generators at some length in both Chapters 4 and 5. After LFOs, envelope generators are probably the next most popular and commonly used internal modulators on a synthesizer. Remember from our previous discussion that an envelope generator creates a multisegmented, rising and falling control signal that is triggered by pressing and releasing keys on a synthesizer. In Chapter 4, we used that rising and falling signal to control the amplitude of an oscillator to give shape to a sound, and in Chapter 5 we used it to create a dynamic timbre for the sound by raising and lowering the cutoff or center frequency of a filter. Those examples, however, were just two of the many uses for envelope generators. As with all the other modulators, the envelope generator's rising and falling control signal may be used to modulate almost every aspect of a synthesizer. As the envelope generator becomes more and more popular as a modulator, synthesizer developers have added new features and capabilities that go well beyond the traditional ADSR envelope generator.

Unlimited-Stage and Looping Envelopes

In Chapter 4, we discussed multistage envelopes containing more than the typical four segments (attack, decay, sustain, release). Many of the newer synthesizers allow users to create numerous breakpoints in the envelope's shape, often providing an unlimited number of envelope stages. Most of these envelope generators also allow each segment to be curved to some degree for either logarithmic or exponential transition between the breakpoints.

We usually think of the sustain segment of an envelope as the part of the envelope where everything remains constant until the key is released, but another way to think of it is that the envelope generator keeps looping from the end of the sustain section back to the beginning of the sustain section until the key is released. In this scenario, breakpoint segments that are added to the sustain section are looped as well. The effect can be somewhat like an LFO that begins only after the attack and decay segments and ends when the synthesizer key is released. Some synthesizers even allow you to synchronize the looping of the sustain section with a tempo to create rhythmic effects.

Figure 6.8
Native Instrument's FM8 synthesizer allows you to create envelopes with numerous curved segments by adding an unlimited number of breakpoints in the envelope. The segments that fall within the sustain section are looped for as long as the key is held down.

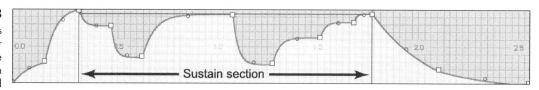

Bipolar Envelopes

Thus far, all of the envelope generators we have examined are unipolar; that is, they represent only values greater than zero. Given that the envelope generator was originally designed to control amplitude, this makes perfect sense, as a sound's output level cannot be less than zero. However, a number of synthesizer parameters can be modulated both above *and* below zero. In fact, we have already done this when we applied an LFO to the pitch of an oscillator. As the LFO wave moves above zero, the pitch is pushed sharp, and as it falls back below zero, the oscillator pitch goes flat.

A bipolar envelope generator works on the same concept of going above and below zero, but like all envelope generators it does so when a synthesizer key is pressed and released. As with most envelope generators, you set the duration in the number of milliseconds that you want each segment to take for its transition, with the penultimate segment usually reserved for the sustain level. The difference in bipolar envelopes is that the amplitude values can be either positive or negative. Bipolar envelopes can be particularly effective when applied to the cutoff or center frequency of a resonant audio filter.

Figure 6.9
In addition to unipolar envelope generators, Avid's Hybrid synthesizer has several bipolar envelopes available as modulation controllers.

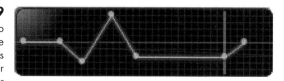

Vector Envelopes

In 1986, Sequential Circuits released the Prophet VS (Vector Synthesis) synthesizer with a new type of modulation envelope called a *vector* envelope. The vector envelope generator was actually two bipolar envelope generators arranged in an X/Y configuration that modulated the levels among four oscillators. As the envelope moved above and below the X-axis, it raised and lowered the levels of the oscillators at the top and bottom; and as it moved left and right of the Y-axis, it raised and lowered the levels of the oscillators at the sides of the graph. Like other envelope generators, pressing and releasing synthesizer keys triggers the vector envelope generator. In this case, however, the envelope can start and end anywhere in the grid, and even double back on itself.

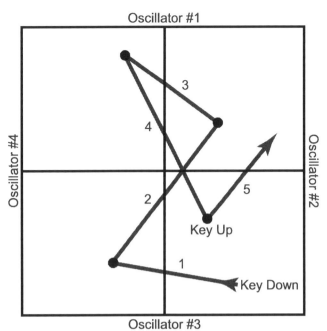

Figure 6.10
The original vector, or X/Y, envelope modulated between four oscillators as a key was pressed and released.

In the years since the Prophet VS release, a number of synthesizer designers have included vector (also known as X/Y and 2-D) envelope generators on their instruments. As happened with the original ADSR envelope generator, these vector envelope generators developed more features, such as multiple and looping segments, and they can be assigned to modulate nearly all of a synthesizer's functions. Typically, the outputs of the two axes would be assigned to different functions. For example, one output might be assigned to the frequency of an oscillator, and the other to the filter cutoff. Then the envelope would modulate between the pitch and timbre of the sound as the synthesizer key is pressed and released.

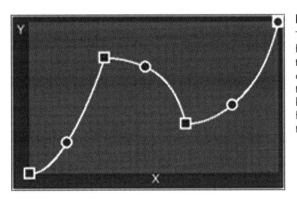

Figure 6.11
The 2D envelope from KVR's SynthMaster is an example of a vector envelope that can modulate between any two functions assigned to its X and Y axes.

Envelope Followers

Instead of timed segments that are triggered by note-on and note-off messages, envelope followers generate their envelope by tracking the amplitude of an incoming signal. The envelope follower creates its rising and falling segments from the rising and falling amplitude of the other sound. In order to use an envelope follower, the synthesizer must either have a way to get externals sounds into the instrument, or be able to follow the sound envelopes of its own internal sounds. Once the incoming audio signal has been selected, the envelope follower usually provides controls allowing the user to adjust the sensitivity and response to compensate for the type of sound source.

Like all envelope generators, the output signal may be used to modulate all manner of synthesizer functions. One of the more popular uses has been to superimpose the rhythm of a drum part onto a synthesized bass sound so that the bass has the same sort of "groove" as the drums. Another common use is to drive the cutoff or center frequency of an audio filter on a synthesized sound with an external sound source.

Figure 6.12

An envelope follower might track the incoming audio signal of a drum part in order to generate an envelope that superimposes the feeling of the drum "groove" onto a synthesized sound.

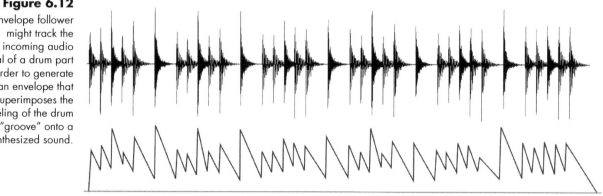

Function Modulators

Demo 6.3

In the early 1990s, Kurzweil introduced a type of modulator in its K2000 line of synthesizers that turned the X/Y modulator on its head. Instead of using a point within an X/Y grid to send control information to the X and Y destinations, Kurzweil's function modulator (or FUN as they called it) received inputs on the X- and Y-axes (labeled "a" and "b") from different synthesizer elements. The data from these two inputs were then manipulated with a mathematical formula to create an output that was used as the actual modulator signal.

Nearly every aspect of the synthesizer could be assigned as inputs for a and b. One input might be a physical controller like the modulation wheel or pitch bend wheel, while the other input got its data from an internal modulator like an LFO or envelope generator. Values such as MIDI note numbers and velocities could also be used, as could a static value on one of the inputs, such as 0.25. Some of the FUNs even have a third input (labeled "y") that allowed the output of the FUN to be fed back into the formula, creating a more random result. You could even assign the output of one FUN as an input to another FUN, as there were a total of four FUNs available.

Though some of the formulae were rather simple (e.g., $a + b$, $a - b$, $|a \times b|$[4]), others were more complex, as with $(a + 2b)/3$, or $a(10^{(2b)}/100)$. And, as mentioned above, some formulae fed the output of the FUN back into itself, as with $a(b - y)$ or $y(a + 1) + b$, to create a more chaotic and random result. Regardless of the inputs or formula, the output was a control signal that evolved in a variety of ways depending on the changing inputs. This control signal, like any other modulator signal, could then be used to modulate other elements on the synthesizer.

The function modulators, or FUNs, on the Kurzweil instruments were incredibly powerful, often complex, and ultimately (pardon the pun) a lot of fun to use. It is prob-

---

4 $|a \times b|$ = the absolute value of $a \times b$. If the value of $a \times b$ is a negative number, it is multiplied by -1. Thus all values for this formula are positive numbers.

ably due to their complexity and steep learning curve that more synthesizer manufacturers have not adopted something similar, but you often find these sorts of capabilities in music programming languages such as Csound, Max, and Pure Data (Pd).

Figure 6.13
The FUN editor on the Kurzweil K2000 series of synthesizers allows you to use up to four function editors (FUNs) and assign their various inputs and formulae. You can even assign the output of one FUN to the inputs of other FUNs. In this example, FUN 3 uses the average of the modulation wheel and aftertouch values to create a control signal.

Step Sequencers

You are probably already familiar with the MIDI sequencer programs found in today's DAWs (digital audio workstations) like Pro Tools, Logic, Cubase, and Digital Performer. These incredibly powerful programs allow you to record and edit a seemingly endless number of notes on hundreds of tracks. Given these capabilities, it is often hard to imagine that these massive sequencer applications grew out of simple eight-step sequencers capable of little more than sending a repeating string of control voltages to an oscillator.

Demo 6.4

Step sequencers were originally hardware modules that produced a limited number of control signals in a steady, pulsed sequence that kept repeating until deactivated.[5] The output of the signal could be sent to some other synthesizer module, such as an oscillator or audio filter. If you sustained a single note while the step sequencer was active, the changing voltage, when assigned to the frequency of an oscillator, would produce a repeating sequence of changing pitches. As step sequencers continued to evolve, their use grew to include such things as triggering synthesized "drum" sounds (often called "pattern sequencers"), modulating the amplitudes of sounds, and controlling the cutoff or center frequency of audio filters. Although the output of a step sequencer these days may be assigned to almost any function on a synthesizer, using them to control oscillator frequency (pitch), amplitude, and filter cutoff are still by far the most popular uses.

The typical step sequencer has a set of controls that allow the user to control the speed at which the sequencer goes through its steps, determine how many steps are used (up to the maximum available), choose which steps are active or inactive, set the control voltage and duration (gate time) for every step, and assign the output to a synthesizer element. Many step sequencers also have several rows of controls for each step. Individual rows can be assigned to different destinations, producing layered patterns within the sets of steps.

---

5 The majority of synthesizer users in the 1960s and 1970s were pop and rock musicians, whose songs were predominantly based on a 4/4 measure with a straight eighth- or sixteenth-note groove. Therefore step sequencers of the time tended to produce enough steps to create a 4/4 measure's worth of eighth notes (eight-step) or sixteenth notes (sixteen-step).

Figure 6.14

The Q960 Sequential Controller by Synthesizers.com is a modern recreation of the original Moog 960 sequencer module from the 1960s. Like the original, it has eight steps with variable control voltages that can be assigned to three destinations. (image courtesy of Roger Arrick, Synthesizers.com, used with permission)

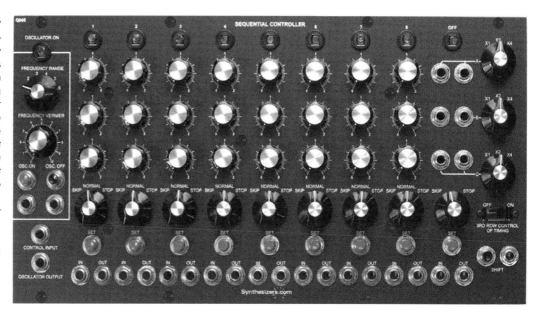

The step sequencer offers a type of modulation source similar to the output of a sample-and-hold LFO, but with much greater control. Whereas the sample-and-hold oscillator can usually synchronize its stepped output to a tempo or rhythm, the output levels of the steps are random and nonrepeating. Step sequencers, by contrast, not only sync to a tempo but allow you to determine the exact output level of every step. You can also activate and deactivate individual steps to create syncopated rhythms from your steps, and by adjusting the gate time or duration of the steps you can create longer and shorter note values.

Figure 6.15

By deactivating individual steps (circled), a syncopated, repeating rhythmic pattern may be created from a sixteen-step sequencer.

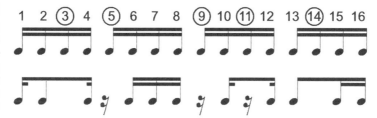

Many step sequencers now provide more than sixteen steps, and some even allow you to create several measures worth of pulses. It is also increasingly common to create more complex rhythms than just eighth and sixteenth notes, either by having more subdivisions within the measure or by creating envelopes on the individual steps. Today, large sequencer programs have mostly taken over the role of recording notes, especially for complete pieces of music, but the step sequencer still remains an important modulator source for creating rhythmically pulsed effects in your sounds.

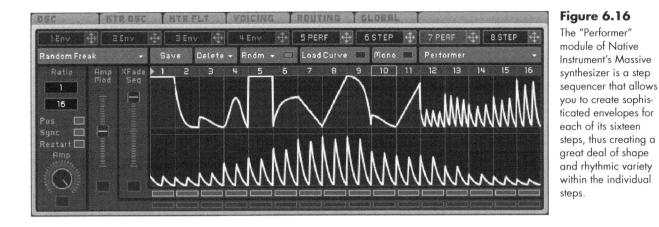

Figure 6.16
The "Performer" module of Native Instrument's Massive synthesizer is a step sequencer that allows you to create sophisticated envelopes for each of its sixteen steps, thus creating a great deal of shape and rhythmic variety within the individual steps.

Arpeggiators

Although arpeggiators share a common lineage with step sequencers, they have evolved along a different path over the years. The original arpeggiators performed much like a sequencer by applying a stepped control voltage to an oscillator thereby causing its pitch to change in a rhythmic fashion. On a modern synthesizer, the arpeggiator function typically examines the notes a player is holding down on the keyboard and separates them into some sort of rhythmic arpeggio according to the settings of the arpeggiator.

Most arpeggiators allow the user to set such options as the rhythmic value of the arpeggio, the direction (up, down, stepped, random, etc.) to read through the individual notes, whether to extend the arpeggio into multiple octaves, and whether to synchronize the arpeggio speed with the tempo of a DAW. Arpeggiators were extremely popular in the 1980s and are currently experiencing a bit of resurgence among synthesizer enthusiasts and performers.

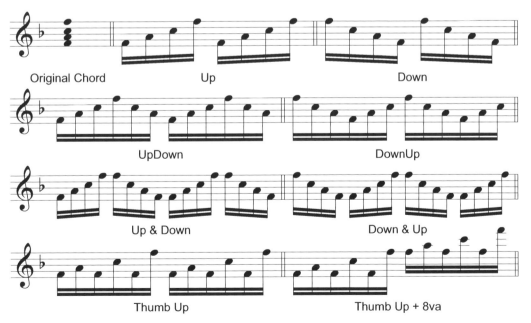

Figure 6.17
A few common arpeggiator patterns created from a basic F major chord.

Modulating the Modulators

So far, we have discussed modulators in terms of their use in controlling primary synthesizer elements such as oscillators and filters. However, as you have already seen, modulators may also be used to modulate other modulators. You can cascade modulators to add another layer of complexity and control to your synthesizer sounds. When modulating other modulators, it is usually best to work backward from the last modulator. Determine how it will affect the synthesizer sound, and then back up to the modulator that controls the final modulator. Continue working backward until you configure the initial modulator. The possible uses of modulators controlling other modulators are nearly endless, but here are a few quick examples to give you a taste of the level of control available on a synthesizer with cascaded modulators.

Shaping an LFO

Assign a sample-and-hold LFO to the cutoff or center frequency of an audio filter. Assign a bipolar envelope generator to the depth of the LFO on the filter and shape the envelope so that it begins very high, slowly (approximately 1,000 ms) drops to zero percent, and then ramps back up to about 50 percent positive before going to zero percent on the key release. When you play long notes, the filter will produce a stepped cutoff effect that diminishes over one second and then increases again, although not to the same level as before. When the note is released, the stepped cutoff effect dies away.

Oscillating an Audio-Rate Oscillator

Assign an audio-rate modulator to the cutoff or center frequency of an audio filter, and assign a slow (0.25 Hz), triangle-wave LFO to the frequency of the audio-rate modulator. As you play notes, the LFO will move the frequency of the audio-rate modulator up and down, creating an FM effect that sweeps up and down. If you set key velocity to control the LFO depth, the effect will be even more pronounced on louder notes.

Making a Hyper-Responsive Vibrato

Assign an LFO with a triangle wave to the pitch of an oscillator and an envelope generator with a delay stage to the depth of the LFO on the oscillator's pitch. Next, assign key velocity to the amplitude and stage times of the envelope generator. Finally, assign pressure (often called aftertouch) to the LFO rate. As you play melodic notes, note that harder velocities cause the vibrato to begin a little later and be a bit more intense. Further pressing of the keys after the note is struck adds even more emphasis to the vibrato.

Modulators are an incredibly powerful and important element of any synthesizer and allow you to add a huge amount of variety and dynamic shape to your sounds. In Chapter 7, we will look at some of the external modulation sources for a synthesizer, but for now it is time to put some of these internal modulators to use.

Your Turn

Working with Crystal

In Chapters 4 and 5, you used envelope generators to modulate the amplitude and timbre of a sound respectively. In addition to those two envelope generators, found on all three voice tabs, the Modulation tab in Crystal provides six additional envelope generators and six LFOs that may be assigned to modulate almost any function in the synthesizer via the modulation matrix.

Modulation tab

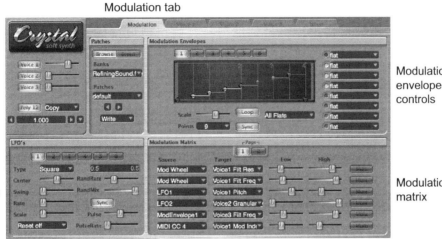

Figure 6.18

In addition to the separate filter and amplitude envelope generators for each of the three voices, the Modulation tab in Crystal contains six additional envelope generators, six LFOs, and a modulation matrix that allows you to assign modulators to nearly every one of the instrument's many control functions.

Modulation envelope controls

Modulation matrix

LFO controls

Modulation Matrix

The lower-right pane in the Modulation tab contains Crystal's modulation matrix. There are two identical "pages" of six modulation slots that allow you to assign a modulator to a destination and control the range of modulation. After assigning a modulator to a control, you will see that the control's knob in the other windows has illuminated, indicating its function is being modulated.

- *Source* selects the desired modulator. Clicking this menu reveals a long list of possible modulators, including the six modulation envelopes and LFOs, as well as numerous external MIDI controls.
- *Target* selects the function to be modulated. Clicking this menu reveals nine submenus that all have a list of functions available to be controlled by the modulator selected in the Source menu.
- *Low* and *High* sliders allow you to set the minimum and maximum amount of modulation effect. The farther apart the two knobs are, the greater the amount of effect.
- *Mute* allows you to quickly disable a Source and Target pairing.

Modulation Envelopes

The six additional modulation envelope generators in Crystal are identical to the filter and amplitude envelope generators in the three voice tabs, with one exception: the amplitude envelope generator has a velocity sensitivity control while the filter and modulation envelope generators do not. Click one of the six numbered buttons at the top of the modulation envelope pane to access an individual envelope generator.

LFOs

Crystal's six low frequency oscillators offer a wide range of shapes, modifications, and controls to provide an extremely sophisticated level of repeating modulation. Select the individual LFOs from the numbered buttons at the top of the LFO pane.

Type

Typically the first setting made in an LFO is the wave type. Crystal has seven LFO waves, some of which reveal two extra control sliders, as described below.

1. *Sine*: a sinusoidal wave.
2. *Random*: a sinusoidal wave that randomly changes speed and direction.
    • *RandRate*: controls how frequently the wave changes speed and direction
    • *RandMix*: controls how far the wave deviates from the value specified by the Rate parameter below
3. *Triangle*: a triangle wave.
4. *Square*: a square wave. By using the RandRate and RandMix controls, you can achieve a sample-and-hold effect.
    • *RandRate*: controls the randomness of how frequently the pulse changes
    • *RandMix*: controls the randomness of the levels to which the pulse jumps
5. *Saw Up*: a standard sawtooth wave that ramps up and drops down.
6. *Saw Down*: an inverted sawtooth wave that ramps down and jumps up.
7. *Heartbeat*: a wave that simulates the beating of a human heart.
    • *Width*: adjusts the time between the primary and secondary beats
    • *Damp*: controls the amount of the secondary "bounce" in the beating

Rate

Whenever the LFO is not synchronized to a tempo, its rate is shown in cycles per second (the same as Hertz) with a range of 0.01 to 60. When synchronized to a tempo, the rate changes to cycles per beat, with the same 0.01 to 60 range of values. When using cycles per beat, a rate of 1 equals a quarter note. For longer note values such as whole and half notes, use rates of 0.25 and 0.5 respectively. To create LFO waves that correspond with shorter note values, simply count the number of those note values in a single quarter note and use this for the LFO rate. For example, a rate of 2 produces a wave that correlates with an eighth note, and 4 with a sixteenth note.

Center, Swing, and Scale

On many synthesizers, the LFOs oscillate to their maximum amplitude on either side of zero (usually down to −1 and up to 1). On those instruments, the actual LFO amplitude is not usually controlled, but the effect of the LFO amplitude is regulated with the depth control in the modulation matrix or on the target function itself. Crystal uses three controls that add a great deal of flexibility to the LFOs amplitude and shape.

1. *Center*: determines the central point around which the wave will oscillate
2. *Swing*: determines how far above and below the center point the wave oscillates
3. *Scale*: creates a multiplier value for the LFO output

All LFOs in Crystal have a maximum output range of 0 to 1. To create a basic oscillation between the values of 0 and 1, set the Center to 0.5, Swing to 0.5, and Scale to 1.0.

Figure 6.19
In Crystal, a full-amplitude LFO oscillates between 0 and 1.

Now the fun begins. Even though the maximum *output* range of the LFOs is 0 to 1, you can use the Center, Swing, and Scale controls to make the LFO wave go outside this range. Doing so can create some interesting rhythmic patterns as only the part of the LFO wave that falls between 0 and 1 will actually be output as a modulation signal (see Figures 6.20 and 6.21 below).

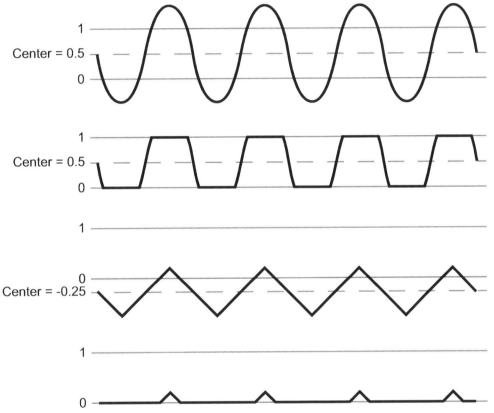

Figure 6.20
Changing the Swing of the LFO in Figure 6.19 from 0.5 to 1 doubles the amplitude of the wave, causing it to exceed the 0–1 output range (top). Thus the actual LFO output begins to take on the shape of a pulse wave, but with sloping transitions (bottom).

Figure 6.21
A triangle LFO wave with a Center value of –0.25 and a Swing of 0.5 spends most of its time below the 0–1 output range (top), producing a small, periodic "bump" as its output (bottom).

Pulse and PulseRate
The Pulse and PulseRate controls apply a secondary pulse wave LFO to the primary LFO, and can be used to create a "wobble" in the LFO signal. The Pulse slider mixes the output of the primary and secondary LFOs with a value of zero being no secondary, and a value of 1 being equal parts primary and secondary. The PulseRate slider controls the rate of the secondary LFO and works exactly like the primary LFO Rate slider.

Reset Menu
The Reset menu at the bottom of the LFO pane controls the free-run versus retrigger mode of the LFO. When **Reset off** is chosen, the LFO is in free-run mode and continues its oscillation regardless of the notes being played. With **Reset on note** selected, the LFO retriggers every time a new note is played.

With so many internal modulator possibilities, the options in a synthesizer such as Crystal can seem a bit overwhelming at first. To help you make sense of these modulators in practice, work through the examples below. They are designed to illustrate the types of modulation controls possible on a contemporary synthesizer while maintaining their transparency so that you can see and hear exactly what is happening in the sound.

Examples

For each example, begin with these settings:

- Select the default patch from the RefiningSound bank and change the oscillator type in voice 1 to **Synthesized:SawSquare**.
- Position the PulseMix slider at 0.500 and the PulseWidth slider at 0.000.
- Create a four-point amplitude envelope with linear breakpoints at:
    1. (Blue) 0.00, 0.00
    2. (Yellow) 0.03, 1.00
    3. (Red) 0.12, 0.60
    4. (Blue) 0.35, 0.00
- Select the **ResLoPass** filter type and set the cutoff to approximately 5,000 Hz and resonance to 0.300.
- Save these settings as a preset called *Modulation* using the instructions from the box entitled "Naming and Storing a New Patch in Crystal" in the Your Turn section of Chapter 3. Now you will be able to quickly return to this configuration as you begin each example.

Cycling Pulse Width

- In the Modulation Matrix pane, select **LFO1** as the first source and **Voice1 PulseWidth** as the first target.
- Select **Sine** as the Type for LFO 1 with Center and Swing both set to 0.500.
- Set the LFO Rate to 0.1 cps, and leave Scale set to 1.000
- Leave Reset, Sync, Pulse, and PulseRate all off.

When you play a note, you will hear that the timbre of the sound changes periodically as the LFO modulates the PulseWidth value.

Now, let's refine the cycling pulse width a bit. In the modulation matrix, raise the Low slider for LFO1 to 0.100 and lower the High slider to 0.900. You should now hear that the pulse width value is not pushed all the way to its minimum and maximum values. You will still hear the oscillation, but it will not be as extreme.

Next, turn the Sync button for the LFO on and set the rate to 0.25 cpb. The LFO will now complete one cycle in the time of a whole note. However, because pulse width modulation sounds quite similar in both positive and negative ranges, the oscillation will sound as if it is changing every half note instead of on the whole note. Unfortunately, the Rate slider resolution does not allow a value of 0.125 to make it sound like it is oscillating on the whole note, but there are several other options for making it do so.

The simplest option for giving this a whole-note oscillation is to reduce the Sync Tempo to half its current value. So long as nothing else is synchronized to the tempo, this option works well. However, if other modulators are tempo driven, changing the tempo will slow them down as well.

Since the half-note sound is a result of the fact that pulse width sounds similar in both upper and lower extremes, another solution is to keep the LFO restricted to either the positive or the negative range of pulse width values. The Low and High sliders in the modulation matrix make this quite easy to do.

- Change the Low slider to 0.500.
- Move the High slider back to 1.000.

Now when you play a note, you should hear an oscillation in the pulse width at the speed of the whole note in the Sync Tempo.

Modulating the LFO

- In the modulation matrix, select **ModEnvelope1** as the second source and **Other:LFO1 Swing** as the second target.
- Leave the Low slider on 0.000 and lower the High slider to 0.500.
- Select a four-point envelope for Modulation Envelope 1.
- Turn the envelope's Sync button on.
- Adjust the Scale slider for the envelope so that you can see five beats.
- Create these breakpoints:
    1. (Blue) 0.00, 0.00
    2. (Yellow) 2.00, 0.00, **curve positive**
    3. (Red) 4.00, 0.50
    4. (Blue) 4.50, 0.00

Now, you still have your modulating pulse width, but the LFO does not begin to take effect until the second beat in the sync tempo and fades in over two more beats.

Swirling Multiwave Oscillator

So far, you have used only voice 1. In this example, you continue to use the settings from the previous example, but with slight modifications to create a dynamically swirling multi-wave oscillator sound.

- Copy voice 1 and paste it to voices 2 and 3.
- Using the FineTune slider, tune voice 2 down to −0.08 and tune voice 3 up to 0.08.
- Apply the settings from LFO 1 to LFOs 2 and 3. Unfortunately, there is no copy-and-paste functionality for LFOs, so you have to set their values manually.
- With the Sync button on, set the Rate of LFO 1 to 0.16, LFO 2 to 0.25, and LFO 3 to 0.35.
- Select LFO 4 and set the Type to **Sine** with the Center at 0.5 and the Swing at 0.4.
- Apply the LFO 4 settings to LFOs 5 and 6.
- With the Sync button on, set the rate of LFO 4 to 0.25, LFO 5 to 0.35, and LFO 6 to 0.16.
- Configure the modulation matrix with these settings.

141

Source	Target	Low	High
LFO1	Voice1 PulseWidth	0.500	0.900
LFO2	Voice2 PulseWidth	0.500	0.900
LFO3	Voice3 PulseWidth	0.500	0.900
ModEnvelope1	LFO1 Swing	0.000	0.500
ModEnvelope1	LFO2 Swing	0.000	0.500
ModEnvelope1	LFO3 Swing	0.000	0.500
LFO4	Voice1 Pan	0.000	1.000
LFO5	Voice2 Pan	0.000	1.000
LFO6	Voice3 Pan	0.000	1.000
ModEnvelope1	LFO4 Swing	0.000	1.000
ModEnvelope1	LFO5 Swing	0.000	1.000
ModEnvelope1	LFO6 Swing	0.000	1.000

Set your sync tempo around 60–70 bpm and sustain a chord on your synthesizer keyboard. You will hear that the notes tend to swirl in somewhat random fashion. Because of the slightly different LFO rates, the six LFOs go in and out of phase with each other. By using the modulation envelope, when the note first sounds, there is no modulation, but it fades in over four beats. Try experimenting with LFO rates and swing amounts and note the differences that are created.

Look Ma, No Sequencer

Crystal does not have a step sequencer or arpeggiator. However, with its numerous multistage and looping modulation envelopes, you can create the effect of one with overlapping, looped envelopes, assigned in this case to pitch.

- Return to the *Modulation* patch you created at the beginning of this Your Turn section.
- In the modulation matrix set the first four sources to **ModEnvelope1, ModEnvelope2, ModEnvelope3**, and **ModEnvelope4**.
- Set the target for all four modulator envelopes to **Voice1 Pitch**. When you select pitch as a target for a modulator envelope, the vertical values in the envelope editor window change. Instead of reading 0 to 1, they read −12.0 to 12.0, with each whole number value representing a half step.
- Turn the Loop and Sync buttons on for the first modulation envelope and adjust the Scale slider so that you can see all the way to beat 4.
- Create a seven-point envelope for the first modulation envelope with all breakpoints set to **flat**.
- Copy the envelope and paste it to envelopes two, three, and four.
- Configure the breakpoints in the four envelopes as follows (use the shift key to set the precise values):
    - Envelope One
        1. (Blue) 0.00, 0.0
        2. (Yellow) 0.00, 0.0
        3. (Green) 0.25, −1.0
        4. (Turquoise) 0.50, −3.0
        5. (Purple) 0.75, −5.0
        6. (Red) 4.00, 0.0
        7. (Blue) 4.00, 0.0

- Envelope Two
    1. (Blue) 0.00, 0.0
    2. (Yellow) 1.00, 0.0
    3. (Green) 1.25, −1.0
    4. (Turquoise) 1.50, −3.0
    5. (Purple) 1.75, −5.0
    6. (Red) 4.00, 0.0
    7. (Blue) 4.00, 0.0
- Envelope Three
    1. (Blue) 0.00, 0.0
    2. (Yellow) 2.00, −6.0
    3. (Green) 2.25, −5.0
    4. (Turquoise) 2.50, −3.0
    5. (Purple) 2.75, −1.0
    6. (Red) 4.00, 0.0
    7. (Blue) 4.00, 0.0
- Envelope Four
    1. (Blue) 0.00, 0.0
    2. (Yellow) 3.00, −6.0
    3. (Green) 3.25, −5.0
    4. (Turquoise) 3.50, −3.0
    5. (Purple) 3.75, −1.0
    6. (Red) 4.00, 0.0
    7. (Blue) 4.00, 0.0

Sustain the note C5 (the C above middle C) on your MIDI keyboard, and you should hear a repeating set of sixteenth notes like that shown in Figure 6.22.

Figure 6.22
Configuring four modulation envelopes as described above creates this repeating passage when sustaining the note C5.

Since the envelope generators do not have enough breakpoints to create sixteen steps, using overlapping envelopes allows you to build up the number of breakpoints. All four envelopes are set to begin at 0.00 and end at 4.00, but they all do their note stepping on different beats. Obviously, this approach is not nearly as easy as using an actual step sequencer, but if you do not have a sequencer and really need the functionality this technique will work. This example also gives you an idea of the power and capabilities of looping envelope generators.

Audio-rate Modulation

Although Crystal does not have audio-rate modulation oscillators, the rate for the LFOs goes up to 60 Hz. Applying a sine wave LFO with such a high rate to the filter cutoff of a resonant filter, or to the pulse width of a square wave, creates some of the FM-like qualities we described earlier. You can even assign key tracking to the LFO rate in the modulation matrix, but you will not get the same type of ratio relationship that usually occurs with true audio-rate modulation oscillators.

With these examples, we have only scratched the surface of the modulation capabilities of a sophisticated synthesizer. Take some time now to go back through the factory presets that came with Crystal (FactoryPresets.fxb) and explore the many modulation controls employed in those sounds. Although creating, shaping, and filtering a synthesizer's sound make up the fundamentals of synthesis, it is the dynamic modulating of these sounds that brings them to life.

Using Your Own Synthesizer(s)

1. What types of internal modulation sources do you have on your synthesizer(s)?
   A. LFOs? What types? How many?
   B. Audio-rate oscillators? How many?
   C. Modulation envelopes? How many? What types?
   D. Function modulators? How many?
   E. Step sequencers? How many?
   F. Arpeggiators? How many?
2. Can your modulators be synchronized to a tempo?
3. How is the modulation matrix designed on your synthesizer?
   A. To which functions on your synthesizer can you assign a modulator?
   B. What modulators can be used to control other modulators?
   C. Can you assign the same modulator to multiple destinations?
   D. Can you assign multiple modulators to the same destination?

In Chapter 7, we will examine external control sources like control voltage and MIDI that may be used to modulate functions on a synthesizer as well as many of the instrument's internal modulators.

7

External Control Sources

Shaping Your Sounds with Playing Techniques

Online materials for this chapter:

http://www.oup.com/refiningsound/Chapter7.html

Up to now, we have focused on the internal workings of a synthesizer with little more than a passing regard for the mechanics of actually playing the instrument. No matter how good the sound-making capabilities of a synthesizer might be, without a way to musically and expressively render those sounds, the device will be of little value to musicians. The ability to play a synthesizer expressively is vital if we wish to include it in the ranks of "musical" instruments.

You no doubt already know that pressing a key on a synthesizer's keyboard triggers a note to sound. You probably also know that on most instruments, the force with which you strike the key will affect the sound's loudness, and that the various wheels, knobs, faders, and other controllers have some sort of effect on the synthesizer's sound. In fact, the ability of synthesizers to be modulated with a number of external physical controllers has spawned a generation of so-called *keyboard controllers*. These devices often make no sound of their own, but provide a host of physical control mechanisms such as knobs and faders to manipulate the sounds of a synthesizer while you play the notes on the piano-style keyboard.

Figure 7.1
Although it makes no sound on its own, the Oxygen49 keyboard controller by M-Audio provides numerous wheels, faders, knobs, and buttons for use in modulating another synthesizer's sound in real time. (photo © copyright 2012 inMusic, used with permission)

With most synthesizers and controllers today, the communication between these external control sources and the synthesizer sounds is handled via a communications protocol known as the *Musical Instrument Digital Interface,* or MIDI (rhymes with *kiddie*). Before MIDI, though, there was another system of communication that involved transmitting changing voltages through wires from one device or module to another. Although that control voltage system has been largely replaced by MIDI, there are still a number of synthesizers that use—or emulate using—the system. So it is with control voltages that we begin our examination of these various external controllers and consider how they, along with playing techniques, may be used to shape your synthesizer sounds in real time.

Electrical Voltage Control (CV/Gate)

If you have ever seen one of the original Moog synthesizers—or even seen pictures of one—you probably noticed all the cables strung across the instrument like so many strands of spaghetti. As synthesizers evolved, many of them replaced their external cables with internal circuit buses. Even though the circuits were internal, they still functioned just like a cable and required the user to designate the input and output destinations of the circuit with some sort or switch, knob, or button.

Although some of those cables and circuits carry audio signals between the various modules, others carry electrical signals that cause the receiving module to change its output in some manner or another.[1] The electrical signals on these early synthesizers generally fell into two categories, known as *gate* (or *trigger*) and *control voltage* (CV).

Figure 7.2
Early analog instruments used "patch" cables to send both audio and electrical voltage signals between the various modules on the synthesizer. In this photograph, Mark Rubel's Moog Modular synthesizer as restored by Mark Smart. (photo courtesy of Mark Smart, used with permission)

---

1 It is important to remember that an audio signal inside an analog synthesizer is just a rapidly oscillating electrical signal. Except for the rapid oscillations, it is nearly identical to all the electrical control signals passed back and forth through the synthesizer.

Gate

Gate signals are simple binary (on–off) voltages typically used to start and stop a note or to trigger an envelope generator. On many instruments, the gate signal is a so-called *V-trigger* ("voltage trigger" or "positive trigger"), where the output voltage from the keyboard unit remains at 0 V until a key is pressed and then instantly jumps to some higher, positive value (often between +2 V to +10 V depending on the synthesizer).

Some instruments, however, use an *S-trigger* ("short-circuit trigger" or "negative trigger"), where the keyboard output voltage remains at some high value until a key is pressed, and then it drops to 0 V. Although both types of gates are on–off triggers, they work in opposite directions. Connecting a V-trigger to an instrument that expects an S-trigger, or vice versa, will not damage anything, but it can cause notes to sound when all the keys are up and to stop sounding when a key is pressed.

Control Voltage (CV)

As opposed to the on–off voltages of gates, control voltage (CV) circuits produce a continuously variable range of electrical voltages that may be used for such processes as changing the frequency of an oscillator, the cutoff of an audio filter, the gain of an amplifier, or the rate of an LFO, to name a few. Although there have been a number of control voltage ranges implemented over the years, some of the more common ranges are 0 V to +5 V, 0 V to +10 V, and −5 V to +5 V. As with gates, connecting a device that outputs one voltage range to a module that expects another range will *work*, but it is likely to produce rather unexpected results.

On the early monophonic synthesizers, there were only a small number of oscillators. These few oscillators were not used to create multiple notes but were combined to create richer, more complex sounds. In order to play different notes, the oscillators had to change their frequency every time a new key was pressed on the synthesizer's keyboard. These original oscillators were "voltage controlled" oscillators (VCO) that responded to a changing CV by raising or lowering their output frequency. As a key was pressed, the keyboard module would output the specific voltage assigned to that key, causing the VCO to jump to the appropriate pitch.

As simple as this concept is, its implementation is a bit problematic. This is due to the two competing and conflicting methods of controlling an oscillator with voltage. One CV system (volts per octave) is based on the concept of every increasing volt representing an octave rise in pitch. In other words, if 1 V equals the pitch A1, then 2 V = A2, 3 V = A3, 4 V = A4, etc. To produce the twelve semitones in an octave, you simply divide the volts into twelve equal increments. Thus, if A3 = 3 V, then Bb3 = 3.084 V, B3 = 3.167 V, C3 = 3.25 V, etc.

The other commonly used system (Hertz per volt) works the same way frequencies do. Just as going up an octave is a doubling of the frequency, it is also a doubling of the voltage. In this system, if 1 V = A1, then 2 V = A2, 4 V = A3, 8 V = A4, etc. Semitone voltages are calculated using the same ratios as with frequency; if A3 = 4 V, then Bb3 = 4.267 V (15:16), B3 = 4.491 V (9:8), C3 = 4.745 V (6:5), etc.[2]

---

2 Ratios are based on the just intonation system, but the actual voltage is altered slightly to compensate for the differences between just intonation and equal temperament.

Again, connecting one voltage system to a device expecting the other voltage system will *work*, but the notes will get further and further out of tune as you go higher on the keyboard. There are, however, commercial products designed to convert from one voltage or tuning system to the other.

In addition to the oscillators, nearly all modules on early analog synthesizers respond to CV signals, and most of the modules output CV signals as well.[3] An envelope generator, for example, outputs a CV signal that can be used to raise and lower the output level of an amplifier to create the amplitude envelope of a sound. An LFO creates an oscillating CV that might be used to raise and lower the frequency of an oscillator to create a vibrato in a sound. In a more complex scenario, the aforementioned LFO could have its oscillation rate modulated by the CV from another envelope generator so that the vibrato changes speed over the duration of the note.

As sophisticated as the CV/Gate system is, it has a few major limitations. One of these is the aforementioned voltage incompatibility between the various systems. Most manufacturers used their own voltage levels, meaning that a module from one manufacturer would likely not be compatible with a module from another.

Many synthesizer performers wanted to be able to layer their sounds so that when they played a note on the keyboard, several synthesizers, often from different manufacturers, would sound simultaneously to produce a richer, more complex sound. Since the voltage output of the keyboard was, typically, correct for only one manufacturer's instruments, this was often impossible. To get around this limitation, many synthesizer performers stood behind large banks of synthesizers so they could play on a number of keyboards at the same time. Even with this so-called *wall of synths* approach, players were still restricted by the fact that they had only two hands, so producing anything more than two layers of sound required either multiple performers or multitrack recording.

Even with these various layering workarounds, the result was often less than satisfactory. It is nearly impossible to play the same passage with both right and left hands and have it sound exactly the same. When one hand is using the thumb, the other is using the pinkie finger, and the articulation difference between the two is quite difficult to overcome. Imagine trying to also do this while lining up with another player, or a prerecorded track. Consequently, the resultant tone, although richer, tended to sound more like an ensemble of sounds that were all slightly different from one another than a single sound with multiple layers to it.

Another limitation to the CV/Gate system is the fact that only one voltage level at a time may be transmitted through a given cable or internal circuit. Although this is often fine for modules like envelope generators and LFOs, it also means that the keyboard module can transmit only one note-frequency voltage at a time. Therefore, synthesizers that rely on CV to transmit frequency information to oscillators are, by design, limited to playing only one note at a time. In order to play two notes, you need two synthesizers; three notes, three synthesizers; etc.

It seems ironic that Cahill's Telharmonium of 1897 could play chords with layered sounds from its keyboard controller, but the typical electronic synthesizer of the 1970s

---

3 Given that audio signals, except for their frequency rate, are very similar to CV signals, it does not take much of a stretch to think about using audio-rate oscillators as control modules, like those described in previous chapters on AM and FM synthesis and audio-rate modulations.

could not. Although the continuously variable voltage of the CV/Gate system had numerous advantages over the electrical dynamo system on Cahill's two-hundred-ton behemoth, the lack of polyphony and layering ability continued to be a source of frustration with electronic synthesizers well into the 1980s.

Given the strong desire for complex layering and polyphony on synthesizers, a number of instrument designers and engineers began experimenting with other ways to control the many modules of the electronic synthesizer in the 1970s and 1980s. However, it was not until they took a radically different approach—one that replaced the analog electrical voltages with digital messages controlled by microprocessors—that they finally solved the problems of layering and polyphony. Furthermore, thanks to the work of a few visionary engineers, they also developed a system that allowed interoperability between synthesizers built by nearly every manufacturer.

MIDI

In the late 1970s, Dave Smith of Sequential Circuits was working to develop a polyphonic analog synthesizer that eventually became known as the Prophet-5. Realizing the limitations of the CV/Gate system, Smith began experimenting with a system that used digital messages of ones and zeroes to control multiple oscillators simultaneously. One of the added benefits of these digital messages was that they could be stored in memory chips or on computer disks as presets, thus eliminating much of the "patching" that had been elemental to synthesizers for so long. It also occurred to him that if these messages could be stored, they could also be transmitted between devices, and thus the seeds of a digital control system were planted.

In 1981, Smith, along with Chet Wood, a fellow engineer at Sequential Circuits, presented a paper at the Audio Engineering Society's (AES) annual conference in which they proposed a Universal Synthesizer Interface that would allow electronic instruments to communicate with each other via a common digital code. In 1983, at the National Association of Music Merchants (NAMM) show, they demonstrated a digital connection between a Sequential Circuits Prophet-600 and a Roland Jupiter-6 via a revised version of their earlier interface. This connection and its underlying code eventually became known as the Musical Instrument Digital Interface (MIDI) version 1.0 and made available, royalty-free, to all synthesizer manufacturers.

Figure 7.3

A photograph of the very first public demonstration of MIDI at the 1983 NAMM Convention shows a Roland Jupiter-6 and a Sequential Circuits Prophet-600 communicating with each other via MIDI connections. (photo courtesy of Dave Smith, www.dave smithinstruments.com, used with permission)

Perhaps the most amazing thing about the MIDI protocol is how forward-looking the original code and design was. As anyone who has ever purchased software knows, the version numbers increment upward nearly every year as upgrades and improvements are made. Yet because of its amazing capability and flexibility, at the time of this writing (three decades after its proposal) we are still using MIDI version 1.0!

Figure 7.4

The typical arrangement of MIDI ports on the back of a synthesizer.

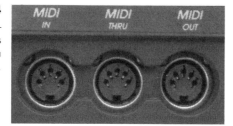

TIP The IN, OUT, and THRU of MIDI

Most instruments with MIDI capability will have a set of three round ports, labeled IN, OUT, and THRU. MIDI is a one-way communication protocol, so data can travel in only one direction through a port and on the MIDI cable. When connecting two devices, you typically connect a MIDI cable between the OUT port of one device and the IN port of the other, and vice versa.

The IN port receives MIDI data arriving from another device. The OUT port transmits MIDI data generated within that device. The THRU port passes a copy of the MIDI data received at the IN port, but it does not send any MIDI data generated within the device itself. The purpose of the THRU port is to allow devices to be "daisy-chained" together.

Consider a scenario where you want to control three MIDI synthesizers from a separate controller keyboard. Since the MIDI data will be generated in the keyboard, connect the OUT port of the keyboard to the IN port of the first synthesizer. That syn-

> **TIP** *continued*
>
> thesizer (along with the other two) will not generate any new MIDI data but merely respond to, and pass along, the original data from the keyboard. Then connect the THRU port of the first synthesizer to the IN port of the second, and the THRU port of the second to the IN port of the third synthesizer. Now, the data generated by the keyboard can control all three synthesizers.

As MIDI has assumed a greater operational role in the control of modern synthesizers, the use of the CV/Gate system has nearly disappeared. There are still some analog instruments that continue to use CV/Gate, often alongside MIDI, and there are even devices that will convert between MIDI and CV/Gate.[4] Just as some people continue to debate the qualities of digital and analog audio, some synthesizer enthusiasts continue to debate the qualities of the analog CV/Gate system versus the digital MIDI system.

Figure 7.5

The Andromeda A6 synthesizer by Alesis has inputs for both CV and MIDI connections. (photo © copyright 2012 inMusic, used with permission)

It is well beyond the scope of this text to explain all the details and inner workings of MIDI. There are numerous sources for further information about MIDI, some of which are listed with the online materials for this chapter. However, to get the most from playing and controlling your synthesizer via MIDI, it is helpful to have a basic understanding of MIDI, MIDI messages, and the physical MIDI controls you will commonly find on synthesizers, keyboards, and other external controllers.

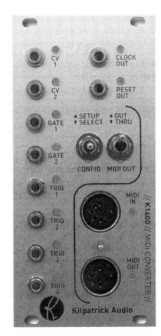

Figure 7.6

The K1600 MIDI Converter by Kilpatrick Audio converts incoming MIDI messages to a variety of CV/Gate messages. (photo © copyright 2012 Kilpatrick Audio, used with permission)

---

4 Many software synthesizers, especially those that attempt to recreate earlier analog hardware synthesizers, emulate CV/Gate functionality. In most cases, though, the CV or gate "inputs" on the synthesizer are virtual inputs that respond to MIDI messages. It is also important to note that since the software synthesizer is running in a computer's operating system, all messages are, by definition, digital.

> ## TIP **Can I Hear the MIDI?**
>
> It is important to understand that MIDI is not an audio signal. When you connect devices through MIDI cables, you are not sending sound; you are sending instructions. Let's say you play middle C on a keyboard that is connected to another MIDI device. You are not sending the sound of that note; you are sending the fact that you pressed a specific key at a certain time, with a specific amount of force, and released that key at some point later. The receiving device uses this information to actually generate the synthesized sound. MIDI is just data passing through a network cable. If you were to actually hear the MIDI, it would sound much like the sound you hear when a fax machine or telephone modem connects to another device.

MIDI Channels

One of the initial goals of MIDI was to allow multiple synthesizers to be controlled by a single keyboard. In order to accomplish this, a system of *channels* was incorporated into the MIDI protocol. MIDI channels allowed as many as sixteen synthesizers to operate on their own, independent channel. When a note was triggered from the keyboard controller, part of the information included in the note message (we will examine MIDI messages in greater detail in the next section) was information about which channel the note was on. For example if it was a "channel-3" note, then only a synthesizer set to receive channel 3 would play the note, and all other instruments would ignore it.

It might be helpful to think of MIDI channels like television channels. If you have multiple television monitors connected to the same cable, it is possible to view different programs on the individual televisions by simply tuning them all to different channels. Remember, all of the TVs are connected to the same cable or antenna, and they are receiving all the channels at once. By tuning a monitor separately, though, a television responds to (or displays) only the channel to which it is tuned at that moment. Similarly, MIDI devices receive messages on all MIDI channels, but they only respond to (or play) the messages that arrive on the channel to which they are set (tuned). One synthesizer might be set to channel 1 and programmed to produce a piano sound, another set to channel 2 and producing a bass sound, and a third set to channel 3 and producing a drum sound. By assigning the appropriate channel to the outgoing notes on the keyboard controller, only the "piano" notes would be played by the first instrument, the "bass" notes by the second, and the "drum" notes by the third instrument.

As we will see below, the format of the MIDI messages made implementation of sixteen channels quite simple. Just as in the early days of television, when few could imagine the need for more than three or four channels, not many people in the early days of MIDI thought there would ever be a need for even sixteen channels. Although we certainly might question the "need" for as many TV channels as we currently have, the need for more than sixteen MIDI channels has been an issue for some time in the synthesizer world.

At the time MIDI was introduced, although many synthesizers had already incorporated their own internal digital system for note polyphony, most instruments were still *mono-timbral*, capable of playing only one sound at a time. One of the biggest developments in the 1980s was the introduction of synthesizers capable of playing not only multiple simultaneous notes but multiple simultaneous sounds as well. Previously, to produce two sounds required use of two synthesizers. However, the newer, digital instruments contained enough processing power to function as multiple synthesizers inside one instrument.

These so-called *multi-timbral* instruments separated their sounds into *parts* or *voices* that responded to different MIDI channels. As computing power increased in synthesizers, it was not long before a single instrument could play multiple notes with different sounds on all sixteen MIDI channels at the same time. By the early 1990s, it was fairly common for synthesizers to be both polyphonic and multi-timbral.

The typical method for connecting multiple instruments together was with a daisy-chain, as described above ("The IN, OUT, and THRU of MIDI"). However, with instruments capable of playing all the MIDI channels, this method no longer worked since a "channel-3" note message would trigger a response from all the synthesizers in the chain.

Since the number of MIDI channels is limited to sixteen, a workaround was developed, using a multiport MIDI interface (sometimes called a MIDI patchbay) to assign MIDI messages to a specific port on the interface. These devices are typically connected to a computer that controls their operation. The synthesizers are each connected to their own, unique port on the interface. The software that drives these interfaces adds a port destination to the MIDI message, so that it looks something like "Port 1: Channel 2," "Port 3: Channel 12," etc. With a multiport MIDI interface, it is possible to have several multi-timbral instruments, each responding to as many as sixteen MIDI channels.

Figure 7.7
The MOTU MIDI Express XT has eight independently assignable MIDI ports, each capable of transmitting 16 channels for a total of 128 (8 × 16) channels. (photo courtesy of MOTU, Inc., used with permission)

MIDI Messages

Like nearly all forms of digital communications, MIDI messages are built from *bits* (zeroes and ones) organized into groups of eight called *digital words*, or more commonly, *bytes*. In MIDI, there are two kinds of bytes, known as *status* bytes and *data* bytes. Every MIDI message begins with a status byte, which informs the receiving device what type of MIDI event is happening and, in many cases, on which MIDI channel it is happening. The status byte is then followed by data bytes that provide further details about the particular MIDI event.

TIP Nybbles and Bits (and Bytes)

In binary calculations, numbers are expressed with zeroes and ones organized into larger groups of eight bits, known as bytes.[5] Since the byte has eight bits, it is said to have *eight-bit resolution*. Each bit represents 2^x power, with the right-most bit (called the *least significant* bit or lsb) representing 2^0 power (1) and the left-most bit (called the *most significant bit* or msb) representing 2^7 power (128).

Byte							
msb							lsb
2^7	2^6	2^5	2^4	2^3	2^2	2^1	2^0
128	64	32	16	8	4	2	1
Nybble				Nybble			

To calculate the decimal value of a byte, simply total the columns that contain a one and ignore the columns with a zero in them. Thus the byte 11111111 has a decimal value of 255 (128 + 64 + 32 + 16 + 8 + 4 + 2 + 1), while the byte 00000000 has a decimal value of 0. The range of values for a single byte is from 0 to 255. Remember that computers consider zero to be a value, so a range of 0–255 is a total of 256 possible values.

For values greater than 255, bytes are grouped together into sets of two, three, and even four bytes. These grouped bytes are treated as a single byte with sixteen-bit (msb = 2^{15}), twenty-four-bit (msb = 2^{23}), and thirty-two-bit (msb = 2^{31}) resolution. By doing so, the decimal value of these grouped bytes reaches into the billions.

In most cases, bytes are treated as a single number. However, in a few special cases—MIDI being one—some bytes are separated into two halves, known as *nybbles*. In this case, the values of the two nybbles are treated as separate message elements.

Status Bytes

The first part of any MIDI message is the status byte, which tells the receiving device what kind of MIDI event is being transmitted. Status bytes always have a one in the msb position, so their range of values goes from 10000000 (128) to 11111111 (255). However, the status byte is really treated as two nybbles, with the left nybble indicating the type of MIDI event and—in most cases—the right nybble indicating the MIDI channel.

Given that a status byte always has a one in the msb position, the left nybble has only eight possible values, and these values are defined in the MIDI protocol as a particular type of MIDI event.

---

5 Since bits and bytes both begin with the letter *b*, it has become common practice to abbreviate bits with a lowercase b and bytes with an uppercase B. In keeping with that tradition, in this text we will also use msb/lsb for most/least significant *bit* and MSB/LSB for most/least significant *byte*.

Since the right nybble can have either a zero or a one in any of its bits, it has sixteen possible values. The first seven types of MIDI events listed in Table 7.1 are sometimes referred to as *channel messages* since they are designed to function on a specific MIDI channel. It is the second nybble that conveys the MIDI channel number for those messages. System messages, by contrast, are sent to the synthesizer's operating system, and not to a specific channel. For these messages, the right nybble is used to convey the specific type of system message and not a MIDI channel.

A MIDI device receiving a byte of 10010110 would know that it is a status byte because there is a 1 in the msb position and interpret it as a Note On message (first nybble = 1001) on MIDI channel 7 (second nybble = 0110). As for which note it is (as well as how hard it was played), this information comes from the second type of MIDI message byte, the data bytes.

Data Bytes

Once the synthesizer receives the status byte telling it what type of MIDI event is occurring and on which channel it is occurring, it usually receives data bytes to provide details about that particular

Table 7.1: MIDI STATUS BYTE EVENT TYPES.

Nybble	MIDI Event Type
1000	Note Off
1001	Note On
1010	Polyphonic Key Pressure
1011	Controller Change
1100	Program Change
1101	Channel Pressure
1110	Pitch Bend
1111	System Messages

Table 7.2: MIDI STATUS BYTE CHANNEL NUMBERS.

Nybble	Channel	Nybble	Channel
0000	1	1000	9
0001	2	1001	10
0010	3	1010	11
0011	4	1011	12
0100	5	1100	13
0101	6	1101	14
0110	7	1110	15
0111	8	1111	16

event. In contrast to status bytes, data bytes always have a 0 in the MSB position. Thus, the values of data bytes range from 00000000 (0) to 01111111 (127). Each data byte is treated as a single value rather than being divided into nybbles.

The number of data bytes, and their meaning, depends on the type of status byte that comes first. For example if the status byte indicates a Note On message, then there will be two data bytes, to identify the MIDI note number (0–127) and the velocity with which the key was struck (also 0–127).[6] If you play the note middle C with a fairly strong velocity, you might generate these three bytes: 10010000 (status byte: note on/channel 1), 00111100 (data byte 1: note number 60), 01011110 (data byte 2: velocity of 94).

---

6 For a review of MIDI note numbers and velocity, see the "Dynamic Envelope Shapes" section of Chapter 4.

Table 7.3: MIDI MESSAGE BYTES.

Status Byte	Data Byte #1	Data Byte #2
Note Off	Note Number	Release Velocity
Note On	Note Number	Attack Velocity
Polyphonic Key Pressure	Note Number	Note Pressure Value
Controller Change	Controller Number	Controller Value
Program Change	Program Number	none
Channel Pressure	Pressure Value	none
Pitch Bend	Fine Value	Coarse Value
System Messages	Varies with Type	Varies with Type

NOTE: an excellent online resource for deciphering MIDI messages may be found on the MIDI Manufacturers Association website, http://www.midi.org/techspecs/midimessages.php.

Note On-Off Messages

As the names suggest, these are messages to start and stop MIDI notes. In both cases, the first data byte specifies the MIDI note number, and the second byte the key velocity. Most of the time we think of velocity as the speed with which the key is depressed (i.e., *attack velocity*), and it is this value that is used in the second data byte of the Note On message. The second data byte of the Note Off message, though, is for a value known as *release velocity*.

Release velocity is the speed with which a key is released or let go. In reality, very few synthesizers implement release velocity, and so the second data byte for the Note Off message frequently contains the default MIDI value of 64. Just as attack velocity might be used to modulate the attack amplitude and times of an envelope generator, instruments that support release velocity often use this value to modulate the release times of the envelope generator as well.

TIP MIDI Crunch (It's Not a Breakfast Cereal!)

Because the MIDI protocol is built on early 1980s networking protocols, the data transfer rate, or *baud rate*, of MIDI (31.25 kilobits per second) is quite slow by modern standards. Even on devices that connect via high-speed interfaces such as USB and FireWire, the MIDI baud rate remains at this slow speed.

In the early days of MIDI, when its use was mostly to send note messages to a handful of monophonic synthesizers, the baud rate was sufficient. However, as instruments developed, the need to send more and more MIDI messages grew exponentially. If too many messages are sent at the same time, the interface cannot accommodate them all and some messages get delayed, or even dropped. This unfortunate occurrence is often referred to as *MIDI crunch*.

> **TIP** *continued*
>
> MIDI crunch may manifest itself in the form of a "stuttering" in the sound, but one of its worst forms is the dreaded stuck note. In this situation, a Note On message is transmitted, but the corresponding Note Off message gets dropped. When that happens, the note continues to sound until it receives another Note Off message. In most cases, simply restriking and releasing the correct key on the MIDI keyboard will solve the stuck note, but many instruments have also implemented a *panic* button that turns all sounding notes off on all sixteen MIDI channels.
>
> ## Running Status
>
> In an attempt to alleviate some of the MIDI crunch problems, the MIDI protocol includes a method of streamlining messages through a concept known as *running status*. Running status allows a stream of the exact same type of MIDI messages (e.g.: Note On) to pass without resending the status byte for each message. It sends the initial status byte and then only the subsequent data bytes, as long as there is no new type of message introduced into the stream.
>
> Since the vast majority of MIDI messages are Note On-Off messages, a further concession was added to make running status even more efficient. Instead of sending a Note Off message to stop a note, running status recognizes a Note On message with a velocity of zero as the message to stop a note from sounding. Thus with running status, a long string of notes may be started and stopped without resending the Note On-Off status bytes every time. The fact that Note Off messages are rarely transmitted anymore is one of the reasons so few synthesizers bother to implement release velocity. Running status may also be used when there are uninterrupted strings of other types of messages such as pitch bend and controller change.

Polyphonic Key Pressure Messages

After you strike a key on many keyboards, you can continue to apply pressure to the key to generate another type of message known as *pressure* or *aftertouch*. Polyphonic key pressure measures the amount of pressure applied to every individual key and transmits the value to the key's corresponding note to modulate its sound in some manner.

After the status byte, the first data byte indicates a specific MIDI note, and the second byte the amount of pressure applied to that note. As you might imagine, the pressure we apply to these notes is likely to change continually as we hold the notes. Any time it changes on a note, a new message has to be sent. The massive amount of MIDI bandwidth required to transmit polyphonic key pressure makes this one of the biggest culprits in causing MIDI crunch. Consequently, this MIDI message type is rarely used, and as of this writing no synthesizers are being manufactured that implement polyphonic key pressure.

Controller Change Messages

As we saw earlier, there are only eight status bytes, yet there are dozens of functions on a synthesizer that can be modulated via MIDI. To accommodate all of these other functions, the MIDI protocol has a "catch-all" category of status byte known as controller change. Every controller change has a specific number that is addressed by the first data byte of this message type. The second data byte provides the actual value for the controller message.

Theoretically, there could be 128 controller types, but many of the available controller numbers are listed as "undefined" in the MIDI protocol, meaning their function has not been specified. There are also numerous controller types that are rarely used, if ever.[7]

For our purposes, we can focus on the handful of controllers that are commonly used with synthesizers. Most of these controllers have a continuous range of values from 0 to 127 (the second data byte). However, a few controllers are known as *switched* controllers; they function as a simple on–off switch. In this case, controller values less than 64 are treated as off messages and values greater than, or equal to, 64 as on messages.

Controller 0: Bank Select

The MIDI protocol already has a program change message for selecting a stored sound from the synthesizer's memory. Program change has only one data byte, meaning it has a limit of selecting from only 128 stored programs. As the internal memory on synthesizers has increased over the years, instruments can now store thousands of programs. In order to access this large number of programs, a system of program banks was developed. Each bank contains 128 programs, and there is a potential for having 128 separate banks, for a total of 16,384 stored programs. The bank select message is used in conjunction, then, with the program change message to first select the appropriate bank and then the correct program within that bank.

Controller 1: Modulation Wheel

Most MIDI keyboards have two control wheels on them: pitch bend and modulation wheel. The modulation wheel is the one that moves smoothly from bottom to top and stays at whatever position it is placed. The actual function of the modulation wheel depends on the programming of the individual synthesizer sound. For example, the modulation, or "mod," wheel might be used to raise and lower the cutoff frequency of an audio filter, or to increase and decrease the modulation depth of an LFO, or to cross-fade between two oscillators. Modulation wheel is one of the handiest controllers for modulating a synthesizer sound in real time.

Controller 2: Breath Controller

Not all MIDI controllers are designed like piano keyboards. There is a *wind controller* that is blown into and fingered, much like a clarinet or a saxophone. The specific pitches are selected by pressing the keys on the device, and the mouthpiece measures and transmits a value based on how hard the player blows into the instrument. This breath controller message is commonly used to modulate aspects of the sound such as articulation and vibrato.

Controller 7: Volume

Many MIDI devices have a knob or fader that transmits volume controller messages. The volume message sets the overall loudness level for a specific MIDI channel and is typically used to balance the levels between multiple sounds when creating a mix.

---

7 For a complete list of MIDI controllers, see the online support materials for this chapter.

Controller 10: Pan Position

Pan position messages place the sounds on a MIDI channel in the left-right stereophonic field. Although most controllers treat the 0 value as the minimum and 127 as the maximum, pan treats 0 as far left and 127 as far right. Values between 0 and 127 locate the sound between the two extremes, and a value of 64 places the sound directly in the center. It should be noted that on many instruments pan changes work only before a note begins sounding. If you attempt to change the pan while a note is sounding, the note will retain its position, and the next note will be at the new pan location.

Controller 11: Expression

Expression messages are another form of loudness control but are primarily used to create dynamic changes such as crescendos and decrescendos rather than to set the mix levels. In common practice, controller 7 (volume) is used to set the mix balance, and controller 11 (expression) is used to shape the dynamics within that balance.

Controller 64: Sustain Pedal

The sustain pedal on a synthesizer causes the note off messages of sounding notes to be delayed until the pedal is released. As opposed to the damper pedal on a piano, there is no in-between value for sustain pedal. It is a switched controller that is either on or off.

In reality, most modern synthesizers allow you to map any controller number—including the ones not listed here—to almost any synthesizer function capable of being modulated. In many cases, the controllers listed above can even be reassigned, but the default settings of your instruments will expect these controller numbers to have these defined functions, so it is usually best to leave the controllers with their default controller numbers.

Program Change (Patch Change) Messages

Look again at Figure 7.2, near the beginning of this chapter. The patch cables strung across the face of the synthesizer connect the various modules in such a way that a particular sound is created. Synthesizer performers in the 1970s routinely kept notebooks full of sketches and diagrams that illustrated every *patch* (all the cable connections, dial settings, knob and switch positions, etc.) so they could recreate their sounds in the future. In fact, many touring musicians had two identical racks of synthesizers on stage with them. While they were performing a song on one rack of instruments, an assistant was frantically repatching the other rack to get it ready in time for the next song.

The development of the digital synthesizer not only allowed all of the connections and settings to be made internally via the circuit board, but also allowed those settings to be stored in the synthesizer's memory. By simply selecting one of the stored programs, the instrument was instantly configured for the new sound. The program change (often called patch change) message is designed to call up one of these stored configurations via the MIDI connection.[8]

8 Technically, a *program* refers to a set of instructions written in computer code, while a *patch* refers to a physical configuration of cables, knobs, dials, etc. Even though the new digital synthesizers created and stored their settings as *programs*, most performers were from the earlier analog world and continued to describe the settings as *patches*. In the synthesizer world, then, the terms *program* and *patch* are considered interchangeable in that they both refer to the settings used to create a sound on a synthesizer.

In the early days of MIDI and digital synthesizers, internal memory was expensive and usually offered a small amount of storage space. Most synthesizers could store only a few dozen programs at one time. In line with the limited storage space, the program change message was designed with a single data byte, limiting its reach to only 128 programs, which was still considerably more than most instruments of the time were capable of storing.

As synthesizer memory increased, so did the desire to store more and more programs. By the mid-1990s, many instruments were able to store hundreds, and even thousands, of programs. The desire to address these large libraries of programs led to the use of a bank select message (controller 0) in conjunction with the program change message as described above.

Channel Pressure (Aftertouch) Messages

Instead of transmitting the pressure being applied to each key, as with polyphonic key pressure, channel pressure (frequently called *aftertouch*) transmits the pressure of only the key that is being pressed the hardest at a given time, and it applies this value to all sounding notes on the channel. Consequently, the MIDI data stream from channel pressure is considerably smaller than that from polyphonic key pressure, and it has been implemented on a large number of synthesizers and keyboards.

Like program change, the channel pressure message uses only a single data byte to transmit the pressure value on a scale of 0 to 127. This value is often used in a similar manner as the modulation wheel to control elements such as audio filters, LFOs, and oscillator combinations.

Pitch Bend Messages

As mentioned earlier, most MIDI keyboard controllers have two wheels on them: pitch bend and modulation. Although the modulation wheel can be freely moved and left at any desired position, the pitch bend wheel always springs back to the center position when released. Play a note with almost any synthesizer sound while you move the pitch bend wheel, and you will hear the pitch rise and fall with the wheel's position.

Figure 7.8
Like most MIDI keyboard controllers, the Oxygen25 from M-Audio has two control wheels for pitch bend and modulation. (photo © copyright 2012 inMusic, used with permission)

You may notice that the amount of pitch bend changes with different sounds. On some instruments, the pitch bend (also called bend or bender) range is set globally for the entire instrument, while on other synthesizers it is programmed into the individual sound.

The pitch bend range is usually set to a number of half-steps. For example, if you set the bend range to a value of 3, pushing the wheel from the center position to the top of its travel will cause the sound to bend up a minor third (three half-steps). Likewise, pulling the wheel down from the center will cause the sound to drop a minor third. Using a large bender range, like 12, will cause the sound to move up and down by an octave (twelve half-steps) from the center position—a total of two octaves from bottom to top. As opposed to other MIDI messages that put 0 at the bottom and 127 at the top, pitch bend puts 0 in the middle with −64 at the bottom and +63 at the top.[9]

Although most MIDI messages use their two data bytes to provide two pieces of information (e.g., note number and velocity), pitch bend uses its two data bytes to yield a much higher degree of resolution to the amount of pitch bend itself. If the bend range is a large value, say, an octave or more, you can sometimes hear a slight "stair-stepping" or "zipping" of the pitch, rather than a smooth glide, when you move the wheel. This happens because the ear is quite sensitive to changes in frequency, and with so few increments (only sixty-three between the center position and top of the wheel's travel), we sometimes hear tiny, stepped intervals rather than a continuous-sounding glide between notes.

To remedy this problem, the MIDI protocol groups the two pitch bend data bytes together to create a high-resolution value. One data byte provides "coarse" resolution of 128 values and the other data byte creates "fine" resolution by further dividing each coarse value into 128 smaller values. Remember that data bytes always have a zero as their msb, and when grouped together those two zeroes fall into the two leftmost positions. This grouped data, as a result, has a fourteen-bit resolution with a range of 0000000000000000 (0) to 0011111111111111 (16,383). Again, pitch bend treats zero as the middle value, so with this high resolution the pitch bend message value range is now −8,192 to +8,191, instead of −64 to +63. With such fine resolution, even wide pitch bend ranges produce a smooth glide between notes.[10]

System Messages

Up to now, all of the MIDI messages we have described are so-called *channel* messages, messages specific to a single MIDI channel. This last set of MIDI messages, system messages, is sent globally to the synthesizer's operating system and not to any specific channel. Because they do not need channel information, the second nybble of the status byte is used to provide further detail on the type of system message being transmitted. Al-

---

9 Even numbers divide symmetrically by two and do not have a "center" value. In MIDI, the standard range of values is 0–127, or 128 values, which means the mathematical "center" of that range is 64½. Since MIDI does not allow fractional values, a compromise is made for values that require a "center" position, such as pitch bend and pan. In these cases, there ends up being one more increment to the lower (or left) side of center than to the upper (or right) side. In common practice, most instruments treat the two lowest (or leftmost) values as if they are the same. Thus, the amount of sonic change from the two sides of the center position remains symmetrical.

10 Although most higher-quality instruments transmit and support this higher resolution for pitch bend, some older or less-expensive instruments support only the lower resolution. In the latter case, the receiving instrument simply ignores the second data byte and uses the coarse pitch bend range of −64 to +63.

though some system messages use data bytes, many do not because there is sufficient information already provided in the second nybble.

Most types of system messages deal with sequencer timing, synchronization, and playback control, and as such they are not particularly germane to our discussion. However, one type of system message, the *system exclusive* message, is extremely important for those wishing to use computers to create, edit, and store programs from hardware synthesizers via MIDI.

System exclusive (or *sysex*, as they are commonly called) messages allow you to perform a variety of programming and control functions on a synthesizer that are not readily available through conventional MIDI messages. Nearly every MIDI instrument has a large number of features that may be addressed and modified via sysex messages, if you know what they are. Many synthesizers include a chart in their manual that describes the parameters available through sysex, and those that do not often have the chart available on the manufacturer's website.

Sysex messages begin with the system exclusive status byte (11110000) followed by a data byte that is "exclusive" to each model of synthesizer. The manufacturer's ID is typically found in the sysex documentation. If the receiving instrument matches the manufacturer's ID byte, it will respond to the rest of the sysex message. Otherwise, the device will ignore the message.

Following the manufacturer's ID data byte will come any number of additional data bytes depending on the parameters being controlled. Since there is no way for the receiving device to know how many bytes to expect, sysex messages end with another status byte called End of Exclusive (11110111). That way the synthesizer knows when the sysex message has finished.

Sysex messages can usually be created, edited, recorded, and transmitted with a MIDI sequencer program. If you open the sysex message editor window on most sequencers, you will probably see a string of two-character alphanumeric text like this: F0 21 08 37 . . . F7. Depending on the number of parameters, the message may contain dozens of such character pairs. Rather than writing sysex messages as bytes of ones and zeroes, these messages are usually written in what is known as *hexadecimal* notation.

TIP **A Hex upon Us?**

In hexadecimal (sixteen-character) notation, a single character represents each of the sixteen possible nybbles. Since the decimal system of counting has only ten characters (0, 1, 2, 3, 4, 5, 6, 7, 8, 9), the hexadecimal notation system adds six letters to our string of numerals to create a total of sixteen characters with which to count (0, 1, 2, 3, 4, 5, 6, 7, 8, 9, A, B, C, D, E, F). Therefore each of the sixteen nybbles can be represented by one of these "numerals," and a complete byte by a pair of characters. For example, F0 represents the initial sysex status message byte (11110000), and F7 the end of exclusive message byte (11110111). When seen in print, hexadecimal pairs are often followed by a lower-case "h" (e.g., F7h) to confirm that the notation is hexadecimal, but when used by computers just the pair of characters is used.

Fortunately, with today's computers, the use of hexadecimal notation and hand-crafted sysex messages has mostly become obsolete. For those who wish to use a computer to create, edit, and store sounds from their hardware synthesizers, there are a variety of computer applications, known as synthesizer editor/librarians, that make this process immensely easier. These programs continue to communicate with the synthesizer via sysex message over MIDI, but in a way that is mostly transparent to the user. They provide a large window on the computer monitor from which you can see and edit multiple parameters on the synthesizer with the same click-and-drag simplicity of most computer applications. As you change any parameter on the screen, the appropriate sysex message is then transmitted to the synthesizer, thus updating the sound.

Editor/librarian programs perform two primary functions. First, they allow you to edit your hardware synthesizer's sounds from the computer rather than trying to navigate through all the knobs and tiny displays found on most instruments. Second, they provide a library for all the sounds you create that is typically much larger than the storage available in the synthesizer itself.

Because every synthesizer has its own architecture and sound-making structure, it is nearly impossible to create a program that can interact with all the models of synthesizers in use. Instead, editor/librarians usually come with a set of "modules" that are specific to individual instrument models, and they have all the various sysex messages programmed into them to address that instrument's capabilities and features. For an editor/librarian program to work with a particular synthesizer, the appropriate module must be installed into the application. Fortunately, most editor/librarian programs come with a large collection of modules already built into them, and the companies that create these programs often make modules for new instruments available for download via the company's website.

Table 7.4: THE SIXTEEN BINARY NYBBLES AND THEIR HEXADECIMAL EQUIVALENTS.

Nybble	Hex #	Nybble	Hex #
0000	0	1000	8
0001	1	1001	9
0010	2	1010	A
0011	3	1011	B
0100	4	1100	C
0101	5	1101	D
0110	6	1110	E
0111	7	1111	F

Figure 7.9

A computer-based editor/librarian program such as Unisyn by MOTU uses system exclusive messages to communicate with hardware synthesizers via MIDI, allowing the instrument's sounds to be created, edited, and stored on a computer.

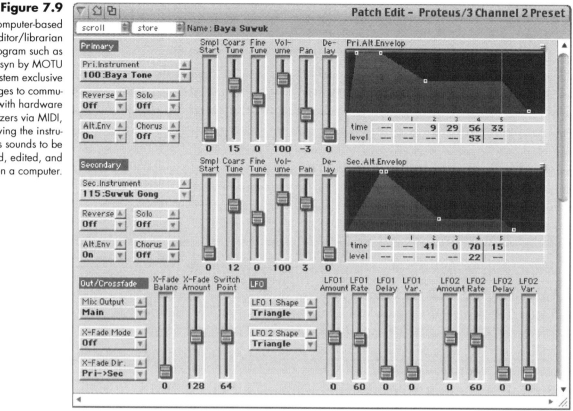

Using Physical MIDI Controllers to Shape Sounds

Whether a synthesizer uses CV/Gate or MIDI (some instruments use both), the purpose of these systems is to manipulate the synthesizer and shape its sounds, often while playing the instrument. Although the possibilities for doing so are nearly endless, here are a few uses of common MIDI controllers to shape the sounds on a synthesizer.

Modulation Wheel

• Filter cutoff: mapping the modulation wheel to the cutoff, or center, frequency of an audio filter is one of the most common uses of this controller. Generally, the more the wheel is pushed to the top, the higher the cutoff frequency goes. This can be quite effective for creating manually controlled timbre shifts and swooshes in a sound. Be careful that pulling the wheel all the way down does not lower the cutoff frequency so much as to actually silence the sound.

• LFO rate: mapping the modulation wheel to the rate of a low frequency oscillator is a great way to make more expressive vibrato and tremolo effects. Set the wheel so that when all the way down there is no LFO, and as the wheel is pushed up the LFO rate increases. Although you can use higher LFO rates at the top end of the wheel's travel, for most "musical" effects set the top end to between 5 and 10 Hz.

Aftertouch

• Filter cutoff: mapping aftertouch to the cutoff, or center, frequency of an audio filter has the same effect as using the modulation wheel. The primary differences are that you do not need to take your fingers off the keys to move a separate controller, and the modulation effect automatically returns to zero when you stop pressing on the keys. This technique is particularly effective for creating momentary "bumps" in a sound's timbre while the note is playing.

• LFO depth: mapping aftertouch to LFO depth is a good way to vary the intensity of a vibrato or tremolo effect. On many acoustic instruments, the player will start the note with little or no vibrato, and then add it with varying amounts of intensity over the duration of the note. Using aftertouch is a nice way to create this effect. Consider mapping aftertouch to both the rate and the depth of an LFO for an even more profound effect.

Pitch Bend

We generally think of the pitch bend control as having only one response: raising and lowering the pitch of a sound. However, many synthesizers allow the user to assign the pitch bend controller to other functions. Be aware that you may need to also unassign the physical controller from the pitch bend effect, as this is a default setting on most instruments.

The advantages of using the pitch bend wheel, as opposed to the modulation wheel, are several, depending on the effect you wish to create. The pitch bend wheel always springs back to the center position when released, so it is good for effects that need to quickly return to zero. The wheel also provides both positive and negative values, so effects that need to deviate on either side of a set value are good candidates for controlling via the pitch bend wheel.

• Filter resonance: mapping pitch bend to the resonance control of an audio filter allows you to raise and lower the resonance amount from its normal setting. Push the wheel up and the filter cutoff frequency becomes more focused. Pull the wheel toward you and the resonance disappears. In both cases, when you release the wheel, it springs back to the middle, returning the resonance to its normal value.

• Oscillator mix: mapping pitch bend to the mix of two oscillators allows you to create temporary changes in that mix. Pull the wheel down and you hear more of oscillator 1, and push the wheel away to hear more of oscillator 2. Release the wheel, and the original mix of oscillators is restored.

These few examples are just a sampling of the many uses of external controls to shape a sound. As mentioned earlier, the possibilities of using physical controllers are nearly endless and are limited mostly by the number of physical controllers available and the modulation mapping capabilities of your synthesizer. Feel free to experiment with mapping any available controller to the synthesizer element of your choice. In doing so, you will likely discover some wonderful ways to manipulate your sounds in real time.

Macro Controls

Many of the newer software synthesizers have the ability to assign an external controller to a so-called *macro control*. These macro controls usually modulate a set of synthesizer elements to create a complex desired effect. For example, the modulation wheel might be assigned to a macro that modulates, by differing amounts (and even directions), the filter cutoff, oscillator mix, amplitude envelope times, and LFO rate and depth. Moving one physical controller causes a complex set of modulations to occur in the sound.

Figure 7.10
The macro controls in Native Instruments' Massive synthesizer allow the user to map a single physical control source to multiple destinations with varying amounts of modulation applied to each destination.

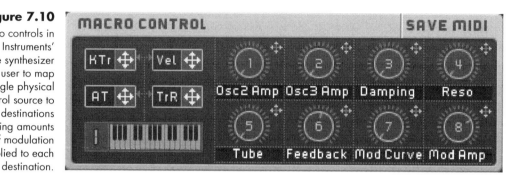

Using a MIDI Sequencer

As sophisticated as macro controls can be, they still impose limits on real-time modulation of events since the user cannot alter individual elements within a macro without reprogramming it. In order to modulate multiple independent controls, a MIDI sequencer program is usually employed. As described earlier, MIDI sequencers record, display, store, and play MIDI messages. They also allow the user to edit and manipulate those messages. Many sequencers display the various controller messages on a number of "tracks" or with uniquely shaped icons, making it quite easy to see and edit the individual controllers. Thus with a MIDI sequencer, you can layer multiple MIDI controllers to create complex modulation effects that it would be impossible for one person to accomplish by moving physical controllers.

Figure 7.11
A full-featured MIDI sequencer such as the one in Avid's Pro Tools software allows the user to see the various MIDI controllers on separate tracks. This type of display makes viewing and editing individual controller messages quite easy.

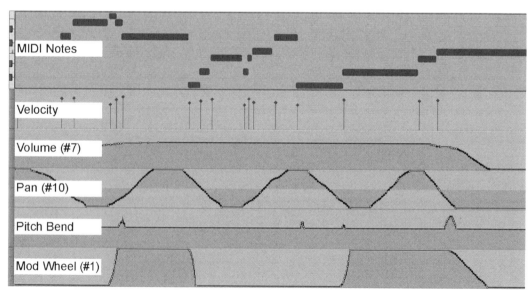

Alternative Controllers

When we mention physical controllers, we normally think of the various keyboards, wheels, knobs, faders, and pedals commonly found on modern MIDI hardware devices. Although these types of controllers are quite common and popular, they are by no means the only ones available to the synthesizer musician. A number of software applications and hardware devices have opened up a whole new realm of alternative controllers, such as light, proximity, pressure, and motion sensors. Other controllers respond to video and audio input, or even to data streams from the Internet. The variety and range of these various controllers is well beyond the scope of this text, but interested readers might enjoy exploring some hardware options such as the I-CubeX from Infusion Systems and Soundbeam from the Soundbeam Project. Software applications such as Max by Cycling '74 and Pure Data are also designed to work with alternative controllers.[11]

Your Turn

Working with Crystal

In the previous chapter, you used a number of the internal modulation sources in Crystal to control various aspects of the synthesizer's sound. Like nearly all synthesizers, Crystal also responds to a wide range of external MIDI controls. By default, key tracking is fixed to the equal temperament system, with A4 tuned to 440 Hz. Pitch bend is also permanently fixed, with a bender range of ±12. Apart from these two, all other MIDI controllers are assigned in the modulation matrix.

To assign a MIDI controller in Crystal, click the Source menu in the modulation matrix to reveal the list of available modulators. Notice that in addition to the internal modulators we examined in the last chapter, there are numerous external modulators. A few of these modulators are named (e.g., Key Velocity, Mod Wheel, Aftertouch, Key Track, and Sustain Pedal), but most are listed only by their MIDI continuous controller number (e.g., MIDI CC 1, MIDI CC 2, etc.). As you did when assigning internal modulation sources in the previous chapter, select an external modulator from the Source menu and a destination function to be modulated from the Target menu, and set the low and high range for the modulation amount.

The possibilities for using MIDI controllers to dynamically shape your sounds are nearly infinite. I hope the demonstrations given here will spark creative ideas of your own. Use the **OscStack** patch you created in Chapter 3 for these examples.

Control Filter Cutoff with Modulation Wheel

Perhaps the most commonly used external modulation control is the Modulation wheel, or "Mod Wheel" as it is often called. In this demonstration you use the Mod Wheel to control the cutoff frequency of a resonant lowpass filter.

1. Select the **XResLoPass** filter with a cutoff frequency around 5 kHz and resonance around 0.3 for all three voices.

---

11 The I-CubeX (http://www.infusionsystems.com) and Soundbeam (http://www.soundbeam.co.uk) systems convert sensor input into standard MIDI controller messages. Both Max (http://cycling74 .com) and its open-source cousin Pure Data (http://puredata.info) provide a graphical interface for programming audio and MIDI controls, including mapping alternative controllers to synthesizers and other sound sources.

2. Select **Mod Wheel** as the Source in the first three rows of the modulation matrix, with the Targets set to **Voice1 Filt Freq**, **Voice2 Filt Freq**, and **Voice3 Filt Freq** respectively.

3. Position the Low and High sliders for all three rows to approximately 3 kHz and 12 kHz respectively.

Play notes on your keyboard as you move the Modulation wheel up and down. The timbre of the combined sounds darkens as the wheel moves to the bottom and brightens as it moves to the top. What happens if you move the three Low sliders all the way to the left?

Reverse the values for the Low and High sliders on voice 2 so that the Low slider is approximately 12 kHz and the High slider is around 3 kHz. Now what happens when you play notes and move the Mod wheel? You should hear that the timbre of voice 2 changes in the opposite direction from voices 1 and 3 as you move the wheel up and down.

Crossfade Voices with Modulation Wheel

1. In the modulation matrix, change the three Target destinations to **Voice1 PreMixerLevel**, **Voice2 PreMixerLevel**, and **Voice3 PreMixerLevel**.

2. Move the Low sliders for voices 1 and 3 all the way to the left and the High sliders all the way to the right.

3. Move the Low slider for voice 2 all the way to the right and the High slider all the way to the left (opposite of voices 1 and 3).

Play notes on your keyboard while moving the Modulation wheel, and you will hear a crossfade between voices 1 and 3 and voice 2.

Pan Sounds Left and Right

1. If your keyboard has a dedicated Pan controller, select **MIDI CC 10** as the Source in the first three rows of the modulation matrix. (If your keyboard does not have a separate Pan control, select the Mod Wheel for this example instead.)

2. Assign **Voice1 Pan**, **Voice2 Pan**, and **Voice3 Pan** respectively in the Target slots of the first three rows.

3. Move the three Low sliders all the way to the left and the three High sliders all the way to the right.

Moving the Pan controller (or the Modulation wheel) on your keyboard will cause the sound to move back and forth from left to right. What happens if you reverse the positions of the High and Low sliders for voice 2? Although Crystal responds to Pan controller messages as a note sustains, many instruments require you to reattack the note to hear the change.

Modulate Vibrato with Aftertouch

1. Create a Sine wave LFO for LFO 1.
   A. Center: 0.500
   B. Swing: 0.250

C. Rate: 6.00 cps

D. Scale: 1.00

2. Select **LFO1** as the Source for the first three rows in the modulation matrix.

3. Set the Targets for the first three rows to **Voice1 Pitch**, **Voice2 Pitch**, and **Voice3 Pitch** respectively.

4. Set all three Low sliders to −1.0 and all three High sliders to 1.0.

5. Select **Aftertouch** as the Source for rows 4 and 5 in the modulation matrix. (If your keyboard does not transmit Aftertouch, select **Mod Wheel** instead.)

6. Select **LFO1 Rate** as the Target for row 4.

A. Low slider: 0.400

B. High slider: 0.600

7. Select **LFO1 Swing** as the Target for row 5.

A. Low slider: 0.240

B. High slider: 0.760

After striking a note on your keyboard, press down on the key to trigger the Aftertouch messages. (If your keyboard does not transmit Aftertouch, use the Modulation wheel instead.) You should hear that the LFO speeds up and also increases its depth, the harder you press the key (or the higher you move the wheel). Experiment with the slider positions for the LFO Rate and Swing values to fine-tune the intensity of your vibrato.

As you are probably beginning to see, the ability to connect numerous internal and external modulation controllers dramatically increases the flexibility of your synthesizer and allows an amazing amount of live, dynamic modulation as you play your sounds. Even if your synthesizer, as with Crystal, does not have a "macro" function per se, you can usually combine several functions on a single modulator via the modulation matrix, thus permitting a macrolike functionality.

Using Your Own Synthesizer(s)

1. Do you have hardware synthesizers, software synthesizers, or both?

2. If you have a hardware synthesizer, can it be used as a controller for other synthesizers?

A. Does it have knobs and sliders that can be independently assigned to MIDI controller messages?

B. Do you have a dedicated MIDI controller?

3. If you have a software synthesizer, does it need to run in a host application, or will it work on its own (standalone mode)?

4. What MIDI messages do your synthesizers transmit and receive?

A. Key velocity?

B. Aftertouch?

C. Pitch bend?

D. Patch change?

E. Patch bank select?

F. Modulation wheel?

G. Volume?

H. Pan?

I. Expression?

J. Sustain pedal?

K. Others?

5. Do you select MIDI controllers by name or by controller number?

6. Can you assign the same controller to multiple functions?

7. Can you combine controllers into a macro? If so, can the macro be modulated by another controller?

8. Do you have a MIDI sequencer program that allows you to record and edit MIDI messages for your synthesizers?

Now that you know how to create sounds and dynamically shape them as you play, let's turn our attention to the final, output stage of a synthesizer in Chapter 8 and examine many of the effects processes that can be used to polish your sounds to a shiny luster.

8

Effects Processors

Polishing Your Sounds

Online materials for this chapter:

http://www.oup.com/refiningsound/Chapter8.html

Effects processing, often called *signal processing*, is usually the final link in the synthesis chain. Technically, everything on a synthesizer after the oscillator stage involves processing the signal, but this final stage is usually considered a separate category where a variety of sonic effects such as reverb, chorus, and delay are applied to the sound to give it a final polish before sending it out to the loudspeakers or recorder.

With the incredible number of effects found on modern synthesizers, not to mention the huge variety of hardware and software effects processors on the market, there are an enormous number of sonic possibilities for the synthesizer programmer and performer. It is well beyond our purpose here to attempt to describe every one of them, but nearly all of the processes are derivatives of the primary effects found in the three main categories of effects processors: time-based effects, frequency-based effects, and amplitude-based effects. Here we examine these three primary categories and the most common effects found in each one. Since our intent is to explore effects that can be used while playing a synthesizer, we deal only with effects that can work their magic in real time, not those that require processing after an audio file has been created. With a basic understanding of how these popular effects work and what they do, it should be relatively easy to understand the many derivations of these effects currently available.

Time-Based Effects

Very simply, a time-based effect manipulates how long it takes for an audio signal to pass through the signal processor. The most common form of this process creates a copy (or multiple copies) of the audio signal to which the time-based effect is applied (the so-called *wet* signal) and then mixes it back with the original, unaffected *dry* signal. The final effect results from the interaction of the wet and dry signals.

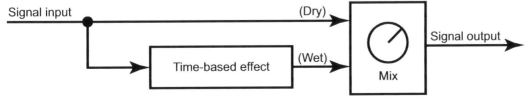

Figure 8.1

Time-based effects processors usually apply the effect to a copy of the audio signal (wet) and then mix it back with the original signal (dry) to create the desired effect.

Feedback

In addition to applying the time-based effect to a copy of the signal, many of these processors provide a feedback control that sends some of the affected signal back through the processor.[1] Depending on the amount of feedback used, the result can range from a subtle thickening of the sound with multiple echoes spread over time to a harmonically rich screeching wail.

Figure 8.2

Time-based effects processors often employ a feedback circuit that loops some of the wet signal back into the effect processor to create a more complex or repeating effect.

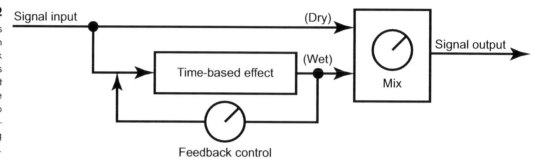

Signal input   (Dry)

Time-based effect   (Wet)   Signal output

Mix

Feedback control

Delay

The most basic of the time-based processors is the delay effect. In its simplest form, a delay makes a copy of the original signal and outputs the copy at a later time, mixing it back with the original signal. Changing the length of time the signal is delayed before being mixed back with the original produces a wide array of outcomes. Delays are therefore often categorized by the length of time, as long, medium, and short.

Demo 8.1

- *Long delays* are usually greater than several hundred milliseconds and can be as much as several seconds in length. With a long delay, the result is a distinct echo of the sound. You hear the initial signal and then a repeat of the signal, often at a lower amplitude level and frequently with some timbral adjustment to make it sound as if it has bounced off a distant surface.

- *Medium delays* are generally considered to fall between 50 and 500 ms. With these delays, a distinct copy of the sound is still heard, but at such a short time interval that the effect is more of a rhythmic doubling than a pronounced echo. In addition to setting the delay time in milliseconds, many medium delays allow the user to set the time interval with a tempo and note value so that the delay fits the rhythm of a musical passage.

- *Tap delays* (often called multitap delays) are frequently found on delay processors that create long and medium delay times. These units produce multiple delayed signals, called *taps*, which may be separated from one another by the same, or varying, amount of delay time. Tap delays often include controls for adjusting the level and the left-right distribution of the individual delays to create stereo, bouncing, or "ping-pong" effects.

1 A few time-based effects have both a feedback and a "feedforward" control. These controls represent two versions of the processed (wet) signal: one without any feedback and one with feedback. The feed *forward* control adjusts the level of the wet signal—without feedback—to the wet-dry mix. The feed*back* control adjusts the amount of signal that is reprocessed in the version of the wet signal that does contain feedback.

Most tap delays also allow the user to synchronize the delay times to a sequencer tempo, creating taps that sound like a succession of rhythmic note values such as sixteenth or eighth notes.

• *Short delays* are typically less than 50 ms, and often in the 1–10 ms range. When a sound is delayed by such a small amount of time, a distinct echo is not heard; instead, the sound takes on a metallic, shimmery quality that is due to phase cancellations occurring when the original and delayed signals are mixed together. This so-called *comb filter* effect of the short delay is used primarily to alter the timbre of sounds. Feedback is commonly used on short delays to increase the harmonic richness of the sound as well. Since most of the phase cancellation in short delays occurs in the upper frequency range (see Figure 8.5), short delays are also frequently used to reduce attack transients and "unfocus" sounds by removing a bit of their crispness.

Demo 8.2

TIP — Kookie, Kookie, Lend Me Your *Comb Filter*

When an audio signal is mixed with a slightly delayed copy of itself, some frequencies in the sound's spectrum remain in phase, creating a reinforcement of the frequency, while other frequencies go out of phase, canceling each other out. These resultant phase reinforcements produce a series of peaks, beginning with the frequency whose wave period equals the delay time and repeating at every harmonic of the first peak's frequency ($2f$, $3f$, $4f$, etc.). For example, a 1 ms delay produces a reinforcement peak at 1 kHz, since a 1 kHz wave completes one wave period in one millisecond.

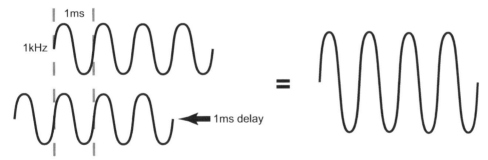

Figure 8.3
A 1 kHz wave delayed by 1 ms creates a phase reinforcement when mixed back with the original, nondelayed 1 kHz wave.

Phase interferences between the two signals produce phase cancellations that create notches in the frequency response, beginning at half the frequency of the first peak (or 500 Hz if we continue with our example above) and repeating between the subsequent peaks.

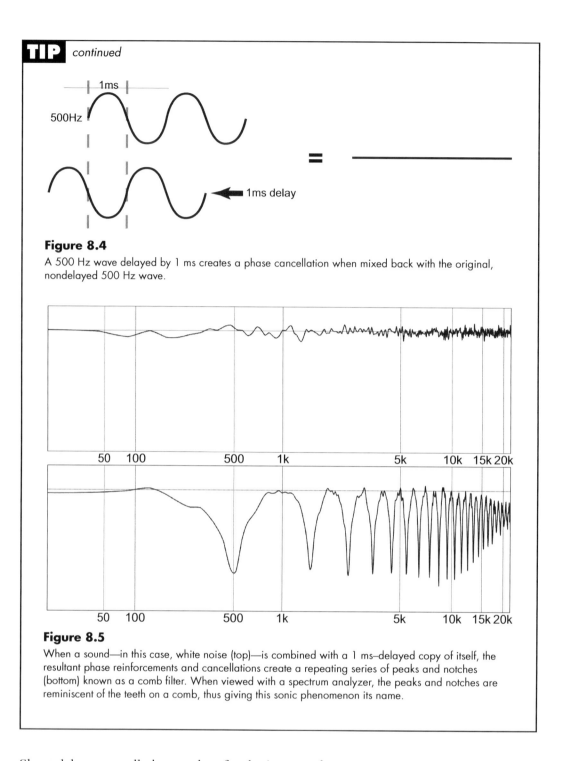

Figure 8.4

A 500 Hz wave delayed by 1 ms creates a phase cancellation when mixed back with the original, nondelayed 500 Hz wave.

Figure 8.5

When a sound—in this case, white noise (top)—is combined with a 1 ms–delayed copy of itself, the resultant phase reinforcements and cancellations create a repeating series of peaks and notches (bottom) known as a comb filter. When viewed with a spectrum analyzer, the peaks and notches are reminiscent of the teeth on a comb, thus giving this sonic phenomenon its name.

Short delays generally have only a few basic controls.

- *Delay time* sets the delay in milliseconds between the two signals.
- *Feedback* controls the level of delayed signal that is sent back through the delay circuit for reprocessing.
- *Wet-dry mix* (often labeled simply as *mix*) adjusts the ratio between the delayed and original signals.

In addition to those listed above, long, medium, and tap delays usually provide controls for the number of taps, the levels and pan positions for the taps, and the ability to synchronize the taps to a tempo or rhythm. More sophisticated units may also have the ability to adjust the timbre of the individual taps and to create differing delay times between the taps. This latter function can be especially effective for creating syncopations or swing rhythms.

Reverb

Demo 8.3

Sounds created by synthesizers—or any type of electronic instrument—originate in the ultimate anechoic chamber, the circuit board. Without an acoustic space in which to resonate, these sounds tend to be quite brash and somewhat abrasive. In early recording studios, engineers would set up a loudspeaker and microphone in a separate room to allow the sound to resonate and be rerecorded with the room's reverberation. Inflexibility in adjusting the room size—not to mention skyrocketing real estate costs—has driven the reverb chamber nearly to extinction. Today, most reverb is created through hardware devices and software applications.

Reverb effects on synthesizers tend to take one of two forms: physical modeling and convolution. Physical modeling reverb processors use a complex set of medium and short delays to create thousands of decaying echoes of the sound that simulate the reverberation of sound in a room. Convolution reverb processors use an actual recorded sample of the reverberation from a physical space and superimpose (convolve) the contours of that reverberation sample onto the synthesizer's sound to create an extremely realistic reverberation.[2]

When a sound is created in a reverberant space, we usually perceive it going through three stages as it reaches our ears: direct sound, early reflections, and reverberation.

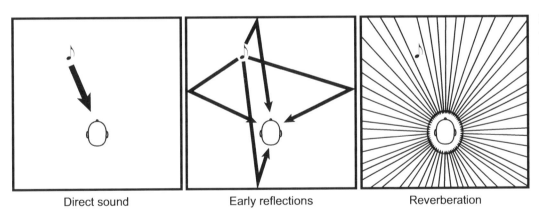

Direct sound   Early reflections   Reverberation

Figure 8.6
The three stages of a reverberant sound.

• *Direct sound* is the sound energy that travels on a direct path from the sound source to us. We use the information in this sound primarily to identify elements such as loudness, timbre, and, to some degree, directionality.

2 Whether it uses physical modeling or convolution, the reverb process is incredibly complex and requires a large amount of computational power to create a high-quality, "good-sounding" reverberation. Because synthesizers also require a large amount of computational power, many instruments provide only a basic reverb so that they can devote the available computational power to the synthesis process. If you need a higher-quality reverb, send your synthesizer's dry sound to an external reverb processor.

- *Early reflections* are the first few distinct echoes of the source's sound as it bounces off various surfaces in the room before reaching us. The information provided in these reflections helps us identify our proximity to the sound source, and it supplies further information on the direction of the sound source from our location.
- *Reverberation* is the final stage, where the sound emanating from the source bounces multiple times off numerous surfaces before reaching our ears. The length and intensity of the reverberation stage helps us identify the size of the reverberant space. The frequency content of the reverberation indicates the acoustic reflectiveness of the room's surfaces. For example, highly reflective rooms (walls, floors, and ceilings made of stone, tile, or glass) produce a reverberation stage with pronounced high-frequency content, while a room with heavy draperies and carpets has very little high-frequency content in its reverberation.

Note that although the reverberation stage yields information on the size of the room, it is primarily the early reflections stage that gives aural cues about distance from the sound source. Many inexperienced reverb users make the mistake of trying to make a sound seem farther away by increasing the amount of reverberation. Instead, they should focus on manipulating the density and amplitude of the early reflections. If you increase only the reverberation size, it sounds as if you are in a large room, but still close to the sound source.

Today, the number and types of controls found on reverb processors seem as vast as the number of processors themselves. Some units feature just a few basic controls while others have an incredible number of detailed controls. However, since the primary function of the reverb processor is to create a series of echoes that follow the contour of a typical room's reverberation, we can make some generalizations about most of the controls you are likely to find. Of course, for specific information about the controls on your reverb unit, consult the user manual that came with it.

Figure 8.7
A plot of the echo amplitudes over time for a typical room reverberation.

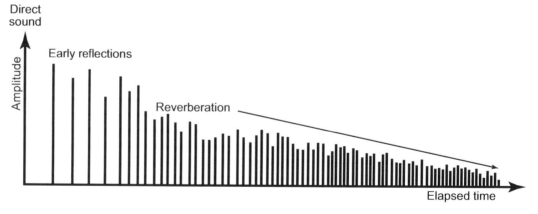

- *Reverb time* (sometimes called RT_{60}) is the length of time it takes for the sound to drop 60 dB in amplitude from its initial direct sound. Large concert halls generally have reverb times in the two to four second range, while smaller rooms may be only a few hundred milliseconds.

- *Pre-delay* adjusts the time between the direct sound and the first early reflection. This control, along with the early reflections controls, imparts a sense of distance from the sound source.[3]
- *Early reflections* controls the first few echoes of the sound before it enters the reverberation stage. There may be separate knobs for controlling the amplitude, density (number of echoes), time, and frequency content of the early reflections. Along with the pre-delay control, adjusting these values affords a sense of distance from the sound source.
- *Reverberation* controls the final stage of the reverberation process. Like early reflections, there may be separate knobs for controlling amplitude, density, time (sometimes called *Size*), and frequency content.
- *High-frequency damping* uses a lowpass filter to control the number of high frequencies in the reverberation. As mentioned earlier, the high-frequency content in the reverberation gives aural cues to the "liveness" of a room. This means the high-frequency damping control can be used to make a room sound live or dry.
- *Early reflections-reverb mix* adjusts the ratio between these two stages.
- *Wet-dry mix* adjusts the ratio between the direct sound and the early reflections/reverberation sound. Both of these last two controls may be used to manipulate the sense of distance from the sound source.

Flanger

Demo 8.4

At some point, many years ago, someone noticed that if you touched the flange (reel) of an analog tape while it was playing, the friction from the finger pressure caused the tape playback to slow down and the pitch of the audio to drop. Later, when audio engineers had the ability to synchronize two tape recorders, they discovered that they could play the same audio on synchronized machines, touch the flange on one machine, and cause the audio to slow down in relation to the other; then, when they released the flange, the audio would speed up as the tape recorder accelerated to stay synchronized with the other machine.

---

3 Pre-delay often confuses first-time users of reverb because the time values work in the opposite direction from what many people expect. Larger pre-delay values create a sense of being close to the sound source, while smaller values create a sense of greater distance from the sound. Remember that pre-delay is the time *difference* between the direct signal and the first early reflection. To illustrate how this works, imagine a scenario where you and a sound source are quite close together in the middle of a room. In this case, the time difference between the direct signal and the first early reflection (pre-delay value) is rather large since it takes considerably longer for the sound to radiate out to the walls and then back to you than it does for the direct sound to reach you. Now imagine that the sound source moves away from you and is much closer to one of the walls. In this scenario, the amount of time for the first early reflection to reach you is much closer to that of the direct sound. Hence the time difference between the two, or pre-delay value, is rather small.

Figure 8.8

Alternately touching and releasing the tape flange on one of two synchronized tape recorders created the original version of the flanger effect.

Synchronized

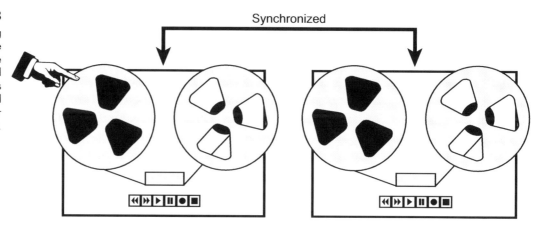

As one tape was slowed down, it fell behind the other tape, creating a delay and a resultant comb filter in the sound. As the tape decelerated and accelerated, the amount of delay between the sounds changed, causing a shift in the timbre of the comb filter. In addition, the slowing down and speeding up of one tape created a Doppler-like pitch shift in the sound. By alternately touching and releasing the tape flange, especially when done in tempo with the music, audio engineers created an interesting—and rhythmically related—sound effect that became known as flanging.

TIP **Why Does Changing Time Change the Pitch?**

You may have noticed that shortening the delay time while a sound is present causes the frequency, or pitch, of the sound to temporarily rise, and lengthening the delay makes it drop. As soon as the delay time stops changing, though, the sound returns to its normal pitch. In the case of a flanger, an LFO continuously increases and decreases the delay time, causing the frequency to constantly rise and fall at the LFO rate.

To understand this effect, it's helpful to think of the delayed sound as emanating from a nearby wall as an echo. As you shorten the delay time, think of the wall moving closer, and as you lengthen the delay, think of it moving away from you. Just as with the famous Doppler effect of a passing train's sound, as the delay moves toward you, the sound's frequency rises, and as the delay moves away the frequency falls. The Doppler pitch shift is an important element in the flanger and chorus (below) effects.

On a synthesizer, flanging is created with a specialized version of the short delay processor. Like the short delay, the flanger creates a comb filter by delaying a copy of the original signal by a small amount and mixing it back with the original. The main difference between a flanger and a delay is that the length of the delay time on a flanger is modulated by an LFO so that it is constantly increasing and decreasing. As with the original tape recorder version, this effect produces both the shifting comb filter as well as the Doppler pitch shift associated with this effect.

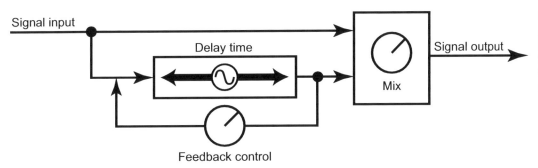

Signal input

Delay time

Signal output

Mix

Feedback control

Figure 8.9
A flanger is created
by applying a low
frequency oscillator
to the delay time of a
short-delay processor.

Most flangers have only a few basic controls.

- *Initial delay* sets the short delay time between the wet and dry signals.
- *Rate* controls the speed of the LFO.
- *Depth* controls how far the delay amount is modulated away from the initial delay time. This value is usually a percentage of the initial delay time. For example, if your initial delay is 6 ms and your depth is 50 percent, then the delay time will swing back and forth between 3 ms and 9 ms (± 50 percent of 6 ms).
- *Feedback* controls the amount of feedback into the flanger's delay circuit. As with the short delay, this boosts the harmonic richness of the sound.
- *Wet-dry mix* adjusts the ratio between the delayed and original signals.

Chorus

Demo 8.5

Have you ever noticed that the sound of a violin section is quite different from the sound of a single violin, or that the sound of one singer is completely unlike the sound of a large chorus? It is not just a matter of the group being louder than the individual. In fact, there often is not much difference in loudness. Instead, there is a substantially different quality to the sound of a group relative to that of an individual.

When a group of (even the very best) musicians all play or sing the same part, there are tiny, subtle differences from one performer to another in pitch, timbre, vibrato, articulation, and so forth. These microscopic individual variations within the group generate small, random phase cancellations in the sound of the combined performers that create a blurring effect on their composite sound. The sound of a group tends to have a much smoother, less focused quality to it than the sound of an individual. This gentle blurring of the sound is the concept behind the chorus effect.

Like the flanger, the chorus effect uses the concept of LFO modulated delay lines to process the sound. The chorus, though, has several major differences from the flanger, beginning with the fact that the chorus often has multiple delay lines instead of just one. Although the delay lines on both processors have feedback capabilities, the amount of feedback used with chorus is generally much less than that used with a flanger. A chorus frequently uses longer initial delay times than a flanger, but the rate and depth of the LFO modulation of that delay time is usually much smaller than that of a flanger. Finally, the chorus frequently uses a random LFO rather than the cyclic LFO found on most flangers.

Figure 8.10

Chorus uses multiple, LFO modulated delay lines to create its blurring effect.

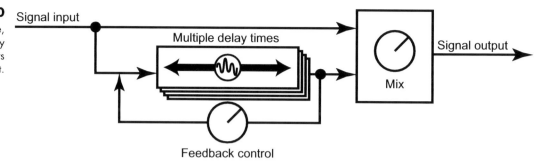

Signal input

Multiple delay times

Signal output

Mix

Feedback control

The result of all these differences is that the chorus produces a number of gently—and randomly—modulating delay lines that produce multiple, tiny, Doppler pitch shifts and comb filter sweeps to blur the sound, as opposed to the obvious timbre and pitch shifts created by the flanger. A chorus will not make you sound as if you are a violin section or a big choir, but it will add a rich, swirling, blurry quality to your sound. It is particularly effective when used on sounds with percussive attacks and quick transients such as those from synthesizer leads, electronic keyboards, and electric guitars, as chorus tends to soften the attack stage a bit on these sounds.

The typical chorus effect has a few more controls than a flanger.

- *Initial delay* sets the short delay time between the wet and dry signals.
- *Width* (also called *Spread*) creates differences between the delay times of the individual delay lines. As you increase the width, the individual delay times draw further and further apart. Be aware that some chorus effects use the label Width to refer to the stereophonic output capabilities of the chorus. Be sure to check the manual for your device if you have a function labeled Width.
- *Rate* controls the speed of the LFO.
- *Depth* controls how far the delay times are modulated away from their initial setting. This value is usually a percentage of the initial delay time. For example, if your initial delay is 6 ms and your depth is 50 percent, then the delay time will swing back and forth between 3 ms and 9 ms (± 50 percent of 6 ms).
- *Feedback* controls the amount of feedback into each delay line of the chorus. As on the flanger, this boosts the harmonic richness of the sound.
- *Wet-dry mix* adjusts the ratio between the delayed and original signals.
- *Stereo* outputs the wet-dry mix as a stereophonic signal so that the original mono input takes on a much wider sound.

Phaser

Demo 8.6

Although the phase shift process used in a phaser does create microscopic delays (on the order of a couple of samples), this is not enough for the process to really be considered a true, time-based effect. However, the sound of the phaser is so closely associated with that of the flanger and chorus that most musicians think of them as being in the same category. So it makes sense to include phaser here. Unlike the time-based effects that create comb filters with short delays, the phaser passes the wet signal through a series of two-pole allpass filters to create a small number of evenly spaced notches in the frequency spectrum.

Remember from our discussion in Chapter 5 that an allpass filter gradually shifts frequencies 180° out of phase. Remember, also, that the effect of an allpass filter by itself is practically inaudible. The ear is not sensitive to phase position, so we notice the effect only when the filtered and unfiltered signals are recombined. With a single (one-pole) allpass filter, a lowpass filter is created since the upper frequencies cancel each other from being out of phase.

Since phase position is circular, once a signal passes through 180°, it begins moving back into phase. Combining two allpass filters in series to create a two-pole filter steepens the transition slope so that the second filter shifts the frequencies back into phase, essentially folding them back up from the 180° phase position. When this happens, a notch is created at the point where the transition slope passes through 180°.

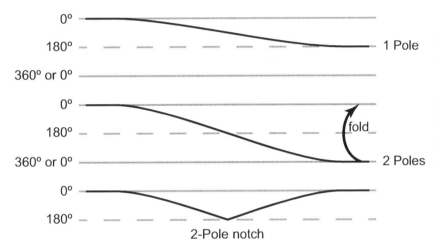

Figure 8.11

A one-pole allpass filter gradually shifts the upper frequencies 180° out of phase (top). A two-pole allpass filter increases the steepness of the transition so that the slope eventually folds the frequencies back around to 0° (middle), producing a notch in the frequencies at the point where the slope passes through 180° (bottom).

Adding more two-pole allpass filters further steepens the transition slope, causing the frequencies to pass through 180° and 0° multiple times. At every point where the slope crosses 180°, a notch is created because of phase cancellation when recombined with the original, unfiltered signal.

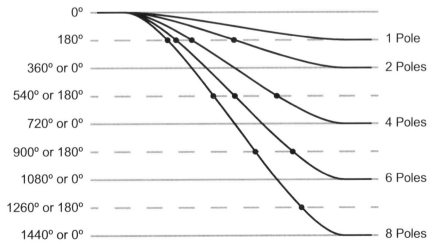

Figure 8.12

As successive two-pole allpass filters are applied to a signal, the steepness and depth of the transition slope increases. Since phase is circular (it always comes back around to 0°), the second allpass filter in each pair brings the phase-shifted signal back into phase. Every time the transition slope crosses 180° (marked with •), a notch is created in the frequency response when the dry and wet signals are combined.

Figure 8.13
The frequency response of white noise processed by a phaser with two-, four-, six-, and eight-pole allpass filters. Each pair of filters (two poles) creates a notch in the frequency spectrum. In this example, the cutoff, or corner, frequency for the allpass filters is 100 Hz, with an extremely wide transition band encompassing more than seven octaves.

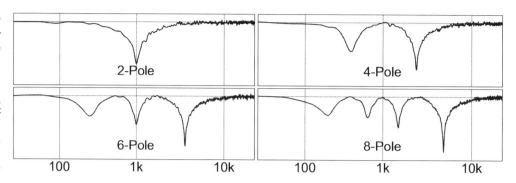

Once the frequency notches have been created, the phaser effect moves them higher and lower in frequency by modulating the cutoff (sometimes called *corner*) frequency of the allpass filters with an LFO. Because there are considerably fewer notches than are created in a comb filter, the frequency-sweeping effect is subtler than the flanger, and more importantly there is no Doppler pitch shift in the sound. Instead, there is only the classic swooshing sound of the phaser.

Figure 8.14
Phasers pass the signal through a series of two-pole allpass filters to create a small number of evenly spaced notches in the frequency spectrum when the wet and dry signals are combined. Modulating the cutoff frequency with an LFO produces an oscillating swoosh in the sound.

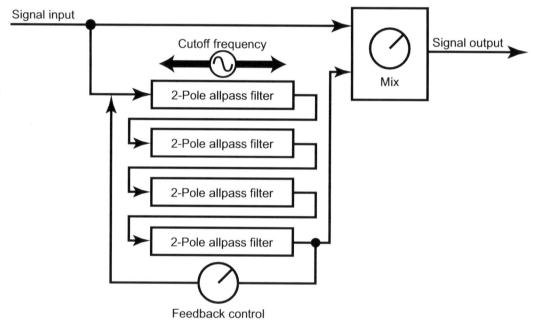

Many phasers are rather spartan when it comes to controls. They assume the user wants the swoosh and so they often furnish controls only for the LFO and the wet–dry mix. More complex and sophisticated phasers may also add controls for creating and adjusting the number and position of the notches.

- *Rate* controls the speed of the LFO as it modulates the allpass filter's cutoff frequency.
- *Depth* controls the distance over which the LFO moves the allpass filters' cutoff frequency above and below their set position.
- *Frequency* sets the cutoff, or corner, frequency of the allpass filters.
- *Poles* determines the number of frequency notches by engaging additional pairs of allpass filters. Remember, every two-pole increase adds one frequency notch.

- *Width* sets the spread of the frequency notches by adjusting the slope of the allpass filters' cutoff.
- *Feedback* controls the amount of wet signal that is reprocessed through the allpass filters. This tends to boost the intensity of the phaser effect.
- *Wet-dry mix* adjusts the ratio between the delayed and original signals.

Frequency-Based Effects

Frequency-based effects are those that manipulate the frequency content of an audio signal. The effect might be something as basic as altering the frequency spectrum of a signal with audio filters, as we discussed in Chapter 5. Audio filters, however, are so intrinsic to the basic sound of a synthesizer that we usually think of them not as "effects" so much as a fundamental link in the synthesis chain. Instead, when we describe frequency-based effects, we are usually referring to processes that dramatically manipulate or alter the primary frequencies in a sound. These effects might use the primary frequencies to generate new frequencies, or they may superimpose the frequency spectrum of one signal onto another.

Frequency Shifters, Pitch Shifters, and Harmonizers

Demo 8.7

Both frequency shifters and pitch shifters are used to raise and lower the frequencies in a sound, but with contrasting methods. Frequency shifters move all the frequencies present in a sound by a specific number of Hertz, while pitch shifters move them all by the same musical interval. Harmonizers work in a similar way to pitch shifters, but they also allow the original sound to be heard so that the pitch-shifted frequencies form a harmony interval such as an octave or perfect-fifth to the original sound.

With all the sophisticated controls found on a synthesizer for manipulating the frequencies of the oscillators, it might be tempting to think that frequency and pitch shifters would not be of much use. Although it is quite easy to shift the fundamental pitch of a sound sound within the oscillator, frequency shifters allow us to alter the relationship of all the overtones in a sound to the fundamental and to each other.

Consider a sawtooth oscillator wave with a fundamental frequency of 110 Hz (the bottom-space A in the bass clef staff). We know from Chapter 2 that sawtooth waves contain all the harmonics (whole-number multiples) of the fundamental, but with decreasing amplitudes. So, in addition to our fundamental of 110 Hz, the next four harmonics of our sawtooth are 220 Hz, 330 Hz, 440 Hz, and 550 Hz. If we use a pitch shifter to lower the A by a major-second interval to G, the fundamental drops 12 Hz to 98 Hz, but the overtones drop by varying amounts to 196 Hz, 294 Hz, 392 Hz, and 490 Hz. Since the overtones maintain their harmonic relationship to the fundamental, the oscillator sound continues to have a strongly pitched quality. By contrast, if we pass our 110 Hz sawtooth wave through a frequency shifter set to lower the frequency by 12 Hz, our fundamental still drops to a G (98 Hz), but our overtones are also lowered by 12 Hz to 208 Hz, 318 Hz, 428 Hz, and 538 Hz. These overtones are now inharmonic to the fundamental, giving the original sound somewhat of an unpitched or noisy quality.

Remember that timbre is the result of the distribution and relative amplitudes of all the harmonic and inharmonic frequencies in a complex sound. When you shift the frequency of the fundamental up and down with the oscillator, those ratios remain relatively constant, thus maintaining the timbre of the sound at different pitch levels. However, when you apply a frequency shifter to a complex sound, not only is the fundamental frequency moved up or down, the quality and timbre of the sound is drastically changed as well. Consequently, frequency shifters are usually not used to change the fundamental pitch of a sound, but to alter its frequency spectrum, and thus its timbre. In fact, some of the best uses of these effects are for creating nonpitched and noisy types of sounds, as the alteration of the frequency spectrum usually produces some wonderfully exotic results.

It is also important to remember that in digital audio and synthesis the data being generated are amplitude values, not frequency values.[4] Frequency is established only by a repeating series of amplitude changes occurring at a regular time interval. Since frequency and pitch shifters must first know all the component frequencies of a sound, they have to be able to examine and analyze a series of amplitude measurements over a period of time. Consequently, it is impossible to calculate the frequency, or pitch, of a sound without a small amount of latency or time delay in the calculation. Until recently, these types of effects were not considered real-time processes. However, the newer computer processors have brought the calculation latency down so low that it is imperceptible in most cases. Still, even though frequency shifting is a wonderfully useful effect, pitch shifting and harmonizing are commonly not included as effects, since they are so easily handled in the oscillator stage.

Audio Filters

We dealt extensively with the uses of audio filters in Chapter 5. In the effects stage of a synthesizer, filter use is generally the same, but with more extreme settings. Filters in the effects stage often use quite narrow pass bands with high resonance values to substantially alter the quality and timbre of the sound. Many of the effects stage filters also have their own built-in modulators, allowing you to create active and dynamic sounds. Rather than repeat all the information here, I encourage you to review Chapter 5, "Audio Filters," bearing in mind that in the effects stage of the synthesizer the settings and resultant sounds are usually much more profound.

Demo 8.8

Vocoder

The vocoder is an amazing process that superimposes the frequency spectrum of one sound—usually a complex sound such as the human voice—onto a synthesizer sound. This effect is frequently used to create the robotic voices heard in popular music and in numerous science fiction films.[5]

The vocoder first passes both the modulator (voice) signal and the synthesizer signal through identical sets of high-Q bandpass filters to separate the two signals into identical

---

4 For a review of digital audio concepts, see Chapter 1, "Digital Audio and Synthesis."

5 The vocoder is often confused with another device known as a "talk box." The talk box is a completely different process whereby the sound from a synthesizer is fed through a small plastic tube that enters a singer's mouth. The singer then "mouths" words in front of a microphone to acoustically shape vocal formants onto the synthesized sound.

multiple frequency bands. It then measures the amplitude of the energy in each band of the modulator signal and applies this amplitude level to the equivalent frequency band in the synthesizer signal. Since the *formants* of speech produce a complex distribution of energy in the frequency spectrum, this process has the effect of superimposing speech formants onto the synthesized sound.

> **TIP** *Formants* are the unique and distinguishing frequency components of the human voice. They allow us not only to identify individual voices but to distinguish among all the vowel and consonant sounds in the voice.

For this process to be most effective, the synthesized sound must contain a broad spectrum of frequencies. Consequently, sounds like modulated pulse and sawtooth waves are quite popular as synthesizer sound sources. To add a bit more realism to the speech quality, most vocoders also have a white noise oscillator, used instead of the synthesizer sound whenever the modulator signal goes above some predetermined frequency threshold. In human speech, consonants tend to produce very high frequencies while vowels produce much lower frequencies. This frequency threshold is used to separate vowels and consonants so that the vowels produce a pitched synthesizer sound while the consonants produce a brief, unpitched, noise sound. By varying the type and frequency of the synthesized sound, as well as the "consonant" threshold, a wide variety of "talking-synth" sounds can be created.

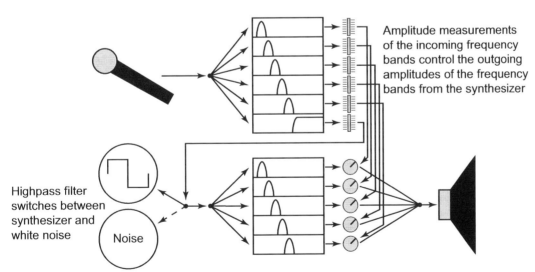

Amplitude measurements of the incoming frequency bands control the outgoing amplitudes of the frequency bands from the synthesizer

Highpass filter switches between synthesizer and white noise

Noise

Figure 8.15

The vocoder measures the amplitude of the modulator signal in each of the many frequency bands and applies that amplitude level to the same frequency band of the synthesized sound. Frequently, noise is used instead of the synthesizer sound when the modulator signal goes above a predetermined frequency to simulate consonants.

Although vocoders are typically designed to use the voice as the modulator input, any type of audio signal may be used. For best results, though, the signal should be one that has a rich, complex set of frequencies that are constantly changing, like those from a drum set or an acoustic guitar.

Figure 8.16
Although many vocoders are software-based, some instruments such as the Korg MicroKORG XL are both hardware synthesizers and vocoders. (photo courtesy of Korg USA, used with permission)

As with all effects processors, vocoder controls vary slightly with the model, but typically have the following:

- *Input select* allows you to choose the sound source for both the modulator and synthesizer sound.
- *Synthesizer controls* on instruments with a built-in synthesizer allow you to manipulate the synthesizer sound and play various pitches from a keyboard.
- *Frequency bands* determines the number of bandpass filters used to separate the sounds into component frequencies. Depending on the sophistication of the vocoder, this option may also allow the center frequency of every band to be set individually.
- *Filter Q* sets the steepness of the passband in each filter. The higher the Q value, the less overlap there is between adjacent bands.
- *Consonants (or noise)* adjusts the sensitivity of the vocoder for deciding whether a sound is a vowel or a consonant, and it injects white noise into the signal as appropriate. Some devices break this control down into two components: high-pass cutoff frequency and amplitude threshold.

Ring Modulator

> **TIP** The *ring modulator* gets its name from the design of the original analog device consisting of four diodes arranged in a circular configuration on a circuit board.

Like the vocoder, the ring modulator is also used to superimpose the frequency response of a complex signal onto a synthesizer sound. The process and the finished product, though, are completely different. In Chapter 3, "Oscillator Combinations," we discussed a method of combining two oscillator signals through a process known as amplitude modulation. As mentioned in that chapter, amplitude modulation is rarely used as a sound source, but a specialized form of it, known as ring modulation, has become quite popular as an effects process.

In ring modulation, as with amplitude modulation, the amplitudes of the carrier and modulator waves are multiplied by each other. The primary difference is that in amplitude modulation, the modulator's amplitude has been modified with a *DC offset* so that its values are always positive (unipolar), while the modulator amplitude in ring modulation remains centered on zero so that it has both positive and negative values (bipolar). The net result is that amplitude modulation produces a pulse in the carrier once per cycle of the modulator, while ring modulation produces two pulses per modulator cycle.

TIP *DC (direct current) offset* is simply a constant voltage added to a changing voltage such as that of an audio signal. It is frequently used to shift a signal so that it remains above the zero crossing line.

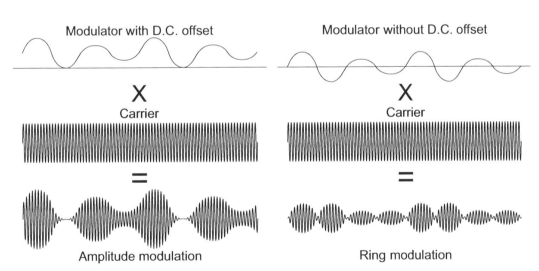

Modulator with D.C. offset

Modulator without D.C. offset

X

Carrier

=

Amplitude modulation

X

Carrier

=

Ring modulation

Figure 8.17

The modulator in AM synthesis has a DC offset so that it never passes the zero crossing line. Thus the amplitude of the carrier rises and falls from maximum to minimum on the basis of the shape of the modulator. In ring modulation, the modulator does not have a DC offset, so the carrier rises to maximum in both compression and rarefaction stages of the modulator and falls to zero only when the modulator passes the zero crossing line.

Just as with amplitude modulation, ring modulation creates sidebands at the sum and difference of the carrier and modulator frequencies ($f_c + f_m$ and $f_c - f_m$).[6] The main sonic difference is that ring modulation also removes the carrier frequency, leaving *only* the sidebands. Consequently any sense of a central pitch in the sound is lost.

Demo 8.9

6 There is a special form of ring modulator known as a *single-sideband* ring modulator, which allows the user to choose only the upper sideband ($f_c + f_m$) or the lower sideband ($f_c - f_m$). If you select the upper sideband and use a fixed-frequency sine wave as the carrier input, the device functions as a frequency shifter by adding the frequency of the carrier to all the component frequencies of the modulator. If you want to shift the frequencies down, just select the lower sideband output. Single-sideband ring modulators are often used for this purpose but have recently lost ground to the newer frequency shifters that actually analyze the frequency content before performing the shift.

When one of the inputs to a ring modulator is a complex sound like a voice, and the other input is a synthesizer sound, the result is somewhat similar to a vocoder in terms of superimposing formants onto the synthesizer sound; but without the pitch of the carrier, the frequency content is completely unpredictable. To make the effect even less predictable, many ring modulators include an LFO to modulate the frequency of the carrier oscillator.

Ring modulators are relatively simple devices. As such, they usually have only a few basic controls.

- *Input level* controls the input trim of the modulator signal.
- *Mix* controls the ratio between the modulator and carrier signal levels.
- *Frequency* sets the oscillator frequency for the carrier wave. Some devices allow selection of an external source for the carrier, but most have a simple sine-wave oscillator.
- *LFO* sets the rate of a low frequency oscillator modulating the carrier frequency.
- *Filter* adjusts the cutoff frequency of a lowpass filter on the output signal to control its timbre.

Amplitude-Based Effects

Having examined effects that manipulate the time and frequency of synthesizer sounds, we now turn our attention to effects that alter the amplitude of sounds. These amplitude-based effects processes fall into two basic categories: those that distort the shape of the sound wave and those that control the dynamic range of a sound.

Distortion Processors

In electronics, the term *distortion* refers to any unwanted change in signal frequency, phase, or amplitude. Because of inherent flaws in materials, electrical components, and circuit designs, every electronic device creates some amount of distortion in the signals that pass through. In most cases, the distortion is so low that it is imperceptible. *Saturation* is a specific type of *amplitude distortion* that occurs when the signal's amplitude is too great for the components attempting to handle it. Although one might be tempted to think of saturation as undesirable, it has actually become quite popular as an effect in a number of popular and electronic styles of music.

In analog audio, there are two common types of saturation: tape saturation and tube saturation. Tape saturation occurs when the signal being recorded onto tape exceeds the capabilities of the magnetic particles on the tape's surface. Tube saturation happens as a result of trying to force too many electrons to pass from the cathode to the anode inside the vacuum tube.[7] Engineers in analog recording studios found that overloading the signal onto an audiotape, or through a tube, produced a pleasingly warm, compressed quality in the sound. Although both tape and tube saturation clipped the peaks off the

---

7 You will occasionally see the phrase "valve distortion" used. In some parts of the English-speaking world, vacuum tubes are called "valves," and so valve distortion or saturation is the same thing as tube distortion or saturation.

waveforms, they did so in different ways, producing contrasting harmonic spectra for the two types of distortion.

Electric guitar players found there were two ways they could overload the tubes in their amplifiers to create saturation in the signal. One technique was to raise the level of the input trim so high that the guitar signal was saturated as it entered the amp, but the level of the main amplifier tube remained at a normal gain. The other method was to bring the signal in at a normal level, but boost the internal amplification of the signal so much that the main amplifier tube became saturated. In the first scenario, clips occurred early in the signal chain. By the time the signal passed all the way through the amp's circuitry, though, the edges of those clips had been smoothed down, and the saturation had a warm, harmonic quality to it. In the second scenario, the saturation occurred late in the signal chain and the clips maintained more of a squared-off shape, producing a harsher, edgier sound.

As audio equipment moved to solid-state components, and eventually to digital microchips, the response of the transistors, and the later DSP chips, produced an even harsher sound when overloaded. The clipping from tape and tube saturation—even if it occurred late in the signal chain—produced a considerably warmer sound than did clipping with transistors and DSP chips. If we look at the clips on an oscilloscope, we will see that tape and tube saturation produce a rounded, "soft" clip, while the transistor and DSP saturation produce a flat, "hard" clip. Over the years, the soft and hard clips—along with their resultant sound quality—have become known as *overdrive* and *distortion*, respectively.[8]

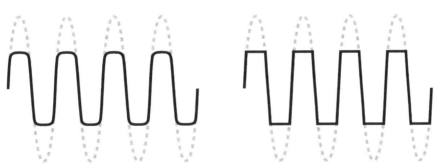

Figure 8.18
The rounded edges of a soft clip (left) produce a warmer tone, often called overdrive, while the "sheared" edges of a hard clip (left) produce a much harsher sound known as distortion.

There still tends to be a bit of confusion and overlap in the meaning and usage of saturation, overdrive, and distortion, but generally, saturation has come to mean a fairly soft clip that also mimics the frequency and compression artifacts of tape and tube saturation. In fact, saturation effects processors usually have specific settings for tape or tube saturation. Overdrive also usually means a soft clip, but with a slightly brighter sound than that of saturation. Distortion tends to be used to describe the sound of hard clips and is the harshest and edgiest of the three effects.

Demo 8.10

Today, engineers frequently use saturation to warm up a sound, or to give it an "analog" quality. Overdrive and distortion are used more as an effect to add some higher-frequency content, edginess, and a bit of "dirt" to sounds. With contemporary equipment, all three of these processes are created not by overloading some electronic component

---

8 Although there are other forms of distortion, most musicians, when using the term *distortion*, are referring to the hard clip type of sound.

but with special analog circuitry, or with some form of digital signal processing such as waveshaping.

The interface on distortion processors is often rather simple, with only a few controls for the user.

- *Distortion type* allows the user to choose from the common categories of saturation, overdrive, and distortion.
- *Input trim* adjusts the incoming signal level. Boosting this value substantially can create additional distortion in the signal.
- *Drive or distortion* adjusts the intensity of the distortion effect.
- *Tone, frequency, or cutoff* adjusts the cutoff frequency of a lowpass filter if the processor has one.
- *Output gain* raises and lowers the amplitude of the finished, processed signal.

Bit Crushers

Bit crushing, or bit reduction, is another form of amplitude distortion becoming ever more popular with digital synthesizers. In this process, the number of bits used to measure the amplitude of the sound wave is reduced. Most digital audio devices use either a sixteen-bit or a twenty-four-bit digital word to measure and store the amplitude of a digital sample. It is this high number of bits that provides the fine resolution of the sample's amplitude.[9] By reducing the number of bits, the quantization error of the sample increases, and the wave becomes more angular, producing a harsher tone. The sound also loses the subtlety of amplitude gradation, creating a noisy sound that jumps from one amplitude level to another.

Figure 8.19
A full bit depth waveform (left) reduced to four-bit resolution (center), and two-bit resolution (right).

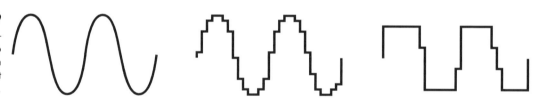

Like the other distortion processors, bit crushers also tend to have a rather simple interface with only a couple of controls. Other than the input and output levels, they frequently have a control only for changing the bit depth. Some processors also have a lowpass filter to remove some of the harshness from the sound.

Dynamics Processors

When musicians use the word *dynamics*, they are usually referring to loudness in a piece of music. On sheet music, the dynamic levels are typically indicated with Italian terms (or their abbreviations), like *forte* (*f*) or *piano* (*p*), loud and soft respectively. With synthesizers, and with audio, we talk about the dynamic range of sounds, referring to the amount of amplitude change between the quietest and loudest sections of a sound or recording.

9 For a review of digital audio fundamentals, see Chapter 1, "Digital Audio and Synthesis."

There is a set of amplitude effects processors known as "dynamics processors" that, as the name implies, modify the dynamic range of a sound. Many people list four processors in this category: compressor, limiter, expander, and gate. As we will see, though, there are really only two processors, since the compressor and the limiter are essentially the same thing, as are the gate and the expander. The primary difference is in their use and settings, not their actual operation. In fact, most manufacturers today describe their products as a compressor/limiter or an expander/gate. Fortunately, the functions and controls of these devices are quite similar. Thus, we will examine the compressor—the most common of the dynamics processors—in some detail, and then look at how the other processes differ in their function and use.

Compressor

Have you ever been driving in a car, listening to the radio, and had to turn the volume up because the outside noise level was high and the music was soft? Probably at some other point, the music got louder and the outside noise quieter, and you had to turn the volume level back down. What you did was compress the dynamic range of the signal: when the music was too soft you turned it up, and when it was loud you turned it down. Narrowing the dynamic range of a signal is exactly what a compressor does, only it does so automatically and very quickly.

A compressor begins by comparing the amplitude of the incoming signal to a user-defined amplitude level known as the *threshold* level. So long as the incoming amplitude remains below the threshold, the compressor does nothing. However, if the amplitude exceeds the threshold, then the compressor begins to turn down the level, or gain, on the incoming audio. Once the incoming signal falls back below the threshold, the compressor turns the audio level back to its original level. Only the audio that exceeds the threshold is compressed. The rest of the signal is unaffected.

The speed with which the compressor engages when the signal crosses the threshold is known as the *attack time*, and the speed with which it disengages as the signal falls back below the threshold is called the *release time*. Both of these values are usually given in milliseconds or fractions of a second. In general, attack times are usually set to be quite short, in the range of 1–20 ms. Release times, on the other hand, are often a bit longer and may extend up to half a second or more. If the release time is set to an extremely short value, the sound of the compressor turning the gain back up often becomes audible, creating what audio engineers frequently refer to as compressor "pumping" or "breathing."

Figure 8.20
The same percussive sound before and after processing by a compressor. Note that only the amplitudes that exceed the threshold are turned down, and they are turned down proportionally to how far they went above the threshold. Also note that the very first peak is nearly identical in both examples. This is a result of the attack time not being fast enough to catch the first impulse. The remainder of the audio that does not exceed the threshold level is left unaffected.

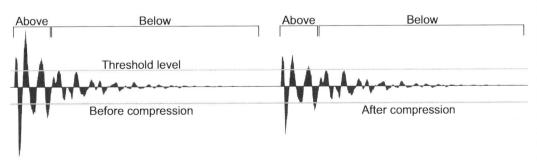

Once the level and speed at which the compressor engages and disengages are established, the amount of gain reduction that is applied to sounds exceeding the threshold is set with a value known as *ratio*. The ratio is a mathematical representation comparing the amplitude level of the incoming audio to that of the outgoing audio, and it is always written as two numbers separated by a colon (e.g., 3:1, 7:1, 20:1, etc.). The left-hand number represents the incoming amplitude and the right-hand number the outgoing amplitude. With compressors, the right-hand number will always be a 1. A ratio of 1:1 means that for every 1 dB by which the incoming audio level exceeds the threshold, the outgoing audio level will also rise 1 dB above the threshold level. In other words, they are maintained at the same level. A ratio of 3:1 means that for every 3 dB by which the incoming audio level goes above the threshold, the outgoing signal will increase by only 1 dB above the threshold level.

The greater the value of the left-hand number, the more the signal will be turned down as it exceeds the threshold. Consequently, small ratios produce a gentle amount of compression while larger values produce more compression. When a compressor's ratio is set to a value greater than 10:1 (some go up to 100:1 or even ∞:1), it is considered to be a limiter instead of a compressor. With ratios this large, for all intents and purposes the incoming audio is prevented from exceeding the threshold.

Figure 8.21

The greater the ratio value, the more the gain is reduced on audio signals that exceed the threshold. Audio levels below the threshold are unaffected.

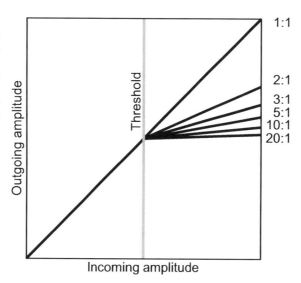

Rather than making an abrupt transition from uncompressed to compressed signal as the audio level exceeds the threshold, many compressors provide a way to soften the transition through a control known as *knee*. A "hard" knee means the compressor has an instantaneous change from uncompressed to compressed output as the incoming signal crosses the threshold. A "soft" knee actually begins applying a small amount of compression as the incoming audio approaches the threshold, and it does not actually reach the full amount of the ratio until the incoming audio has gone a bit over the threshold. Some compressors merely allow you to switch between hard and soft knees, while others provide a continuous control between hard and soft so that you can set something between the two extremes. Soft knees are particularly good for sounds that are smooth and legato, while percussive and staccato sounds often work better with a hard knee.

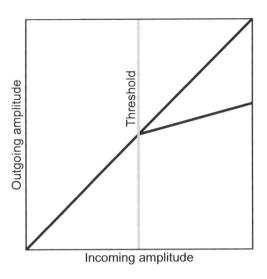
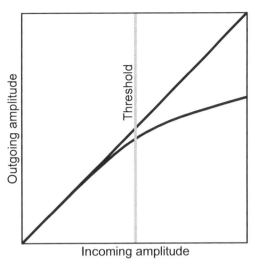

Figure 8.22
A hard knee (left) causes the compressor to instantly change from uncompressed signal to compressed signal as the incoming audio crosses the threshold. A soft knee (right) provides a smoother transition between uncompressed and compressed signal as the incoming audio approaches and crosses the threshold.

The final element of most compressors is the output level control, often called *makeup gain* or simply *gain*. The makeup gain is typically used to compensate for the loss of the louder signals by boosting the entire output of the compressor.

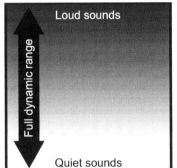
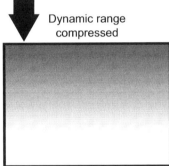
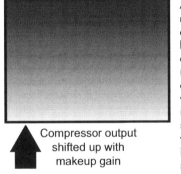

Figure 8.23
A compressor reduces the full dynamic range (left) by lowering the level of the loudest sounds (center). The entire output is then boosted with makeup gain (right) so that the loud sounds are back where they were initially, and the quiet sounds are raised to a louder level.

Demo 8.11

Compressor Usage

Many newcomers to electronic music and recording find themselves unsure of how to use compression on their sounds. Although the outcomes of the effects we have previously discussed are usually quite obvious, compression can often be subtle in its result. Synthesizer players and audio engineers often think of the other effects as a way to dramatically alter the sound, while thinking of compression as a way to make things sound "better." Obviously, we hope that everything we do makes our sound "better," but in this sense they are usually referring to the idea of making things easier to hear in the overall mix of sounds. With this concept in mind, here are a few common uses of compression in the synthesis process. The first two are used to make a sound stand out in a mix, and the third to add some sustain richness to a sound.

Make It Louder

Sounds on a synthesizer can have a wide dynamic range between the loudest and softest notes, often as a result of the player's technique or some sort of modulator. As a result, when the sound is combined with other sounds in a mix, it often becomes difficult to hear the softer notes. If the level of the sound is turned up so that the soft notes are audible, then the louder notes often clip or distort. Compression helps to solve this problem by reducing the level of the loud notes and then boosting the overall level with makeup gain. You can hear the softer notes better, and the louder notes do not clip.

Clarify the Attack

It is a well-known fact that we tend to identify a sound in the first few milliseconds of the sound's attack stage. With a complex mix of sounds, it can often be difficult to hear all the sounds as they have a tendency to mask each other, especially when coming from just two loudspeakers. Compression can help to clarify the attack of a sound—what audio engineers often call creating a "punchy" sound—by reducing the amplitude of the sound during the sustain stage. Normally we think of using compression to control the loudest potion of a sound, the attack stage. In this scenario, the attack time is set to a longer value so that the attack triggers the compressor, but the actual compression effect is slightly delayed. So instead of turning down the attack stage, the compressor turns down the sustain stage. Reducing the sustain level on many sounds often helps us hear all the sounds more clearly.

Add Sustain

Because compressors change the balance between the loud and soft sounds, compression can be used to increase the perceived sustain level between notes. Apply a moderate ratio with a fast attack and a fairly quick release to a sound; then boost the makeup gain to create the sense of more sustain between notes. This is particularly effective on sounds that have a percussive attack and a quick decay.

Limiter

As mentioned earlier, a limiter is essentially a compressor with a large ratio value. By setting the ratio so high, the outgoing signal is prevented from exceeding the threshold level, thus limiting the amplitude. Limiters are often used to prevent clipping on a signal that might have an occasional large peak in amplitude. The attack time needs to be as fast as possible, because it is often the very first peak in a sound that clips.

Limiters have also become quite common in the final mixdown and mastering stage of a recording. They are used to increase the perceived loudness of a recording by setting the threshold rather low and then boosting the makeup gain by a comparable amount. In recent years, numerous audio engineers have pushed this practice to extremes in what is known, pejoratively, as *the loudness war*.[10] With such massive amounts of limiting and makeup gain, many contemporary recordings have little or no dynamic range in them.

Specialty Compressors

In addition to the limiter, the use of a few specialty compressors has become rather common with synthesizers. One type allows you to use one audio signal to compress a second signal, and another separates the signal into multiple frequency bands, allowing the bands to be compressed individually.

Side-Chain Compressors

The standard compressor examines the amplitude of the incoming signal and applies compression to the signal as needed. Side-chain compressors, by contrast, examine the ampli-

---

10 There are numerous articles, both online and in print, about the loudness war, but a good summary, with audio examples, may be found in Wikipedia, at http://en.wikipedia.org/wiki/Loudness_war.

tude of one incoming signal, known as the side-chain input (also called the *key input*), and use that signal to trigger compression on another incoming signal, the *main input*. Side-chain compressors are frequently used in two common scenarios: *ducking* and *de-essing*.

Ducker

In the broadcast world, the main input to a ducker is often a music track and the side-chain a voice-over announcer. When the announcer speaks, the side-chain compression causes the level of the music to "duck" underneath the level of the announcer. Duckers have become quite popular in the electronic dance music genre. In this style, the main input to the compressor is the entire electronic music mix, and the side-chain input is usually the kick drum sound. Every time the kick "thumps," the overall mix makes a quick drop in amplitude to produce the "pumping" sound so common to this style of music.

De-Esser

The de-esser is designed to remove the sibilance, or *s* sounds, from speech, but it can also be used to remove high-frequency noises from any sound. Like the ducker, this device is also a side-chain compressor. However, instead of using a separate source for the side-chain input, a copy of the main signal is used after being sent through a highpass filter. Then, whenever there is substantial energy in the high frequency range, the compressor quickly reduces the amplitude of the main signal to lower the presence of sibilance and other harsh noises.

Multiband Compressor

The multiband compressor passes the incoming signal through a bank of lowpass, high-pass, and bandpass filters to separate the signal into multiple frequency bands. Each band is then compressed individually, allowing much greater control over the balance of the entire frequency spectrum than what is available with just an EQ filter. Although multi-band compressors may be used on individual sounds, they are most frequently used on the entire mix to create a sonic balance of all the frequencies.

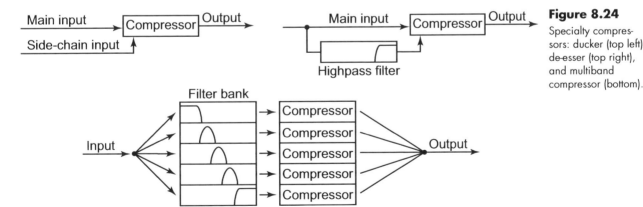

Figure 8.24
Specialty compressors: ducker (top left), de-esser (top right), and multiband compressor (bottom).

Expander

Demo 8.12

As opposed to a compressor, which turns down the levels on sounds that go above the threshold, the expander (often called a downward expander) reduces the levels on sounds that fall below the threshold, thus creating a wider, expanded dynamic range. In practice, the expander is used to turn the level down on a sound when it is not playing. This most commonly occurs in the recording studio when an instrument or vocalist is being recorded with a microphone. During the time the musician is not playing or singing, the expander will automatically reduce the level of the audio signal to help eliminate background noise that might be captured by the microphone.

Gate (Noise Gate)

A gate, or noise gate, is nearly identical to an expander except that rather than turning the outgoing audio down when it falls below the threshold, it simply mutes the audio (closes the gate). Because gates operate so abruptly, they are often noticeable when they open and close. For this reason, most people prefer to use an expander rather than a gate.

Since synthesizers, especially digital ones, tend to be extremely quiet, the use of expanders and gates is usually unnecessary for noise control purposes. Rather, these processors are often used to create "choppy" and pulsing sounds by setting the threshold high enough to trigger while the incoming sound is still audible.

In many regards, the expander/gate controls work just like those on a compressor/limiter, but with a few primary differences. As mentioned already, the expander engages when the incoming signal falls below the threshold rather than when it rises above it. This often leads to a bit of confusion regarding the attack and release time controls. Opposite to a compressor, attack controls how quickly the signal turns back up, and release controls how quickly it turns down after falling below the threshold.

Another difference between expanders and compressors is the way the ratio is expressed. On some expanders, the ratio is reversed and indicated as Outgoing:Incoming rather than the Incoming:Outgoing ratio used on compressors. Thus, a ratio of 5:1 means that the outgoing signal drops 5 dB for every 1 dB by which the incoming signal falls below the threshold. Other expanders, rather than reversing the order of the ratio, indicate it as either 1:5 or 0.2:1. In both cases, the signal is reduced to one-fifth of its amplitude. Regardless of how the ratio is expressed, though, the larger the difference between the two sides of the ratio, the more the signal is reduced.

Because many sounds have a long decay, expanders and gates frequently have additional controls that allow sounds to die away naturally, rather than be chopped off when the amplitude falls below the threshold. This process is handled in two ways. Most expanders and gates will have one of these controls, and a few provide both for even greater control.

- *Hold time* is an additional delay after the sound drops below the threshold before the release time begins.
- *Release threshold* is a second threshold level below the attack threshold level. When the incoming sound rises above the attack threshold, the expander/gate opens to allow the sound to be heard. As the sound dies away, it has to fall below the lower release threshold before the expander/gate begins to turn the gain down.

Compound Effects

Because of the large amount of processing power and memory required to create sounds on a synthesizer, it is important to understand that most synthesizers allocate a specific number of memory blocks to handle effects processing. If a synthesizer says it can run two simultaneous effects, this means it can load and operate two separate effects processes at the same time in addition to all the synthesis processing. So you might have a Chorus in one memory block and a Reverb in the other.

Look through the effects list on many synthesizers, and you will often see compound or "chained" effects like "Delay+Reverb," "Chorus+Reverb," and "Flanger+Chorus." It is tempting to believe that you can load Flanger+Chorus into one block and then Reverb into the other and magically create three effects memory blocks. Unfortunately, this is not the case. What happens with compound effects is that the synthesizer has "light" versions of the two chained processes, so that they still use only one block of memory. This may be adequate for your needs, but you should be aware that the quality of the two items in the compound effect is likely not as good as it is in the individual items if loaded separately.

Internal vs. External Effects

As mentioned at the beginning of this chapter, in addition to the effects built into synthesizers, there are an incredible number of external software and hardware effects processors available today. Synthesizer manufacturers tend to place their emphasis on the sound-making capabilities of their instruments and often treat effects processing as somewhat of an afterthought. As a result, it is not unusual for the effects processes built into a synthesizer to be inferior to the sound-making quality of the instrument.

Many synthesizer performers bypass the effects stage altogether on their instruments and use external processors on their sounds. A hardware, or dedicated, software effect will almost always be superior to the one in the instrument. If your hardware synthesizer has multiple outputs, you can assign different sounds to individual outputs and process them separately with hardware effects units. If you are working with a software synthesizer inside a digital audio workstation (DAW), you can route the sounds to various channels in the DAW and process them separately. Another advantage of working in a DAW is that you can simply record the synthesizer output with the effect process applied and then free up the memory needed for that sound to make it available for other processing.

Regardless of whether you use internal or external effects, these processes afford a wide array of sonic possibilities for polishing your synthesizer sounds. The sheer number of effects can seem overwhelming at first, but if you group them into the categories we have used in this chapter, it will help you make sense of them. It will also help, as you begin your exploration of effects, to use a simple sound such as a basic sawtooth wave. This way, you will be able to easily ascertain what the effect is contributing to the sound. As you experiment with your effects, be sure to frequently turn the effect bypass on and off so that you can hear the difference every little change in effect has on the sound.

Your Turn

Working with Crystal

The final output stage and effects processing for Crystal is found on the Mixer tab. In addition to the effects processing controls, the mixer provides sliders for sending signals to four delay lines and to a four-band frequency splitter as well as providing output pan and level controls for all signals. The sheer number of controls on this tab can be overwhelming at first, so before you begin working with effects take a look at the arrangement and controls in this window. Refer to Figure 8.25 as you read the descriptions of the controls below.

Figure 8.25

The Mixer tab is divided into three panes, labeled Mixer, Delays, and Splits. Refer to this figure for the location of the controls as they are described and explained below.

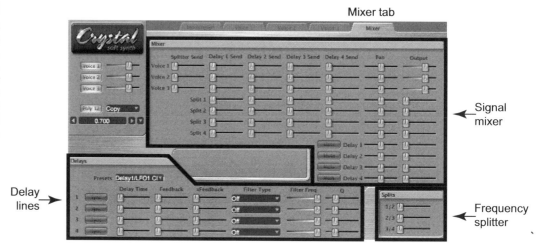

Frequency Splitter

In the bottom-right corner of the Mixer tab is a pane labeled Splits, with three sliders for adjusting the crossover frequencies of a four-band frequency splitter (see Figure 8.26). The frequency splitter uses bandpass filters to separate a signal into four frequency bands, and the sliders adjust the frequency of the crossover point between two adjacent bands (e.g., the 1/2 slider controls the crossover between bands one and two). The frequency splitter allows you to apply effects and delays to specific ranges of frequencies in the sound.

Figure 8.26

The three sliders in the Splits pane adjust the position of the crossover frequency between adjacent bands in a four-band frequency splitter.

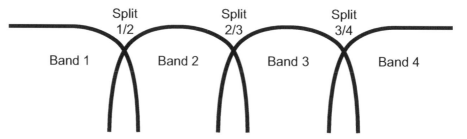

Delay Lines

In the lower left of the Mixer tab, you find the four delay lines and their controls in a pane labeled Delays.

- *Presets* allows you to select from a list of preset delay line configurations.
- *Sync* synchronizes the delay time to the tempo of the host application.
- *Delay Time* sets the initial amount of delay.
    - With Sync off, the delay time is in milliseconds.
    - With Sync on, the delay time is in beat subdivisions.
- *Feedback* controls the amount of feedback within the delay line.

- *xFeedback* produces a cross-feedback between pairs of delay lines.
  - Delay 1 and 2 are paired together. Increasing the xFeedback on delay 1 sends its delayed signal into delay 2, and vice versa.
  - Delay 3 and 4 are paired together. Increasing the xFeedback on delay 3 sends its delayed signal into delay 4, and vice versa.
- *Filter Type* selects a filter for the delay line.
- *Filter Freq* sets the cutoff-center frequency for the delay line's filter.
- *Q* controls the steepness of the transition slope(s) in the filter.
  - Filters can also be used without any delay by setting the delay time to zero.
  - If a filter type is set to Reverb, the other controls change their function.
    - Delay Time controls reverb pre-delay.
    - Feedback controls reverb room size.
    - Filter Freq controls the cutoff frequency of the reverb's lowpass filter.

Mixer

The largest pane on the Mixer tab contains numerous sliders for sending signals to the frequency splitter, the delay lines, and the main synthesizer output.

- *Splitter Send* controls the amount of each voice sent to the frequency splitter.
- *Delay Send* controls the amount of each voice and frequency split sent to the four delay lines.
- *Pan* positions each signal in the left-to-right stereophonic field.
- *Output* controls the level of each signal in the final synthesizer mix.
- *Mute* quickly removes a delay line from the final mix.

Applying Effects

Crystal does not have amplitude-based effects, and the only frequency-based effects are audio filters. However, with four separate delay lines, its ability to apply time-base effects to sounds is quite powerful. As with the demonstrations in previous chapters, what I present here is merely a sampling of the kinds of effects processes that can be added to a synthesized sound.

For the sake of making these examples as direct and obvious as possible, let's use a single pulse wave oscillator. Load the default preset and change the sine wave oscillator for voice 1 to a pulse wave (Type: **Synthesized:SawSquare**, PulseMix: 1.000, Pulse-Width: 1.000). Leave the filter turned off, and the amplitude envelope set to the flat default. You will use only voice 1 for these demonstrations. Unless specified, assume all controls are at their default positions.

Comb Filter
- *Mixer*
  - Voice 1: Delay 1 Send at 1.000
  - Voice 1: Output at 0.760
  - Delay 1: Output at 0.760
- *Delays*
  - Delay 1: Delay Time 27 ms (0.027 sec)

> • *Splits*
> > • Not used

A short delay mixed back with the original signal creates the metallic sound of the comb filter. Turn the Mute button for delay 1 on and off to compare the difference between the original sound and the comb-filtered version.

For variations on this effect, try different delay times up to around 50 ms. (Delays longer than this become noticeable as a second sound.) Raise the feedback slider, and notice the high-frequency tone that begins to enter the sound. Apply a resonant lowpass filter and experiment with a number of cutoff frequency and Q settings. If you push the filter into uncontrolled self-oscillation, either move the Q slider to the left or select **Off** as the Filter Type to stop it.

Tap Delay

> • *Mixer*
> > • Voice 1: Delay 1 Send at 1.000
> > • Voice 1: Output at 0.760
> > • Delay 1: Output at 0.760
> • *Delays*
> > • Delay 1: Delay Time 220 ms (0.220 sec)
> • *Splits*
> > • Not used

Instead of a comb filter, this longer delay time creates a secondary echo. As before, experiment with different delay times and filter settings. However, now when you raise the feedback slider, instead of generating a high-frequency tone a repeating set of echoes is produced.

Move the feedback slider all the way to the right, and play a quick single note. The note will continue to repeat for a long time, eventually dying away after more than a minute or so. With the feedback slider set at 0.500, the echoes die away much more quickly as more of a decaying rhythmic passage.

Rhythmic Tap Delay

Many synthesizers allow you to easily create rhythmic patterns by synchronizing the delay to a tempo and choosing note values for the delay times. The beauty of this approach, for instance, is that if you choose an eighth note for your delay time, the delay time will always be an eighth note, even if the tempo speeds up or slows down. For this example, keep all the settings from the previous multitap delay example.

> • *Mixer*
> > • Voice 1: Delay 1, 2, and 3 Sends at 1.000; Pan at 0.000; Output at 0.760
> > • Delay 1: Pan at 0.340; Output at 0.400
> > • Delay 2: Pan at 0.660; Output at 0.340
> > • Delay 3: Pan at 1.000; Output at 0.200
> • *Delays*: Turn the Sync button on for delay 1, 2, and 3.
> > • Delay 1: Delay Time 3/16 (delay by a dotted-eighth note)
> > • Delay 2: Delay Time 1/4 (delay by a quarter note)
> > • Delay 3: Delay Time 7/16 (delay by a quarter + a dotted-eighth note)

- *Splits*
    - Not used

Notice that this setting produces a dotted-eighth/sixteenth note pattern that is synchronized to the tempo in the Crystal Player keyboard window. Instead of your having to recalculate all the delay times whenever the tempo changes, the duration of the delays automatically adjusts to maintain the rhythm.

Shimmering Slap Delay

In this next example, you will use the frequency splitter to create a ping-pong, slap delay that gets brighter with every echo. Begin with your settings from the Rhythmic Tap Delay example above, and change only the sliders indicated below.

- *Mixer*
    - Voice 1: Splitter Send at 1.000; Delay 1, 2, and 3 Sends at 0.000; Pan at 0.000
    - Split 1: Delay 1 Send at 1.000
    - Split 2: Delay 2 Send at 1.000
    - Split 3: Delay 3 Send at 1.000
    - Delay 1: Pan at 1.000
    - Delay 2: Pan at 0.000
    - Delay 3: Pan at 1.000
- *Delays*: All Sync buttons turned off
    - Delay 1: Delay Time 0.106
    - Delay 2: Delay Time 0.220
    - Delay 3: Delay Time 0.328
- *Splits*
    - 1/2: Approximately 4,000 Hz
    - 2/3: Approximately 8,000 Hz
    - 3/4: Approximately 12,000 Hz

Now, instead of a dotted-eighth/sixteenth rhythm, you hear a rapid back-and-forth echo that gets brighter with every "slap." To accomplish this, you send the original signal to the frequency splitter and use its output to create the delayed echoes. As before, experiment with delay times, split frequencies, feedback amounts, and delay filters. This type of delay is quite effective for creating sounds that seem to bounce around the room.

Flanger

Remember that a flanger is a comb filter with an LFO modulating the delay time. For this example, go back to the setting you used in the initial Comb Filter example.

- *Mixer*
    - Voice 1: Delay 1 Send at 1.000; Pan at 0.500; Output at 0.760
    - Delay 1: Output at 0.760
- *Delays*
    - Delay 1: Delay Time 5 ms (0.005 sec)
- *Splits*
    - Not used

- *Modulation matrix* (Modulation tab)
  - Source 1: **LFO1**
  - Target 1: **Delay1 Time**; Low = 0.400; High = 0.600
- *LFO 1*
  - Type: **Triangle**
  - Center: 0.500
  - Swing: 0.500
  - Rate: 2.00 cps
  - Scale: 1.000

When you first play a note, the flanger effect will be rather subtle. To produce the "classic" flanger sound, raise the delay 1 feedback slider above 0.500. The higher the feedback is raised, the more pronounced the pitch shift of the flanger becomes. Control the wet-dry mix by adjusting the balance between the voice 1 Output and the delay 1 Output.

Stereo Chorus

For this example, you will create two modulated delay lines. Begin with your settings from the Flanger you have just created.

- *Mixer*
  - Voice 1: Delay 1 and 2 Sends at 1.000; Pan at 0.500; Output at 0.760
  - Delay 1: Pan at 0.240; Output at 0.600
  - Delay 2: Pan at 0.760; Output at 0.600
- *Delays*
  - Delay 1: Delay Time 27 ms; Feedback at 0.100
  - Delay 2: Delay Time 41 ms; Feedback at 0.100
- *Splits*
  - Not used
- *Modulation Matrix*
  - Source 1: **LFO1**
  - Target 1: **Delay1 Time**; Low = 0.440; High = 0.560
  - Source 2: **LFO1**
  - Target 2: **Delay2 Time**; Low = 0.560; High = 0.440
- *LFO 1*
  - Type: **Sine**
  - Center: 0.500
  - Swing: 0.500
  - Rate: 0.10cps
  - Scale: 1.000

For a more random chorus effect, set up LFO 2 just like LFO 1, but with a rate of 0.08 cps, and assign it to **Delay2 Time** instead of using LFO 1. This will cause the two LFO sweeps to slowly go in and out of phase with one another. By leaving the original sound panned to the center and the two delay lines panned to opposite sides, you create a rich stereo chorus. Widening the Low and High sliders in the modulation matrix will increase the depth of the chorus effect. As with all of these examples, experiment with delay times, feedback amounts, filters, etc.

Stereo Reverb

As mentioned earlier, to create a reverb processor in Crystal you change a delay line's Filter Type to Reverb and use the other controls to shape the sound of the room. For this example, you send the signal to a pair of delay lines panned left and right to create a stereo reverb.

- *Mixer*
    - Voice 1: Delay 1 and 2 Sends at 1.000; Pan at 0.500; Output at 0.760
    - Delay 1: Pan at 0.000; Output at 0.260
    - Delay 2: Pan at 1.000; Output at 0.260
- *Delays*
    - Delay 1 Time: 17 ms
    - Delay 2 Time: 18 ms
    - Feedback: 0.500
    - Filter Type: **Reverb**
    - Filter Freq: Approximately 8,000 Hz
    - Q: 0.500
- *Splits*
    - Not used

Adjusting the Delay Time controls the ratio between the distance of the sound source and the reflective surfaces. Shorter delay times create the effect of being much closer to the sound source and farther from the reflective surfaces, while longer delay times sound as if you have moved farther from the sound source and closer to the reflective surfaces. Feedback controls the perceived size of the reverberant room. As you increase the feedback amount, the room size increases.

Time-based effects processors are some of the most versatile and commonly used effects on a synthesizer. Merely mixing the delayed copy of a signal back with the original can create profound changes in the synthesizer sound. Learning to use delay lines and other time-based processes will give you a huge array of effects to use in polishing your sounds. Although reverb is quite complex to create, if your synthesizer does not have a dedicated flanger or chorus you can easily build one by modulating delay lines as you did above.

Using Your Own Synthesizer(s)

1. Does your synthesizer have an effects stage?
    A. Is it part of the output stage?
    B. Do you have the capability of applying effects earlier in the synthesis process, or only at the end?
2. Do you have time-based effects?
    A. Delay?
    B. Flanger?
    C. Chorus?
    D. Reverb?
    E. Phaser?
    F. Others?

3. Can your time-based effects be synchronized to a tempo?

4. Do you have frequency-based effects?

    A. Equalization?

    B. Frequency or pitch shifter?

    C. Harmonizer?

    D. Vocoder?

    E. Ring modulator?

    F. Others?

5. Do you have amplitude-based effects?

    A. Distortion and saturation?

    B. Bit crusher?

    C. Compression?

    D. Limiter?

    E. Expander?

    F. Gate?

    G. Others?

6. What modulation sources can you use with your effects processors?

7. How many effects can you use at the same time?

8. Can you apply effects individually to the sound sources, or are they global to the entire synthesizer output?

Throughout this text, we have been examining every stage of the synthesis process in detail as if we were taking a synthesizer apart. Now it is time to put the instrument back together. In Chapter 9, you will use all of these stages and processes to create some of the more popular types of synthesizer sounds by starting with the raw materials of oscillators and refining those sounds to a polished finish.

9

Putting It All Together

Creating *and* Refining *Your Own Synthesized Sounds*

Online materials for this chapter:

http://www.oup.com/refiningsound/Chapter9.html

In each chapter of *Refining Sound*, we have focused on a single element or stage in the synthesis process. Now, it is time to put all of those elements together so that you can begin creating and refining your own synthesized sounds. This chapter is essentially one big Your Turn section, as you use Crystal to create some of the most common types of synthesizer sounds.

With each of the sounds below, the indicated settings are suggestions. In every case, you are encouraged to try settings other than those given, to explore a number of possibilities and get the most out of your experience. Because Crystal combines different functions under the same tab, we first present an overview of the various synthesis stages for each patch and then provide step-by-step instructions for creating the sound according to the layout of each tab in Crystal.

Lead Patch

Audio 9.1

Listen to the sound of the Lead Patch example on the Companion Website (Audio 9.1). Much like the lead guitar in a rock band, lead synthesizer sounds usually have a timbre that allows them to be easily heard even in the midst of a dense sonic texture. Their brilliance and "edginess" make them the perfect synthesizer patches for prominent melodic or monophonic solo parts. To create that edginess, leads tend to feature bright, basic waveforms like sawtooth and square, and they often have extremely quick attacks and releases when triggered. Use the descriptions and step-by-step instructions below to create this "funky" lead patch, suitable for a number of punchy melodic and rhythmic voices.

Oscillators

As mentioned above, lead sounds require a certain edginess to cut through a sonic texture, and they frequently rely on sawtooth and square waves to do so. For this patch, you combine synced versions of both sawtooth and square waves, with the "reediness" of the square wave being slightly more prominent than the buzzy sound of the sawtooth wave.

Envelope Generators

To give the sound a more percussive quality, the amplitude envelope for this sound has quick attack and release stages with no decay so that the sound sustains at 100 percent. You will also create multiple copies of a modulation envelope that causes the sound to have a quick wow at the beginning of every note.

Filters

Both oscillators will have a resonant lowpass filter with the filter's cutoff frequency being modulated by the modulation envelope described above. To add a bit of "dirt" to the sound, distortion will also be applied to both oscillator sounds.

Modulators

In addition to the modulator envelopes already mentioned, you will set up an LFO to create a subtle vibrato and another LFO to modulate the delay time for a chorus effect. Keytracking, velocity, and the modulation wheel are also used as modulation sources.

Effects

To give the sound a bit of echo, a medium delay is used along with both chorus and reverb to provide some "space" in the patch.

Step-by-step Instructions

Modulation Tab

Images 9.1

Load the default preset, rename it "Lead" in the control value display, and then write it to one of the unused preset slots.[1] Ensure that voice 1 is active in the voice mixer and turn its volume slider all the way up to 1.000. Since we want this to be a monophonic sound, click the Poly button until it turns off. Select **Legato portamento** from the dropdown menu next to the Poly button, so that you will get a new attack even if the old note is still being held and there will be a slight slide to the new note. We will return to this tab later, but for now, switch to the Voice 1 tab.

Voice 1 Tab

Create a pulse wave oscillator by selecting **Synthesized:SawSquare** from the Type menu, sliding the PulseMix slider all the way to the right, and the PulseWidth slider to 0.780. Lower the oscillator pitch by one octave (**–1**), and turn on "hard sync" by moving the Mogrify slider to a setting of 0.720. Feel free to experiment with the values for both the PulseWidth and Mogrify sliders.

Create a nearly square amplitude envelope by first selecting **Flat 4 pt** from the amplitude envelope preset menu. Slide the third handle (red) to the right so that it is almost, but not quite, directly above the fourth (blue) handle. This envelope will cause the sound to have an extremely quick attack and release, such that it has an almost per-

---

1 If you have forgotten how to name and store a new patch, see the box entitled "Naming and Storing a New Patch in Crystal" in the Your Turn section of Chapter 3.

cussive quality. To give the amplitude envelope a velocity response, move the VelSen slider to 0.420. If you make the amplitude envelope too sensitive to velocity, you run the risk of notes with softer velocities not being heard as those notes will have a lower envelope amplitude.

You will now begin creating the wow in the sound by selecting **ResLoPass** as the Type in the Filters pane. Turn the filter envelope on and set the LoFreq slider to 374 Hz and the HiFreq slider all the way to the right. Give the filter a substantial resonance peak by sliding the Resonance slider up to 0.760, and create a little grunginess in the sound by moving the Saturation and Shaper sliders to 0.120 and 0.740 respectively.

Select **Flat 4 pt** from the filter envelope preset menu. You will use this envelope to make the filter cutoff quickly sweep up and back down at the beginning of every note. To do so, move the Scale slider all the way to the right and set the four breakpoints as follows:

- (Blue) 0.00, 0.37 kHz[2]
- (Yellow) 0.05, 17.1 kHz
- (Red) 0.15, 2.97 kHz
- (Blue) 0.50, 0.37 kHz

When you play notes on your MIDI keyboard, you should now hear a somewhat edgy timbre with a fast filter sweep creating a wow in the sound. Since we want to use most of the same settings for voice 2, select **Copy Voice1** from the menu next to the Poly button, and then select **Paste to Voice2** from that same menu.

Voice 2 Tab

By using the copy and paste function, you will see that voice 2 is now configured exactly the same as voice 1. Because our goal here is to have two oscillators with similar, not identical, timbres, you will make only a few changes to voice 2.

In the Oscillator pane, turn the pulse wave into a sawtooth wave by sliding the PulseMix slider all the way to the left (since it is now a sawtooth wave, the PulseWidth control has no effect). This oscillator will also be synced, but with a different frequency master oscillator, by moving the Mogrify slider all the way to the right.

Since the primary sound of this patch will come from the pulse wave, turn the level of voice 2 down to 0.640 in the voice mixer. With the addition of the sawtooth oscillator, you should now hear a bit more edge to the composite sound of the two oscillators. With our basic sound now created, let's bring it to life with modulators and effects.

Modulation Tab

Switch back to the modulation tab and assign Key track as the Source in the first two rows of the modulation matrix. Set the targets of the two rows to **Voice1 Filt Freq** and **Voice2 Filt Freq** respectively. For both rows, set the Low slider to approximately 3 kHz and the High slider to around 12 kHz. This will cause the filter cutoff frequency for both voices to move higher and lower with the notes you play on your keyboard. Without this setting, higher notes begin to sound darker as they approach the filter cutoff frequency because more and more of their harmonics are being filtered.

---

2 As before, if a breakpoint type is not specified, it should be set to **linear**.

Create a small vibrato in the oscillators by setting LFO 1's Type to a triangle wave with both the Center and Swing sliders at 0.500. Set the LFO Rate slider to 5.11 cps. In the modulation matrix, set **LFO1** as the Source in rows three and four with the targets set to **Voice1 Pitch** and **Voice2 Pitch** respectively. For vibrato, you generally want only a small amount of pitch change, so set the Low and High sliders for both rows to –0.2 and 0.2 respectively. When you play a note, you should now hear a small amount of vibrato in the sound.

Now intensify the timbral shifting effect of this sound by modulating the frequency of the master oscillator for both of the synced oscillators. However, you will modulate the pulse wave sync with the same envelope that the filter is using, and you will modulate the sawtooth sync with the modulation wheel.

Since Crystal does not allow you to assign the filter envelope to anything else, go to the Voice 1 tab and choose **Copy** from the filter envelope preset menu. Switch back to the Modulation tab and select **Paste** from the preset menu of Modulation Envelope 1, and set the Scale slider all the way to the right. You now have the same envelope for your first modulation envelope generator as for your filters. Select **ModEnvelope1** as the Source in row 5 of the modulation matrix, with **Voice1 Mogrify** selected as the target. The goal here is to enhance the wow of the filter sweep, not overpower it. Therefore, set the Low and High sliders to a narrow range of 0.500 and 0.740 respectively. To hear the difference this modulation makes, alternately mute and unmute this row in the modulation matrix as you play notes on your keyboard.

In the sixth row of the modulation matrix, select **Mod Wheel** as the Source and **Voice2 Mogrify** as the Target. Since moving the Mogrify control lower makes the sound brighter and vice versa, reverse the positions of the Low and High sliders so that the Low slider is all the way to the right and the High slider is lowered to 0.340. Now when you push the modulation wheel up, the timbre will brighten, as we normally expect it to do. You will make one more visit to the Modulation tab in a moment, but for now switch to the Mixer tab to create your effects for this sound.

Mixer Tab

Up to this point, the sound has been dry and quite forward-sounding, or what audio engineers often call "in your face." Using the delay lines in the mixer, you will give your sound a greater sense of space and life by adding some echoes, a bit of chorus, and some reverberation.

Turn the Delay 1 Send all the way up for both voices. In the Delays pane, turn the Delay Time for the first delay up to a medium delay length of 304 ms (0.304 sec). To hear this delay, turn up the Output slider for delay 1 in the Mixer pane. You now hear a single echo of your sound. What we want to do, though, is create a soft, decaying slap echo. To do so, turn the Feedback control up to 0.140 and the delay 1 Output level down to 0.100. To alter the timbre of the delay, set the Filter Type for this delay to **XRes-LoPass** with the cutoff frequency around 9 kHz and a Q of 0.260. Now your sound has a "bounce" to it that decays rather quickly so it does not get in the way of other notes.

To "fatten" the sound, add some chorus by sending both voices to delay 2 and modulating the delay time with an LFO. Send both voices to the second delay line by turning the Delay 2 Send sliders all the way up. Set the second delay time to a short value of 41 ms with a small feedback amount of 0.100. You will not use the filter for this line, so leave it turned off. In order to make our short delay into a chorus, we need to modulate the delay time with an LFO. So switch back one more time to the Modulation tab.

Modulation Tab

In the LFO's pane, click the "2" button to configure LFO 2. Set the Type to **Sine** with the Center and Swing sliders both set to 0.500. For this LFO, you want a rather slow oscillation, so move the Rate slider to a value of 0.10 cps. Since you have already used all six rows of page 1 in the modulation matrix, change to page 2 and select **LFO2** as the first Source with **Delay2 Time** as the Target. And since you do not want a large LFO sweep in a chorus, position the Low and High sliders to narrow values of 0.400 and 0.600 respectively; then switch back to the Mixer tab.

Mixer Tab

In the Mixer tab, you now see that the Delay Time slider for the second delay has turned orange, indicating it is being modulated. If you have not already done so, turn up the Output slider for delay 2 in the mixer to hear the chorus effect you have created. Try turning the delay 2 Mute button on and off to hear the difference the chorus produces in the sound.

Although the sound has more life to it now, it still feels a bit as if it's in your face. Use the third delay line to add reverberation to the sound. As before, turn the Delay 3 Sends for both voices all the way up. Select **Reverb** as the Filter Type for delay 3. As you will recall, selecting Reverb changes the functions of several of the delay controls to suit the needs of a reverb processor. Move the Delay Time slider to 17 ms as the "pre-delay" value. Adjust the room size to a small-to-medium size by moving the Feedback slider to 0.280. Roll off a bit of the higher frequencies in the reverberation tail by lowering the Filter Freq to around 7 kHz with a Q value of 0.280. Turn up the Output level of delay 3 in the mixer, and you should now hear that your sound has reverberation applied to it.

To fine-tune the balance of these effects, adjust the ratio of the Output sliders of the two original voices and the three delay lines. You already have delay 1's Output set to 0.100 to create a soft echo. Turn delay 2's Output slider all the way up to really fatten the sound. Set the delay 3 Output slider to 0.700 to create a fairly reverberant sound. Try lowering the two voice Output sliders so all that remains is the processed sound. Simply changing these Output sliders can have a huge impact on the overall sound.

You should now have a punchy lead sound with a quick wow at the beginning of each note. Be sure to save this sound by writing it to the same location you have been using in the Patches pane of the Modulation tab.

Harmony Patch

Audio 9.2

Listen to the sound of the Harmony Patch example on the Companion Website (Audio 9.2). As opposed to the in-your-face quality of lead sounds, harmony sounds tend to be the "shrinking violet" of the synthesizer world. These voices are typically used to play chords, and otherwise support the harmony of the primary voices. Because harmony sounds are used as background to the primary sounds, they tend to be created with softer timbres and rather gentle envelopes. Furthermore, because they are often stacked to create chords, harmony sounds usually have very little activity in them, as layering multiple dynamic sounds together generally creates a rather cacophonous sound.

Because most synthesizers are designed to make their sounds as dynamic as possible, creating these simpler harmony sounds that fit into the background can be surprisingly difficult. The trick is to create a sound that has some motion and energy in it, but not so much that stacking the notes into chords causes the patch to move into the foreground. These types of sounds often employ subtle delays and modulations of timbre to keep them interesting. Use the descriptions and step-by-step instructions below to create this "glistening" harmony voice suitable for playing sustained chords.

Oscillators

For the Lead sound, you used sawtooth and pulse waves to give the sound a bright edge. Although it might be tempting to use darker waves like sine and triangle for a harmony voice, you will have more options by continuing to use brighter waves, but with substantial lowpass filtering. For this patch, you will use two pulse wave oscillators and a sawtooth oscillator tuned in a three-octave stack.

Envelope Generators

The amplitude envelope shape for this kind of sound often has a slow attack and release. Because the goal is to create a small amount of energy in the sound, you can use slightly contrasting attack times so that the three voices fade up at different times.

Filters

Filters play a large role in this patch. They warm up the sound of the pulse wave oscillators as well as the multiple delay lines in the mixer. An envelope-modulated resonant highpass filter is employed to add the glistening effect to this sound.

Modulators

As mentioned above, modulators are employed subtly to keep the patch interesting without become too busy a texture. In addition to the modulator envelopes already mentioned, you will use the modulation wheel and three LFOs to create gentle timbral shifts in the voices as well as a chorus effect and a sweeping pan effect.

Effects

Although a small amount of chorus is used, the primary effects on this patch will be successive delays to create the effect of overlapping envelopes between the voices.

Step-by-step Instructions

Modulation Tab

Images 9.2   Load the default preset, rename it "Harmony" in the control value display, and then write it to one of the unused preset slots. Ensure that voice 1 is active in the voice mixer and turn its volume slider all the way up to 1.000. You will eventually turn on all three voices, but for now leave voices 2 and 3 turned off. Since you will use this voice to play chords, you want a large polyphony setting. Click the Poly button until it indicates **Poly 24**.

Voice 1 Tab

Voice 1 will be the middle voice of our three-octave stack. Select **Synthesized:SawSquare** as the oscillator Type and push the PulseMix slider all the way to the right to create a pulse wave. Set the PulseWidth slider about three-quarters of the way to the right (approximately 0.740) to create a slightly reedy pulse wave sound. Leave the Mogrify slider all the way off, and ensure that the tunings for Octave, Semitones, and FineTune are all set to zero.

Give the sound a slow attack and release by setting a four-point amplitude envelope as follows:

- (Blue) 0.00, 0.00
- (Yellow) 1.31, 1.00
- (Red) 1.50, 1.00
- (Blue) 3.00, 0.00
- VelSen slider at 0.400

In the Filters pane, select **Low Pass** as the Type with a cutoff frequency of approximately 2 kHz. Since the cutoff is so low, make the transition slope as shallow as possible by moving the Q slider all the way to the left. Leave the Saturation, Shaper, and Envelope turned off.

You should now have a somewhat nasal sound that slowly ramps up and down when you press and release a key on your MIDI keyboard. You will configure the second voice similarly to the first voice, so to save some time select **Copy Voice1** from the menu next to the Poly button, and then select **Paste to Voice2**.

Voice 2 Tab

Lower voice 2 by an octave by selecting **−1** from the Octave menu, and give it a slightly different timbre by moving the PulseWidth slider to a setting of approximately 0.260.

Shorten the attack stage of this voice so that the lower tone enters first by adjusting the amplitude envelope as follows:

- (Blue) 0.00, 0.00
- (Yellow) 0.50, 1.00
- (Red) 0.75, 1.00
- (Blue) 2.00, 0.00
- Turn the VelSyn slider all the way off. Since lower frequencies are harder to hear, you probably do not want much velocity sensitivity on this voice.

Since this voice is an octave lower, lower the cutoff frequency of the filter to around 1.3 kHz to maintain a similar frequency spectrum to voice 1. With both voices active, you should now hear the sound in octaves, with the upper octave entering slightly later than the lower one.

211

Voice 3 Tab

This voice will create the glistening sound in the patch. So that you can focus exclusively on this sound for the moment, turn the first two voices off in the voice mixer and activate voice 3 by clicking its button and raising its level.

Again, choose **Synthesized:SawSquare** as the oscillator type, but turn it into a sawtooth wave by moving the PulseMix slider all the way to the left. Turn oscillator sync on by moving the Mogrify slider to 0.160, and raise the pitch an octave by selecting **+1** from the Octave menu. You should now hear a somewhat edgy, high-frequency sawtooth sound.

The glisten effect needs to fade in after the two main voices have been established. It also helps if, once the voice fades in, the effect recedes a bit to prevent overwhelming the other two voices. When you release the MIDI key, this voice will fade down at a faster initial rate to create another timbral shift in the sound. To create this envelope, adjust a four-point envelope as follows (note that this envelope uses curved transitions):

- (Blue) 0.00, 0.00, **curve positive**
- (Yellow) 1.50, 1.00, **curve positive**
- (Red) 2.00, 0.85, **curve negative**
- (Blue) 3.50, 0.00
- VelSen slider at 0.280

For the sound of this voice, you will exaggerate the harmonics and minimize the fundamental with an envelope-modulated resonant highpass filter. Select **ResHiPass** as the filter Type and turn the filter envelope on. So that the filter envelope tracks with the amplitude envelope, select **Copy** from the amplitude envelope's preset menu and then **Paste** from the filter envelope's preset menu. The two envelopes should now be identical.

If you leave the LoFreq and HiFreq sliders set to their respective low and high extremes, you will hear that the sound of this voice disappears as the envelope pushes the cutoff frequency all the way up to 17 kHz. Therefore, make the sweep of the envelope narrower by lowering the HiFreq slider to around 8 kHz. To focus the ears on this sweep, raise the Resonance slider to 0.240. You should now hear a high-frequency tone that sweeps in and settles when you press a key and then drops in level and timbre when you release the key.

Reactivate the other two voices, and you will quickly notice that voice 3 tends to dominate the other two. In the voice mixer, leave the sliders for voices 1 and 2 all the way to the right, but lower the slider for voice 3 to around 0.160. The upper voice should have a subtler effect that adds the glistening quality to the overall sound. Now that the basic sound has been created, give it a subtle dynamic quality with some modulation and delay effects.

Modulation Tab

Recall that you used different PulseWidth settings for voices 1 and 2. You will now add a bit of LFO modulation to those settings to create a subtle timbral shift in the two voices. Configure LFO 1 as a triangle wave with its Center and Swing both set to 0.500. Give it a moderate Rate of .5 Hz (0.50 cps). In the modulation matrix, select **LFO1** as the source in the first two rows with the targets being **Voice1 PulseWidth** and **Voice2 PulseWidth** respectively. Remember, you want the modulation amount to be subtle, so narrow the Low and High sliders for both rows such that they are a little to either side of the position of the Pulse Width slider on that voice's tab. For example, you positioned the Pulse Width slider on the first voice at 0.740. Therefore, in the first row of the modulation matrix, put the Low slider a little below that (0.600) and the High slider a little above (0.880). Similarly, set the Low and High sliders for the second row to 0.120 and 0.400 respectively (the Pulse Width slider on the voice tab is set to 0.260). You should now hear a small, cyclical timbre shift in voices 1 and 2 as the pulse width of each wave is subtly modulated back and forth. You will return to the modulation tab in a few minutes, but for now switch to the Mixer tab to begin creating the delay lines that add more depth to this patch.

Mixer Tab

In the mixer, you will send the three voices through two delays to thicken the sound. However, you will also add a tiny bit of chorus to voice 1 before it enters the delay lines.

Configure delay 2 as a medium feedback delay with a Delay Time of 270 ms and Feedback set to 0.500. You will come back to delay 1 in a few minutes, but for now skip it. Since the goal is to keep the darker timbre of the sound, select **Low Pass** as the Filter Type with a cutoff around 2 kHz and a medium Q of 0.500.

Configure delay 3 as another medium feedback delay, but with a longer Delay Time of 549 ms and a lower Feedback amount of 0.320. Again, choose the **Low Pass** filter, but make it even darker with the cutoff set to around 1.3 kHz and a Q of 0.500.

Now, configure delay 1 as a chorus similarly to what you did in the Lead patch. Set the Delay Time to 41 ms with a small amount of feedback (0.100). You will need to switch back to the Modulation tab to configure the LFO for the chorus.

Modulation Tab

Configure LFO 2 as a sine wave with a Center and Swing of 0.500 and a Rate of .25 Hz (0.25 cps). In the modulation matrix, assign **LFO2** to **Delay1 Time** with a narrow oscillation range of 0.400 and 0.600 for the Low and High sliders respectively.

Mixer Tab

You will now see that the Delay Time slider for the first delay line shows it is being modulated, creating a chorus effect. Assign voice 1 to this chorus by turning the Delay 1 Send all the way up for voice 1. The idea here is to send the output of the chorus to delay 2 rather than directly to the output of the mixer. To do so, turn the xFeedback control of delay 1 all the way up and the Output of delay 1 all the way down. Remember that in Crystal the delays are paired, so turning the xFeedback of delay 1 up sends that signal to delay 2. Thus, with the Output of delay 1 turned down, the chorused sound is not heard directly but mixed into delay 2. *Note:* do not mute delay 1 in the mixer as that prevents the delay line from working. Send voice 2 to delay 2 by moving its Delay 2 Send slider all the way to the right, and add a little of voice 3 to delay 2 by raising the voice's Delay 2 Send to 0.280.

Now send all three voices to delay 3 by setting the Delay 3 Send sliders for voices 1 and 2 to 0.500 and voice 3 to 0.280. With the long release stages in the envelopes you created for the three voices, the two delays will cause the sounds to overlap each other, creating an extremely smooth texture.

Set the Output sliders for the three voices to 0.500, 0.500, and 0.160 respectively, and turn the Output of delay 2 up to 0.760 and delay 3 to 0.500. You should now have a nice, rich blend of the voices and their delay lines. Adjust the ratio between the direct voice outputs and the delay line outputs to control the amount of ambience in the sound.

Modulation Tab

Switch back to the Modulation tab to add two final touches to your sound, an LFO modulated pan position for the second delay line, and a modulation wheel control for the level of voice 3. Configure LFO 3 as a triangle wave with a Center and Swing of 0.500 and a slow Rate of 0.1 Hz. Assign it to **Delay2 Pan** in the fourth row of the modulation matrix. Sounds that swing to the extreme left and right pan positions often sound odd to our ears, so narrow the range of the oscillation by setting the Low and High sliders for this row of the modulation matrix to 0.200 and 0.800 respectively.

Set **Mod Wheel** as the source in the fifth row of the modulation matrix with **Voice3 Level** as the Target. Since you want to always have a little of the glistening sound in the mix, set the Low slider to the same value as the voice 3 Output slider in the mixer (0.160), but push the High slider all the way to the right.

You should now have a rich, but warm, harmony voice with a glistening effect that can be modulated on top of the sound. Be sure to save all your changes by once again selecting **Write** from the menu in the Patches pane of the Modulation tab and saving it to the same location you have been using.

Audio 9.3

Percussive Patch

Listen to the sound of the Percussive Patch example on the Companion Website (Audio 9.3). As the word implies, percussive sounds share sonic characteristics with percussion instruments like drums. They tend to have extremely short attacks with quick decays and releases and are often unpitched. Even when these sounds do have a pitched quality, the pitch is often secondary to the attack and duration qualities of the sound. Use the descriptions and step-by-step instructions below to create this lightly pitched, drumlike sound suitable for a variety of rhythmic patterns and ostinatos.

Oscillators

Because percussive sounds are typically quite short in duration, their timbre comes mostly from the attack stage of the sound. Accordingly, these sounds frequently combine timbres to create an interesting attack. In this patch, you will use a frequency-modulated pulse wave for the primary percussive sound, with a frequency-modulated sine wave to provide a little bit of pitch and a ring-modulated granular wave to create a bit of depth to the sound.

Envelope Generators

Envelope generators for percussive sounds usually have extremely short attack times along with quick release times. For this sound, you will use nearly identical "spike" envelopes to create the fast attack and release.

Filters

The combination of frequency- and ring-modulated oscillators produces a wonderfully rich and bright sound that works quite well for a percussive patch. You will do a bit of filtering on the granular sound, but the other two voices will not use filtering at all.

Modulators

As already mentioned, because these types of sounds are short, modulators like LFOs and looping envelopes are usually unnecessary. Other than a bit of envelope shaping on the granular sound's filter and the sine wave oscillator's pitch, modulators will not be used in this patch.

Effects

You will use a comb-filter delay to thicken the sound of the granular voice, and to give the patch a bit of rhythmic vitality, you will add a bit of synchronized delay to create a sixteenth-note rhythm that quickly fades away.

Step-by-step Instructions

Modulation Tab

Load the default preset, rename it "Percussive" in the control value display, and then write it to one of the unused preset slots. Ensure that voice 1 is active in the voice mixer, and turn its volume slider all the way up to 1.000. You will eventually turn on all three voices, but for now leave voices 2 and 3 turned off. Click the Poly button until it turns off.

Images 9.3

Voice 1 Tab

Voice 1 will be the basis of your sound and the bottom voice of a three-octave stack. Select **Synthesized: WarmSaw** as the oscillator Type. Create a mixed sawtooth-square wave by moving the PulseMix slider 0.400 with a PulseWidth of 0.620. Leave the Mogrify slider all the way off, and lower the Octave tuning by one octave (**−1**). Ensure that Semitones and FineTune are both set to zero. You should have a fairly bright, "buzzy" sound when you play on your keyboard.

Engage frequency modulation for this voice by clicking the Ring/FM button until it illuminates **FM**. If the ModIndex slider is all the way to the left, frequency modulation will have no effect, so move that slider to the middle (0.500). If you now play a note, you will hear the pitch of the oscillator rising and falling because the rate of the modulating oscillator is in the LFO range. Move the ModFreq slider up to 0.260, and the modulating oscillator's frequency rises into the audio-rate range, producing a growl in the voice's oscillator sound.

Give the sound an instantaneous attack and a quick decay by creating a four-point "spiked" amplitude envelope as follows:

- (Blue) 0.00, 0.00, **spike 1.0**
- (Yellow) 0.37, 0.00
- (Red) 0.50, 0.00
- (Blue) 0.50, 0.00
- VelSen slider at 0.660

This voice will not use a filter, so set the Type menu to **Off** and turn the envelope off as well. You should now have a percussive sound with a bright, buzzy quality. You will configure the other two voices similarly, so select **Copy Voice1** from the menu next to the Poly button, and then select **Paste to Voice2** and **Paste to Voice3**. As you work on each of the two voices below, turn the other voices off in the voice mixer so that you can focus exclusively on the one you are editing.

Voice 2 Tab

You will use voice 2 to thicken the sound and create some depth in the patch. Begin by turning frequency modulation off by clicking the Ring/FM button until it turns gray. Select **Sampled:Rough** as the oscillator Type for this voice, and raise the tuning up to the original Octave level (**0**). This oscillator type creates a grainy-sounding tone, but you will make it even more granular by raising the Granular slider to 0.740. With the Wave-Dens slider all the way to the left, the grains that are created are rather far apart, and you hear a pulsing in the sound. Raise the WaveDens slider to the middle point (0.250) and the grains overlap each other, producing a sustained sound but with more variation in timbre than the original Rough sound.

Thicken the harmonic content of this sound by engaging ring modulation to create sidebands. Click the Ring/FM button until it illuminates **Ring**. As with frequency modulation, with the ModIndex slider all the way off, you will not hear any result from ring modulation. Turn the ModIndex up to 0.160 and the ModFreq to 0.500 to create a rich set of sidebands in this oscillator's sound.

Since you are using this voice to create depth in the sound, you will make a slight modification to the amplitude envelope so that it decays a little more slowly than the other voices. Simply move the yellow handle to the right until it is also at 0.50, like the red and blue breakpoint handles.

This voice will also use an envelope-modulated filter to add some timbral shift to the attack of the sound. Select **XResLoPass** as the filter Type, and turn the envelope on. Copy the envelope from the Amplitude pane and past it into the Filters pane. Raise the LoFreq slider to 158 Hz and push the HiFreq slider all the way to the right. To emphasize the timbral shift, move the Resonance slider to 0.500. Add some Saturation (0.240) to create a bit of warm distortion in the sound.

Voice 3 Tab

This voice will add a little pitched "boink" to the sound. Turn the Ring/FM button off, and this time select **Synthesized:Sine** as the oscillator Type; tune it up one octave to the default (**0**) setting. With the amplitude envelope copied from voice 1, you should hear a quick, almost marimbalike sound from this oscillator.

You will give this sound even more of a wooden-bar quality by adding some frequency modulation to the sound. Click the Ring/FM button until it is on **FM**, and set the ModFreq to 0.800 and the ModIndex to 0.240. The oscillator for this voice should now sound even more like a marimba.

Now, let's add the boink. Begin by reshaping the amplitude envelope to these settings:

- (Blue) 0.00, 0.00, **linear**
- (Yellow) 0.01, 1.00, **curve negative**
- (Red) 0.15, 0.00
- (Blue) 0.25, 0.00
- VelSen slider at 0.660

Rather than using the "spike" setting, this envelope has a slightly longer attack so it has a bit less click. Copy this envelope and switch to the Modulation tab.

Modulation Tab

Paste the envelope you just copied into modulation envelope 1. Select **ModEnvelope1** as the source for the first row in the modulation matrix and assign **Voice3 Pitch** as the target. Leave the Low slider all the way to the left, but lower the High slider a bit to 9.0. Now, when you play a note, you will hear an extremely quick rise and fall in the pitch of this voice to produce the boink sound.

Mixer Tab

Turn all three voices on and switch to the Mixer tab. With the input sliders in the voice mixer turned all the way up for all three voices, adjust the Output levels for the three voices so that voices 1 and 2 are both at 0.760 and voice 3 is a little quieter at 0.660. The combined sound should have a slightly pitched percussive quality with a bright, buzzy timbre.

To polish this sound somewhat, you will first use a short delay to add some comb filtering to voice 2, and a rhythmic tap delay to create a decaying sixteenth-note pattern to the sound. You will use delay 1 for the comb filtering and delay 2 for the rhythmic taps.

Turn voice 2's Delay 1 Send slider all the way up and its Output slider all the way down. Rather than sending voice 2 directly to the mix, you will instead send its comb-filtered version by raising the Output slider for delay 1 to 0.760.

In the Delays pane, set the Delay Time for the first delay to 10 ms with a substantial amount of feedback (0.720). Voice 2 should now have a metallic quality to it.

Click the Sync button for delay 2, and set the Delay Time to 1/16 with a Feedback amount of 0.500 to create a sixteenth-note rhythm. Send voice 1 to this delay by turning the Delay 2 Send slider on voice 1 all the way up. Again, you want to send the comb-filtered version of voice 2 to the rhythmic delay instead of the original voice. To do so, move the xFeedback slider for delay 1 all the way to the right. Now delay 2 will receive equal amounts of voice 1 and comb-filtered voice 2. To keep the delay taps from being too bright, engage the **XResLoPass** filter on delay 2 with a cutoff frequency around 7,890 Hz and a Q of 0.300. To hear this rhythmic delay, add it to the mix by raising the delay 2 Output slider to 0.220.

Now, when you play notes, you should hear that your percussive sound has a rhythmic quality to it that changes with the tempo of your host application. Be sure to save your finished Percussive patch as you will use it as the basis for the next sound type.

Ostinato Patch

Audio 9.4

Listen to the sound of the Ostinato Patch example on the Companion Website (Audio 9.4). Synthesizers are frequently used to create sounds that produce a rhythmic ostinato. These ostinato patches are often based on some sort of percussive sound. For this next example, use the descriptions and step-by-step instructions below to modify your previous Percussive patch to create a driving ostinato. Because most of your sound is already built, very little will be changed in the mixer tab, and only the envelopes and filters are changed in the voice tabs. You will, however, use multiple modulators to create the rhythmic interest in this ostinato patch.

Images 9.4

Step-by-step Instructions

Modulation Tab

Load the Percussive patch you created in the previous example. Rename it "Ostinato" in the control value display, and write the patch to a new unused location. Select your Ostinato patch in the Browse pane and switch to the Voice 1 tab.

Voice 1 Tab

The oscillator pane will remain as it is, but you will use a filter envelope to create the rhythmic pulses of this voice. So that the filter envelope can work while the note is sustained, change the Amplitude envelope to the **Flat 4 pt** preset and turn the VelSen slider all the way down.

In the Filters pane, select **XResLoPass** as the filter Type, turn the envelope on, and push the LoFreq and HiFreq sliders full left and right respectively. Next, Set Resonance at 0.500, and create a six-point envelope with these settings:

- (Blue) 0.00, 0.05 kHz
- (Yellow) 0.00, 0.05 kHz, **spike 1.0**
- (Green) 0.25, 0.05 kHz, **spike 0.75**
- (Turquoise) 0.50, 0.05 kHz, **spike 0.5**
- (Red) 1.00, 0.05 kHz
- (Blue) 1.10, 0.05 kHz
- Both Loop and Sync turned on

With only voice 1 sounding, you should hear a repeating rhythm in this voice of two sixteenth notes followed by an eighth note.

Voice 2 Tab

Just as you did in voice 1, set the Amplitude envelope to the **Flat 4 pt** preset and turn the VelSen slider all the way down. Leave all the filter settings as they are from the Percussive patch, but change the filter envelope to this six-point shape:

- (Blue) 0.00, 0.16 kHz, **linear**
- (Yellow) 0.00, 0.16 kHz, **spike 1.0**
- (Green) 0.50, 0.16 kHz, **spike 0.75**
- (Turquoise) 0.75, 0.16 kHz, **spike 0.50**
- (Red) 1.00, 0.16 kHz
- (Blue) 1.10, 0.16 kHz
- Both Loop and Sync turned on

Similarly to what you created in voice 1, you should again hear a repeating rhythm, but this time an eighth note followed by two sixteenth notes.

Voice 3 Tab

Leave the Oscillator and Filters panes as they are, but change the Amplitude envelope to a seven-point shape:

- (Blue) 0.00, 0.00
- (Yellow) 0.00, 0.00, **spike 1.0**

- (Green) 0.25, 0.00, **spike 0.75**
- (Turquoise) 0.50, 0.00, **spike 0.9**
- (Purple) 0.75, 0.00, **spike 0.5**
- (Red) 1.00, 0.00
- (Blue) 1.10, 0.00
- Both Loop and Sync turned on
- VelSen turned all the way off

As with the other two voices, this envelope creates a sixteenth-note pulse when a note is sustained.

Mixer Tab

The controls in the Mixer tab can remain mostly as they were with only a few exceptions to reduce some of the metallic timbre in the sound. In delay 1, lower the Feedback slider to 0.500, and add a **ResLoPass** filter with the cutoff frequency set around 4 kHz and a gentle Q value of 0.100. You might also lower the delay 1 Output slider to 0.500.

Modulation Tab

The modulation controls are used to create a filter and pan position sweep and to make the voices change pitch on the sixteenth-note subdivision. Begin by setting up LFO 1 as a sine wave oscillator with a Center and Swing of 0.500 and a Rate of 0.1 Hz. Select **Reset on note** from the menu so that the LFO begins anew every time a note is pressed.

You will use this LFO with four targets, so select **LFO1** as the Source in the first four rows of the modulation matrix. The LFO will slowly sweep the cutoff frequency of the filters and the pan positions in both voices 1 and 2. Set the Target for the first two rows in the modulation matrix to **Voice1 Filt Freq** and **Voice2 Filt Freq** respectively. Set the Low slider for both rows to around 500 Hz and push both High sliders all the way to the right.

Set the Target for row 3 to **Voice1 Pan**, and set the Low and High sliders to 0.200 and 0.800, respectively. As mentioned earlier, moving a sound all the way to one side or the other often creates an odd, hollow sound, so it may be better to not go all the way to the left or right extremes with pan. Since the output of voice 2 is heard only after passing through the first delay line in the mixer, instead of assigning the fourth row of the matrix to voice 2's pan position, assign it to **Delay1 Pan**. If you turned down the Output slider of delay 1 in the mixer, you may need to expand the outward movement of the delay's pan position by positioning the Low and High sliders to something like 0.140 and 0.860 so that it sounds as if both pans are going to the same position.

In the three voice tabs, you created a sixteenth-note pulsing rhythm. Now use modulation envelopes to make those voices change pitch as well. Before configuring the envelopes, select **ModEnvelope1** as the Source for rows five and six in the modulation matrix and **ModEnvelope2** as the source for the first line on the second page of the matrix (row 7). The Targets for these three rows, in order, are **Voice1 Pitch**, **Voice2 Pitch**, and **Voice3 Pitch**. To modulate the pitch of voices 1 and 2 in opposite directions, set the Low and High sliders of the fifth row to −12.0 and 0.0, respectively, and the Low and High sliders of the sixth row to (+)12.0 and 0.0, respectively. The Low and High sliders for row 7 should be full left and right, respectively.

Select modulation envelope 1 and choose the **Flat 4 pt** preset. Set the envelope breakpoints and controls as follows:

- (Blue) 0.00, 12.0 (in this case, a value of 12.0 puts the breakpoint at the bottom)
- (Yellow) 0.00, 12.0 (at the bottom), **pulse 1.0**
- (Red) 0.25, 12.0 (at the bottom)
- (Blue) 0.31, 12.0 (at the bottom)
- Both Loop and Sync turned on

With this envelope assigned to the pitch of the first two voices, yet with the Low slider set in opposite directions for the two, voice 1 will begin at its defined pitch and alternate with the note an octave lower when the envelope drops to the bottom. Inversely, voice 2 will move to the note an octave higher when the envelope drops to the bottom position.

Copy the amplitude envelope from voice 3 and paste it into modulation envelope number 2, and change the first two breakpoints to **pulse 1.0,** and the third and fourth breakpoints to **pulse 0.50.** This modification will create a stronger sense of pitch in the ostinato pattern.

With all three voices sounding and their pan-modulated delay lines and filter sweeps active, your previous Percussive patch has become a dynamic ostinato patch with sixteenth-note pulses synchronized to the external tempo. Experiment with the output levels in the mixer to adjust the balance between the three voices. For more variety, use different rhythmic values of the various envelopes as well as other intervals for the pitch shift.

Pad Patch

Audio 9.5

Listen to the sound of the Pad Patch example on the Companion Website (Audio 9.5). Perhaps the most complex—and the most enjoyable—patches to create on a synthesizer are the so-called pad sounds. Pads are usually designed to sustain a note for a long time while undergoing continuous evolution in the sound. Pads typically employ numerous modulation sources and effects processes to create their dynamic evolution. Many synthesizers include a Pads subset in their menu of patch presets. Whether with Crystal or any other synthesizer, listen to the amazing variety of these sounds and the types of modifications the sounds undergo as they sustain.

To create the Pad sound in this example, you will use the majority of modulation resources available in Crystal, including four LFOs, a complex looping modulation envelope, the frequency splitter, and all four delay lines. The finished pad will have a rich sustaining quality to it, but with both gradual and quickly pulsing modulations in the sound.

Oscillators

As with the oscillator sounds you created for the harmony patch, lowpass–filtered sawtooth and pulse waves provide the raw materials of this patch. To thicken the spread of these oscillators, you will use precisely tuned FM modulators to add a lower-octave doubling. You also detune one of the oscillators to create a perfect-fourth shimmer in the sound.

Envelope Generators

Envelope generators are used to fade the three voice layers in and out of the composite sound. A complex, looping, multipoint modulation envelope is also used to create a swirling pan effect in the patch.

Filters

All three voices are processed with lowpass filters to shape their harmonic content before they are mixed together. LFO-modulated filters on the delay lines are also used to create a pulsing effect in the sound.

Modulators

As with most Pad sounds, modulators play an extremely important role in this patch. In addition to the modulation envelope mentioned above, four LFOs are used to modulate the filter frequencies and output levels of the delay lines.

Effects

This patch uses the four delay lines for modulated frequency filtering, and to create echoes. The delays also take advantage of their ability to be both in parallel and in series via the xFeedback control.

Step-by-step Instructions

Modulation Tab

Images 9.5

Load the default preset, rename it "Pad" in the control value display, and write it to one of the unused preset slots. Ensure that voice 1 is active in the voice mixer and turn its volume slider up to 0.880. You will eventually turn on all three voices, but for now, leave voices 2 and 3 turned off. You want your pad sound to be monophonic, so click the Poly button until it turns off, and select **Legato mono** from the dropdown menu next to the Poly button to smooth the transitions between notes.

Voice 1 Tab

Voice 1 is the basis of your sound and the middle voice in a three-octave stack. Select **Synthesized:WarmSaw** as the oscillator Type. Slide the PulseMix and PulseWidth sliders all the way to the left to create an "analog-sounding" sawtooth wave. Leave the Mogrify slider all the way off and ensure that Octave, Semitones, and FineTune are all set to zero. Your sound should be that of a basic sawtooth waveform.

You will now use an FM modulator to add a lower octave to the oscillator sound. Click the Ring/FM button until it illuminates **FM**, and move the ModFreq slider to exactly 0.250 (use the Shift key). As you slowly raise the ModIndex, you will hear the tone of an additional frequency one octave lower than the original oscillator. Setting the ModIndex slider at 0.080 should produce a nice balance between the two octaves.

Since you are applying a number of modulation effects to this sound as it sustains, you need to leave the sustain level all the way up. The simplest way to do this is to choose the **Flat 4 pt** envelope from the preset menu in the Amplitude envelope generator pane.

Extend the release of the envelope by changing the red breakpoint to a **curve negative** shape and moving the final blue breakpoint out to 1.00, 0.00.

Finally, warm up the sound of this oscillator by applying a basic lowpass filter in the Filters pane with a cutoff frequency set to around 5 kHz. You should now hear a somewhat nasal tone in two octaves that begins instantly when you press a key but gradually fades out after the key is released. Voice 2 will use many of the same settings as this voice, so copy voice 1 and paste it to voice 2 using the menu next to the Poly button.

Voice 2 Tab

Voice 2 will produce a shimmering effect in the sound by being tuned a perfect fourth higher than the upper note of voice 1. To do so, first turn frequency modulation off by clicking the FM button until it turns gray. Doing so removes the lower octave from the sound. Next, raise the pitch of this oscillator by choosing **+5** (five half-steps) from the Semitones menu. Since you want the sound of this oscillator to have more of an overtone quality, reduce its level in the voice mixer to 0.300.

In the Amplitude envelope generator pane, create a moderate fade in and a long fade out for this voice with a four-point envelope using these settings:

- (Blue) 0.00, 0.00, **curve positive**
- (Yellow) 0.50, 0.50
- (Red) 1.00, 0.50, **curve negative**
- (Blue) 2.00, 0.00
- VelSyn slider all the way to the left

Give this sound a bit more edge by changing the filter Type to **ResLoPass** and moving the Resonance slider up to 0.300. As with voice 1, leave the filter envelope turned off. You will create plenty of filter modulation for these voices with the delay lines in a few minutes.

Voice 3 Tab

Just as you did in voice 1, you will use frequency modulation to make an octave stack with this oscillator, but with a different oscillator sound to make a more interesting texture. Turn voice 3 on and raise its level in the voice mixer to 0.880, as with voice 1.

Select **Synthesized:SawSquare** as the oscillator Type, and create a hybrid sawtooth-pulse wave by setting the PulseMix slider to 0.660 and the PulseWidth slider to 0.140. Again, create the lower octave in the sound by engaging FM synthesis with a ModFreq of 0.250 and a ModIndex of 0.080. Next, lower the sound an additional octave by selecting **–1** from the Octave dropdown menu.

One of the common characteristics of pads is the fact that layers of sound often fade in and out at different times and rates to create an evolving timbre in the overall sound. You will recall that voice 1 enters instantly and voice 2 ramps up over a period of a half-second. Voice 3 will take even longer to enter, so that you hear the voices join the sound individually. Begin by selecting the basic **Flat 4 pt** amplitude envelope and adjust it as indicated below:

- (Blue) 0.00, 0.00
- (Yellow) 1.00, 1.00

- (Red) 1.12, 1.00, **curve negative**
- (Blue) 1.75, 0.00
- VelSyn off

You will also give this voice a harmonic shift that corresponds with the amplitude envelope by using a resonant lowpass filter with the same envelope as that of the Amplitude pane. Select **ResLoPass** as the filter Type, turn the filter envelope on, and copy and paste the envelope shape from the Amplitude pane into the Filters pane. Since this is the bottom voice of this patch, you do not want the filter sweep to go to high, so set the LoFreq slider to 50 Hz and the HiFreq slider to go only to around 5 kHz. Give the filter some edginess by raising the Resonance slider to 0.420 and the Shaper slider to 0.340.

With all three voices activated, you should hear a multioctave sound with a gentle perfect-fourth overtone when you play a note. You should also notice that all three voices fade in and out at their own times and rates.

Mixer and Modulation Tabs

So many elements of the mixer are modulated in this patch that it makes more sense to treat the Mixer and Modulation tabs together as an integrated set of modulated effects, and not write a distinct section for each tab. In this patch, you will create two pairs of modulated filters and delays to create the final output of the sound. You will hear only the delayed outputs of the voices, not their direct outputs, so turn the Output sliders for the three voices all the way down.

Even though Crystal has an individual filter for each voice tab, you can also create a "global" filter that affects all three voices in the Mixer tab. To do so, simply add a filter to a delay line and turn the delay time to zero. You can also add an actual delay after the sound has been filtered by using the xFeedback control in paired delay lines. In this patch, Delays 2 and 4 will be used strictly as modulated bandpass filters with their outputs sent to Delays 1 and 3, respectively, to create tap echoes. Since voices 1 and 2 are a similar timbre, one paired set of delay lines (delays 1 and 2) will be used for those voices, while delays 3 and 4 will be used on different frequency bands of voice 3.

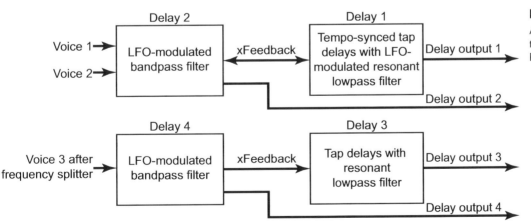

Figure 9.1
A block diagram of the delay lines in the Pad patch.

Send both voices 1 and 2 to the second delay line by turning the Delay 2 Send all the way up for both voices. Since delay 2 is being used only as a filter, leave the Delay Time and Feedback sliders turned off. Select Band Pass as the Filter Type and set the

FilterFreq to approximately 1 kHz and the Q slider to 0.500. To hear this sound, turn the delay 2 Output slider up to 0.700.

In the modulation matrix, assign LFO 1 to modulate the filter frequency of delay 2, and limit the Low and High range to approximately 500 Hz and 2.5 kHz respectively. Configure LFO 1 as a basic sine wave oscillator (Center and Swing both set to 0.500) with a moderately slow rate of .16 Hz. With the LFO modulating the center frequency of the bandpass filter, the sound should slowly sweep up and down in timbre. To make the perfect fourth tone less prominent, set the Delay 2 Send for voice 2 a little lower than for voice 1.

Next, raise the xFeedback slider on delay 2 to 0.500, causing the output of this line to be sent to the input of delay 1. You will use delay 1 to create a tempo–synced set of echoes that are also frequency modulated.

Enable the Sync button for delay 1 and set the Delay Time to an eighth note (1/8). To create a few repeating echoes, move the Feedback slider for this delay up to 0.260, and raise the delay 1 Output to 0.700. If you also raise the xFeedback slider on delay 1 to 0.280, you will feed some of the echoes back into the bandpass filter to be frequency modulated again.

You are now going to create a gurgling quality in this sound by applying a rapid and random modulation to the cutoff frequency of a highly resonant lowpass filter. First, select **ResLoPass** as the delay 1 Filter Type and put the slider for the cutoff frequency somewhere in the middle. Since you will be modulating this control, its initial position is unimportant. Move the Q slider up to 0.860. If you play a note at this point, you are likely to send the delay line's filter into uncontrolled self-oscillation; should this happen, mute Delay 1 in the Mixer. You will need to leave it muted for several seconds to allow all the feedback to die away, or the filter will start self-oscillating again. Before you play any more notes, you need to assign another LFO to modulate, and control the self-oscillation, of this delay.

To modulate this filter, you will create a pseudo sample-and-hold oscillator by using a "square" LFO with random settings.[3] Assign LFO 2 to modulate the filter frequency of Delay 1 and push the Low and High sliders full left and right, respectively. Configure LFO 2 as a square wave with the Center and Swing sliders set to 0.500. Click the Sync button to engage tempo synchronization, and set the LFO's Rate slider to 4.00 cpb (four cycles per beat equals a sixteenth-note pulse). Leave the RandRate slider at 0.000, but move the RandMix slider up to 0.700. If you look at the LFO's display, the little purple indicator will look as if it is rapidly jumping to different values. Now, when you play a note, the rapidly moving cutoff frequency of the filter produces a bubbling, or gurgling, in the sound. With the Output sliders of both delays turned up, you get a mix of the filtered steady tone and its gurgling version.

Voice 3 is processed in a similar manner to what you have done with the first two voices. However, before processing it, you will use the frequency splitter to separate the sound into four bands. You will use the splitter here to allow the lowest frequencies of

---

3 As described in Chapter 6, many synthesizers do not have an actual sample-and-hold LFO, but simulate the effect with a random pulse wave LFO.

the tone to pass, block the middle frequencies, and permit just a small amount of the upper frequencies to pass to create a harmonic shimmer in the tone.

Split the frequencies of voice 3 by raising its Splitter Send to 0.600 and positioning the 1/2, 2/3, and 3/4 sliders in the Splits pane at 610 Hz, 2,010 Hz, and 5,370 Hz respectively. Instead of sending voice 3 directly to a delay, send different amounts of the four frequency splits. To create the distribution of frequencies described in the previous paragraph, raise the Delay 3 Send sliders for the individual splits as follows:

- Split 1: 0.600
- Split 2: 0.000
- Split 3: 0.200
- Split 4: 0.300

Configure Delay 3 exactly the same as you did for Delay 2, except with the xFeedback slider on Delay 3 turned all the way up. To hear this sound by itself, mute the first two delays and turn the delay 3 Output up to 0.700. Your sound should have a thin, reedy quality that ramps up in both amplitude and timbre when you press a key. In the modulation matrix, assign LFO 1 (the same one that is modulating the frequency of delay 2) to also modulate the filter frequency of delay 3. In this case, though, make the filter sweep move in the opposite direction from the sweep in delay 2 by moving the Low slider all the way up and the High slider all the way down. If you unmute delay 2, you will hear that as one sound is modulated to a brighter timbre, the other one grows darker.

Since voice 3 has such a slow attack to its envelope, a medium tap delay creates more of a swelling in the sound than distinct echoes. Earlier, you pushed the xFeedback slider of delay 3 all the way to the right, sending its output to delay 4. Now, raise the Output level of delay 4 to 0.820, and move the Delay Time slider to 176 ms with a Feedback of 0.500. This produces a bit of a springlike "boing" in the sound, especially when a note is released. To heighten the intensity of the effect, select **ResLoPass** as delay 4's Filter Type and set the cutoff frequency to around 2,800 Hz with a moderate Q value of 0.250. In this patch, the filter on delay 4 will not be modulated.

When you unmute all the delay lines and play a note, the result is a sustaining, yet constantly evolving, drone sound with a flurry of gurgling activity in the upper register that is synchronized to the host tempo. In addition to echoes and frequency shifts, many pads also include modulated levels between layers and changing pan positions. Because none of the voices are heard directly, the outputs of the delay lines will be modulated instead.

In the modulation matrix, assign LFO 3 to modulate the level of delay 1. Since you do not want the sound to disappear completely, raise the Low slider a little to 0.120 and move the High slider all the way to the right. Configure LFO 3 as a basic sine oscillator with a moderately fast tempo-synced rate of 2.00 cpb (two cycles per beat equals an eighth-note pulse). This produces a slow tremolo effect in the output of delay 1.

Next, assign LFO 4 to the level of both delay 2 and 3. Again, raise the Low slider to 0.120 to prevent the sound from disappearing, and set the High slider all the way up. For LFO 4, choose **Saw Up** as the Type to produce a repeatedly upward moving ramp. Set the Center and Swing sliders to the 0.500 position to produce the full range of travel for the LFO, and synchronize it to the quarter note by clicking the Sync button and setting the

Rate to 1.00 cpb. Now, in addition to all the earlier modulations, the output levels of three of the delay lines are modulating at the rate of either an eighth note or a quarter note.

For the final bit of polish on this patch, you will use a looping and tempo-synced modulation envelope to change the pan position of the upper frequencies in the sound. Begin by configuring the first modulation envelope with a somewhat random-sounding nine-point shape as follows:

- (Blue) 0.00, 0.00
- (Yellow) 2.00, 1.00, **curve positive**
- (Green) 3.25, 0.15
- (Turquoise) 4.50, 0.85, **curve negative**
- (Purple) 6.75, 0.15
- (Rose) 7.50, 1.00
- (Brown) 10.0, 0.65
- (Red) 11.5, 0.95
- (Blue) 16.0, 0.00
- Loop and Sync buttons turned on

On the second page of the modulation matrix, assign this newly created envelope to the pan position for both delay 1 and delay 2. However, flip the pan motion of the two delays by setting the Low and High sliders for delay 1 to full left and right, respectively, but use the opposite extremes for delay 2. Now you should hear that a lot of the motion in the sound also jumps around in the left-right stereophonic field as you sustain a note.

As with all of the patch examples in this chapter, think of these steps merely as suggestions. Please feel free to experiment with your own settings. Quite frequently we make wonderful discoveries by selecting a single control or setting in a patch and begin modifying it as we listen to the results. When you create something that you really like, be sure to save a copy of it so you can quickly return to the sound in the future.

For all of the patches above, I intentionally used basic waveforms to show you how much can be done just with those. In addition to the basic waves, Crystal provides a number of other oscillator sounds, including sampled sounds, that are already much more complex than the basic waveforms. Try using some of them as raw material and see how much farther you can go as you refine your sounds.

Thinking Like Your Synthesizer

I hope these five demonstration patches have given you an idea of both the sonic power of a modern synthesizer and the structure involved in creating sound on these instruments. One of the secrets to successful sound creation on a synthesizer is learning to "think" like your synthesizer. For example, you might want to design a sound with a bell-like quality. Bells have a quick, percussive attack and a long decay. They also have a fundamental pitch with a relatively strong set of both harmonic and inharmonic partials that decay at different rates as the sound dies away.

Chances are that your synthesizer has envelope generators that can be used to shape the amplitude envelope to create the quick attack and long decay. However, do you have to do it on a voice-by-voice basis, or is there a global envelope that can control the entire sound? Is there a "bell" sample or hybrid oscillator type that you can use? How does your synthesizer create harmonic and inharmonic partials? Is it done with additive synthesis, FM synthesis, subtractive synthesis, or something else?

The point is that you need to spend some time learning how your synthesizer handles the numerous aspects of the sound-making process. It is tempting to just go with the presets found on most instruments, but if you really want to create your own unique sounds, then you will need to understand how your synthesizer implements the various synthesis stages like oscillators, envelopes, filters, and effects. Every instrument does these things a little differently from the others, so take the time to learn how your synthesizer works. Then, when you have an idea for a sound you will be able to think through the elements of the sound and visualize how your instrument is designed and configured to create those elements.

Your Turn

Now, it really *is* your turn. Through the course of this text, we have examined all the stages of the synthesis process and shown how each stage takes the raw material of the oscillator and refines it into the rich, wonderful sounds produced on a modern synthesizer. I hope that these explanations, along with the online materials and demonstrations in this book, have brought you a much deeper understanding of the synthesis process as a whole—and inspired you to create your own sounds. As you begin to expand your synthesizer programming capabilities, I would like to suggest a couple of approaches that may make the process easier.

First, listen carefully to the presets that are already on your synthesizer. Too often, people call up a patch, quickly play a couple of notes, and move on to the next patch, where they repeat the process. Synthesizer sounds rarely reveal themselves with just a few quick notes in the middle of the keyboard. For each sound, play long notes, short notes, loud notes, soft notes, single notes, and chords. Play in the upper and lower registers of the instrument as well as the middle. Quite often a synthesizer sound works best with a particular playing technique. You need to spend some time going through your preset sounds with multiple playing techniques to find where those presets are the most effective. As you do so, be sure to also try manipulating the various external controllers such as Aftertouch, Mod Wheel, and Pitch Bend.

Once you find a sound that is particularly appealing to you, dissect it. Save a copy of the sound to an alternate location so that you do not ruin the original, and begin systematically isolating the elements of the sound and manipulating them. Turn off all the effects processes, the modulators, the filters, and the envelopes until you are left with just the oscillators. At that point, examine how the oscillators are interacting with each other. Is their output combined, or are some oscillators controlling other oscillators? Once you understand what the oscillators are doing, turn the envelope generators on to see what effect they are producing with the sound. Progressively turn each stage back on as you examine its role in the composite sound. As you work your way back to the full sound, consider whether some of the elements in the sound might have been done differently, yet with the same or similar results. For example, could a repeating pattern in a sound have been done with an LFO, or a looping envelope, or even a step sequencer?

See if you can use your own instrument(s) to recreate the sounds you just built in Crystal. As already mentioned, every synthesizer is unique, yet they all have similar elements of oscillators, envelope generators, filters, modulators, and effects. Can you accomplish results similar to those you have created here by modifying the specific steps for Crystal to suit your synthesizer?

Synthesizers are amazing and wonderful instruments that offer the potential for a vast palette of new sounds. You now have the knowledge and understanding of these instruments to begin using the synthesis process to refine their sonic raw materials into unique, custom gems of sound. All you need to do is start. So, go forth and synthesize!

APPENDIX | Further Reading and Information

No text of this nature can completely cover all the various topics related to synthesis and synthesizers. Although there are numerous print and online resources related to the subjects in this book, readers wishing to delve deeper into them may find these books and websites particularly helpful.

Sound, Audio, and Digital Audio

Aldrich, Nika. *Digital Audio Explained*. Fort Wayne, IN: Sweetwater Sound, 2004.

Benade, Arthur H. *Fundamentals of Musical Acoustics*. 2nd ed. New York: Dover, 1990.

Burk, Phil, Larry Polansky, Douglas Repetto, Mary Roberts, and Dan Rockmore. "Music and Computers." http://music.columbia.edu/cmc/musicandcomputers/.

Huber, David Miles, and Robert E. Runstein. *Modern Recording Techniques*. 7th ed. Oxford, UK: Elsevier/Focal Press, 2010.

Maury, C., M. C. M. Wright, and P. A. Nelson. "Sound Waves: Institute of Sound and Vibration Research." http://resource.isvr.soton.ac.uk/spcg/tutorial/tutorial/StartCD.htm.

National Institutes of Health: Noise-Induced Hearing Loss website. https://www.nidcd.nih.gov/health/hearing/pages/noise.aspx.

Rossing, Thomas D., F. Richard Moore, and Paul A. Wheeler. *The Science of Sound*. 3rd ed. San Francisco: Addison-Wesley, 2002.

Russell, Dan. "Acoustics and Vibration Animations." http://www.acs.psu.edu/drussell/demos.html.

Scavone, Gary P. "MUS 150: Musical Acoustics." https://ccrma.stanford.edu/CCRMA/Courses/150/index.html.

History of Electronic Music and Synthesizers

Chadabe, Joel. *Electric Sound: The Past and Promise of Electronic Music*. Upper Saddle River, NJ: Prentice-Hall, 1997.

Friedman, Matt. "Vintage Synth Explorer." http://www.vintagesynth.com/.

Manning, Peter. *Electronic and Computer Music*. Revised and expanded ed. Oxford: Oxford University Press, 2004.

Schrader, Barry. *Introduction to Electro-Acoustic Music*. Englewood Cliffs, NJ: Prentice-Hall, 1982.

Synthmuseum.com website. http://www.synthmuseum.com.

Vail, Mark. *Vintage Synthesizers: Groundbreaking Instruments and Pioneering Designers of Electronic Music Synthesizers*. San Francisco: Miller Freeman, 1993.

Weidenaar, Reynold. *Magic Music from the Telharmonium*. London: Scarecrow Press, 1995.

Synthesis Concepts and Techniques

Aikin, Jim. *Power Tools for Synthesizer Programming: The Ultimate Reference for Sound Design*. San Francisco: Backbeat Books, 2004.

Cann, Simon. *Becoming a Synthesizer Wizard: From Presets to Power User*. Boston: Course Technology, 2010.

Chowning, John, and David Bristow. *FM Theory and Applications by Musicians for Musicians*. Tokyo: Yamaha Music Foundation, 1986.

Cipriani, Alessandro, and Maurizio Giri. *Electronic Music and Sound Design: Theory and Practice with Max/MSP*, vol. 1. Translated by David Stutz. Rome: ConTempoNet, 2010.

Moore, F. Richard. *Elements of Computer Music*. Upper Saddle River, NJ: Prentice-Hall, 1990.

MIDI Manufacturers Association website. http://www.midi.org/.

Puckette, Miller. *The Theory and Technique of Electronic Music*. Singapore: World Scientific, 2007.

Reid, Gordon. "Synth Secrets." http://www.soundonsound.com/sos/allsynthsecrets.htm.

Roads, Curtis. *The Computer Music Tutorial*. Cambridge, MA: MIT Press, 1996.

APPENDIX II Suggestions for the Instructor

Although *Refining Sound* was written for anyone wishing to learn more about synthesizers and the synthesis process, it was originally conceived as a textbook for an introductory synthesis course taught over a typical fifteen- or sixteen-week semester. The following sixteen-week schedule is a suggested approach to using this text and its related materials throughout the course. Feel free to modify this schedule as needed.

WEEK 1: HEARING, SOUND AND ACOUSTICS REVIEW
- Reading: Foreword, Preface, pp. vii–10
- Website materials: Audio Driver Configuration, Crystal Player, Demos 1.1–1.3

WEEK 2: HISTORY OF SYNTHESIZERS, DIGITAL AUDIO REVIEW
- Reading: pp. 10–32
- Website materials: Demo 1.4

WEEK 3: OSCILLATORS AND SOUND SOURCES
- Reading: pp. 33–57
- Website materials: Sine Wave Animation, Demos 2.1–2.5

WEEK 4: OSCILLATOR COMBINATIONS
- Reading: pp. 58–80
- Website materials: Demos 3.1–3.6, Amplitude Modulation vs. Frequency Modulation Animation

WEEK 5: AMPLITUDE ENVELOPE GENERATORS
- Reading: pp. 81–98
- Website materials: Demos 4.1–4.4

WEEK 6: AUDIO FILTERS I: FILTER TYPES AND CONTROLS
- Reading: pp. 99–112
- Website materials: Demos 5.1–5.2

WEEK 7: AUDIO FILTERS II: DYNAMIC FILTERS AND SUBTRACTIVE SYNTHESIS
- Reading: pp. 113–119
- Website materials: Demos 5.3–5.4

WEEK 8: MIDTERM EXAM

WEEK 9: MODULATION MATRIX AND LOW FREQUENCY OSCILLATORS
- Reading: pp. 120–128
- Website materials: Tempo to LFO Rate Calculator, Demo 6.1

WEEK 10: AUDIO-RATE OSCILLATORS AND OTHER INTERNAL MODULATION SOURCES
- Reading: pp. 128–144
- Website materials: Demos 6.2–6.4

WEEK 11: EXTERNAL CONTROLS AND MIDI
- Reading: pp. 145–170
- Website materials: Mega MIDI Monitor, MIDI Note Numbers and Frequencies, MIDI Messages, MIDI Controller Numbers and Names

WEEK 12: TIME-BASED EFFECTS PROCESSING
- Reading: pp. 171–183
- Website materials: Demos 8.1–8.6

WEEK 13: FREQUENCY- AND AMPLITUDE-BASED EFFECTS PROCESSING
- Reading: pp. 183–204
- Website materials: Demos: 8.7–8.12

WEEK 14: CREATING SYNTHESIZED SOUNDS I: LEAD AND HARMONY SOUNDS
- Reading: pp. 205–214
- Website materials: Audio and Images 9.1–9.2

WEEK 15: CREATING SYNTHESIZED SOUNDS II: PERCUSSIVE AND OSTINATO SOUNDS
- Reading: pp. 214–220
- Website materials: Audio and Images 9.3–9.4

WEEK 16: CREATING SYNTHESIZED SOUNDS III: PAD SOUNDS
- Reading: pp. 220–228
- Website materials: Audio and Images 9.5

All of the synthesis demonstrations and examples in *Refining Sound* are done with either the demonstrations from the companion website or the Crystal software synthesizer. If you teach in an electronic music lab or classroom, you may wish to use a software synthesizer other than Crystal. Although it is strongly recommended that you use the website demos to illustrate the specific points and concepts in the text, feel free to use whatever synthesizer you wish for the Your Turn sections at the end of the chapters. You will, of course, need to modify the instructions for the particular synthesizer you use.

To facilitate organization of the website demos, it may be helpful to download all of the demos from the companion website and place them in folders corresponding to each week's topics. The folders can then be placed on a server for the class or in a learning management system such as Blackboard or Moodle.

Although the website demos cover a wide range of topics, you may wish to expand on them by creating your own. Max by Cycling '74 (http://www.cycling74.com) is an excellent tool for creating these demos. As a resource for building your own demos, be sure to see V. J. Manzo's excellent text *Max/MSP/Jitter for Music*, also available from Oxford University Press.

INDEX

additive synthesis, 11, 46, 65–68, 87, 114

ADC (analog-to-digital converter), 26, 49

ADSR. *See* envelope generator

algorithm, 28, 74–75

aliasing, 28, 45

allpass filter, 104, 106–107, 180–183

amplification, 11–13, 189

amplifier, 8, 11–13, 16, 83, 148, 189

amplitude, description of, 6–10

amplitude modulation synthesis, 71–73, 75, 120, 128, 187. *See also* ring modulation

amplitude versus loudness, 6–7, 9

amplitude-based effects, 188–196

AM Synthesis. *See* amplitude modulation synthesis

analog audio

    compared to digital audio, 24–25, 73, 149

    components, digital emulation of, 23, 44–45, 100, 124–125

analog-to-digital converter, 26, 49

anode, 12, 188

arpeggiator, 135

attack

    adding noise to, 41

    note, of a, 51, 126, 194

    stage (envelope generator), 83–93, 129–130

    stage (sound envelope), 81–83, 180, 194

    time (dynamics processor), 191, 194, 196

    time (envelope generator), 84–85

    transient, 173, 180

    using a sample for, 48

    velocity, 92, 156

audio filter. *See* filter

audio-rate oscillator, 37, 123, 128–129, 136, 148n3. *See also* modulation oscillator

average frequency, 61, 65

Babbitt, Milton, 18

bandpass filter, 101–103, 106, 112, 184–186, 195

bandreject filter, 101–103, 106–107, 112

bandwidth, filter, 109–110

beat frequency, 60–62, 63. *See also* combination frequency

Bell, Alexander Graham, 7

bit

    definition of, 26

    digital audio, use in, 25–27, 49, 190

    MIDI, use in, 154–155, 161

bit crushing, 190

bit depth, 26–28, 190, 154, 161

bit rate, 26n14

bit resolution. *See* bit depth

blue noise, 44

brown noise. *See* red noise

Brownian noise. *See* red noise

byte, 26, 153–158, 160–162

Cahill, Thaddeus, 10–11, 18, 24, 66, 148–149

Carlos, Wendy, *Switched-On Bach*, 17, 18n8

carrier, 71

cathode, 12

center frequency. *See also* cutoff frequency; filter

    calculating Q with, 110

    definition of, 106–107

    modulation with

        aftertouch, 164

        amplitude envelope, 113

        audio-rate oscillator, 129, 136

        envelope follower, 132

        function modulator, 132

        key velocity, 113

        LFO, 128, 136

        modulation envelope generator, 129–130

        modulation wheel, 164

        step sequencer, 133

Chebyshev, Pafnuty, polynomials, 47

chorus (effects processor), 179–180

Chowning, John, 72–73

CMI. *See* Computer Music Instrument Fairlight

Columbia-Princeton Electronic Music Center, 18, 83

comb filter, 105, 173–174

combination frequency, 60–62. *See also* beat frequency

compound effects, 196–197

compression, sound wave, 6, 9, 25, 27, 45, 59, 123, 187

compressor (dynamics processor), 191–194

Computer Musical Instrument Fairlight, 20

control switch, 52

control voltage/gate, 146–149

    converters, 151

corner frequency. *See* allpass filter

crackle noise, 44

cutoff frequency. *See also* center frequency; filter

    calculating bandwidth with, 109

    definition of, 106–107

    modulation with

        aftertouch, 164

        amplitude envelope, 113

        audio-rate oscillator, 129, 136

        envelope follower, 132

        key tracking, 113

235

Printed in Great Britain
by Amazon